About the Author

Zanemvula Kizito Gatyeni ('Zakes') Mda was born in Herschel, South Africa in 1948. He was educated in Lesotho, Switzerland, the USA and South Africa. In 1990 the University of Cape Town awarded him his Ph.D. on the utilisation of theatre in development communication.

Professor Mda has taught at various institutions. In 1985 he joined the National University of Lesotho where he was Director of the Theatre for Development Project, and later Professor of Literature and Head of the English Department. He is currently a Fellow at the Southern African Research Program, Yale University, in the USA where he also produces and directs plays.

In addition to his academic career, Professor Mda is a well-known South African poet, playwright and painter. His work has been hung at art exhibitions in the United States, Canada, Britain and Lesotho. His poetry has appeared in various literary journals, including *Staffrider* and *Classic*, as well as in the anthology *Summer Fires* (London, Heinemann Educational Books, 1983). In 1990, Ravan Press brought out *The Plays of Zakes Mda*. His plays have been widely performed in Southern Africa as well as several of them being put on in the USA, the UK, the former Soviet Union (in a Russian translation) and in France (in French). His play, *The Hill*, was televised on West German Television and *Banned* was broadcast on radio by the BBC. In 1979 he was awarded the Amstel Playwright of the Year Award for *The Hill* and in 1984 the Christine Crawford Award of the American Theatre Association for *The Road*.

His busy intellectual and cultural activities also include a wide range of consultancy work and teaching about communications in the field of rural development. Since 1988 he has served as a UNICEF consultant on social mobilization.

Books by Zakes Mda

We Shall Sing for the Fatherland and Other Plays (Johannesburg: Ravan Press, 1980)

Bits of Debris (Lesotho: Thapama Books, 1986)

The Plays of Zakes Mda (Johannesburg: Ravan Press, 1990)

When People Play People: Development Communication through Theatre (London: Zed Books, 1993)

When People Play People

Development Communication
Through Theatre

To my father A. P. S. Mda

ZAKES MDA

When People Play People

Development Communication
Through Theatre

WITWATERSRAND
UNIVERSITY PRESS
Johannesburg

ZED BOOKS
London & New Jersey

When People Play People: Development Communication Through Theatre
was first published by Zed Books Ltd, 57 Caledonian Road, London
N1 9BU and 165 First Avenue, Atlantic Highlands, New Jersey 07716, USA;
and in South Africa by Witwatersrand University Press, PO Wits,
Johannesburg 2050, South Africa.

Cover designed by Andrew Corbett

Typeset by EMS Photosetters, Thorpe Bay, Essex
Printed and bound in the United Kingdom by
Biddles Ltd, Guildford and King's Lynn

A catalogue record for this book is available
from the British Library
US CIP is available from the Library of Congress

ISBN 185649 199 4 Hb
ISBN 1 85649 200 1 Pb ✓

SA ISBN 186814 223 X Pb

Contents

Preface

The focus of this study is on rural communities because they form the vast majority in the Third World, and are the most disadvantaged and oppressed. In the course of my work as a practitioner of theatre-for-development and as a researcher in the field of communication, I have encountered wide gaps in the distribution of services and of wealth between rural areas and towns — and between the centre and the periphery in both urban and rural areas. I have also encountered the lack of dialogue between the centre and the periphery, and within the periphery itself.

It is my hope that this study will contribute to the creation of a mutual body of knowledge in the fields of development communication and theatre-for-development, the application of which will lead to a process of dialogue. The assumption is that dialogue within the periphery itself, and between the periphery and the centre, will in turn lead to a social transformation. With this study, therefore, I also wish to correct the large discrepancies that exist between the theoretical aspects of communication research, and their practical applications in development work.

My interest in theatre began when I was at junior high school. There I started writing plays, some of which were performed by the students. I later gained wider recognition as a playwright when my plays were performed on the professional stage in South Africa, Europe and the United States of America.

After studying fine arts, followed by a spell of teaching at various high schools in Lesotho, I went to the USA, where I obtained a master's degree in theatre, and a second master's in mass communication (with emphasis on telecommunications — radio and television), both at Ohio University, Athens.

My stay at Ohio enhanced my interest in the combination of theatre and communication studies. Since then I have travelled to many countries where I observed at first hand the work that theatre practitioners are doing in development. Early in 1989 I was in Mali, where I listened to the *griots*, who have put into their songs messages on immunisation, breast-feeding and oral rehydration therapy. *Griots* are praise singers who sing of lineages and history, and act as chroniclers in an oral tradition. However, since they have a big following among all sectors in the country, they have decided to use their art to reinforce campaigns on child survival and development.

There is a growing interest in the role that artists can play in development communication. Communication researchers and practitioners have realised the failure of the mediated technological media in effecting change, particularly in rural areas. Hence the big conferences that are held in some part of Africa every year, with the intention of mobilising artists of all kinds to render their services to development communication. One such conference that I attended in 1988 in Zimbabwe was organised by UNICEF, an organisation which has been at the forefront in rallying artists for child survival and development. Among the participants were some Hollywood celebrities, and high-powered politicians and other celebrities of all types from Africa, Europe and the Americas. The whole conference was characterised by glamour, pomp and ceremony. We dined like the 'stars' we were, and drank imported wines at numerous mayoral and presidential cocktail parties — all in the name of the poor. (I do not mean to be an ungracious guest; I would welcome further invitations.) The conference in Mali (also organised by UNICEF), on the other hand, had a different tone, with people like Julius Nyerere not only engaged in the usual ceremonies of opening or closing the conference, but actually participating in workshops in the villages.

Interest in theatre-for-development is not confined to Africa, or to the Third World. I spent the latter part of 1988 on a lecture tour of what was then West Germany. In every city I was approached by 'alternative' theatre groups keen to learn the method of theatre-for-development. In the north of England I have met such groups as Them Wifies, who are involved in the utilisation of theatre as a medium for development communication in that region. All these practitioners feel that even in the developed world there is need for community dialogue that will lead to critical awareness in the various communities. It is not only the rural poor of the Third World who are in need of conscientisation.

Throughout these travels I have been collecting information for this book. For this research I did not engage in any formal methods or procedures. My main data sources were fellow theatre-for-development practitioners in various countries, and personal impressions and observations. When I came back from the United States in 1985, I lived for six months in the mountain village of Sehonghong in Lesotho, where I collected data on folk media. There I participated in the production and enjoyment of traditional performance modes. The major data, however, comes from the work of Marotholi Travelling Theatre, a group with which I was intimately involved as director. Unfortunately this group no longer exists. But other groups have emerged, and theatre-for-development continues in Lesotho.

Zakes Mda

Acknowledgements

I would first of all like to thank Professor Mavis Taylor, head of the Department of Drama at the University of Cape Town, Mr M. L. Fielding of the Professional Communication Unit, also at UCT, and Dr Chris Dunton of the English Department at the National University of Lesotho, for their informed criticism and encouragement.

I would also like to thank my parents, A. P. and Rose, for their understanding, and for looking after my children while I roamed the world in search of theatre. I am also indebted to my children Nduku, Thandi, Dini and Zukile.

I am especially grateful to A. B. Thoahlane and Dr Mosebi Damane with whom I had lengthy discussions on the pre-colonial communication media in Lesotho; to Professor Andrew Horn, who began the theatre-for-development work in Lesotho; to David Kerr who shared with me some unpublished work in his possession; to Dr Chris Kamlongera with whom I had fruitful discussions in Zimbabwe; and to Felicité Train who typed my manuscripts.

Finally I sincerely thank my wife, Adele, who was my greatest support in every possible way, and who also helped to read and correct my manuscripts.

1. Introduction: Development Communication in Africa

One of the major questions in development communication studies today concerns how communication can be organised so as to increase participation, achieve self-reliance, promote equity, and close communication gaps. (Hedebro 1982 p. 126.) There is a growing feeling among communication researchers that existing media systems have failed to serve the needs of development in Africa. The failure is due mostly to the undemocratic structures of the media institutions, which operate in 'an extremely centralised fashion with a sharp concentration of the power, resources and services of the media in urban areas' (Boafo 1988, p. 38). Communication systems in Africa therefore serve the needs of a few urban inhabitants while neglecting those of the vast majority of the population living in rural areas. These media transmit the values and the ideology of the ruling elites.

> Communication patterns and processes in African societies are basically synchronic: patterns and processes in which a few people transmit information to the majority of the people who have minimal or no participation in information generation and dissemination. (Boafo, 1985, p. 86.)

There is, therefore, a need to democratise the structures of communication systems, because in their current authoritarian form they are non-conducive to and dysfunctional for development. Communication technologies need to be decentralised and located among the rural people, who form the majority of the populations in African countries. This will give the rural population access not only to the messages produced by others, but to the means to produce and distribute their own messages.

Another concern in development communication today is the perceived failure of current paradigms — particularly the diffusion of innovations paradigm — to effect development. These paradigms do not take into consideration the structural causes of underdevelopment. They restrict development to improvement in gross national product and other economic indices, without taking into account the fact that 'the function and impact of communication strategies in development are prescribed by the larger social system and that the main inhibitions to development are more structural than informational' (Boafo 1985, p. 83). We shall discuss the failure of current paradigms in greater detail in chapter 2.

As an attempt to remedy the situation outlined above, communicologists are exploring new paradigms significantly different from the old dominant paradigm.

> The new paradigm seeks to emphasise the quality of life — integration of traditional and modern systems of communication — labour-intensive and appropriate technology — self-reliance — user-oriented strategies — popular participation in development planning and implementation. (Wang and Dissanayake, 1982, p. 7.)

Theatre has been identified as one medium the use of which could lead towards the realisation of these objectives. The reasons advanced are that it has the potential for being a democratic medium, in which the audiences may play an active role in medium-programming, and therefore in producing and distributing messages. It is not centralised like the technological media, and is capable of integrating indigenous and popular systems of communication that already exist in the rural areas. It has appropriate technology, since all it needs is human resources, which are plentiful in the villages. It is capable of being more effective since it uses interpersonal channels that have been found to have more impact than the mediated channels of electronic and print media.

> Research on the news-dissemination patterns in sub-Saharan Africa has indicated . . . that audiences use *interpersonal* and *traditional* media sources more often than they use the modern mass media and that mass media content accords closely with elite preferences but not at all well with those of the mass public. (Pratt and Manheim, 1988, p. 79.)

Theatre is now being used widely in many African countries, and every year there are workshops in various countries which aim to initiate theatre practitioners and development extension workers into the use of theatre-for-development. Organisations like the Union of African Performing Artists, the African Council on Communication Education, and UNICEF are in the forefront of this movement, and have supported many such projects in Africa.

Although the use of theatre as a medium for development communication is receiving increasing recognition among theatre practitioners and development extension workers in Africa, scholarship in this area has lagged behind. Only a few works have been published, and most of this literature concentrates on case studies of theatre-for-development campaigns and workshops in various countries. These studies are descriptive, and the research is undertaken from the perspective of theatre practitioners and extension workers. Although the authors claim that theatre is being used as a communication medium, none of this literature examines how theatre functions as communication. What emerges clearly is that theatre-for-development research has been the domain of theatre scholars and practitioners, and of non-formal educators, and not of communicologists.

It is this state of affairs that this book attempts to correct. The study investigates the nature and function of theatre-for-development. The objectives are twofold: firstly, to place theatre-for-development in the context of either development communication theory or development communication paradigms; secondly, to examine how theatre functions as communication, and therefore arrive at a new model of theatrical communication in theatre-for-development. We do not aspire to create a new model of development communication, but to place theatre in the context of existing paradigms, perspectives and theories.

To achieve these objectives the study uses a critical methodology rather than an empirical one. It is therefore not concerned with the operationalisation and measurement of concepts, or with statistical treatment of data. Rather, it is a theoretical enquiry into the phenomenon of theatre-for-development. It is nevertheless a scientific study, in that it is a systematic enquiry that leads to generalised results or explanations that can be applied to reality. It organises and systematises existing knowledge in the two fields of humanities (theatre) and social sciences (communication), and in the process evolves new perspectives and paradigms.

The existing knowledge in these two fields that is relevant to the study is reviewed in the next chapter. The study builds on this literature. Its uniqueness however lies in that by putting theatre-for-development in the context of development communication theory, it can examine how the aesthetics of theatre function as a communication code. The major case study is the Marotholi Travelling Theatre, a theatre-for-development collective that was based in Lesotho. I shall examine other theatre-for-development projects and workshops in Africa briefly, for the purpose of comparing and contrasting aspects of the work of Marotholi.

Although the study will examine the *text* — in this case an individual play or a collection of plays created by the collective in performance — and interpret it, the emphasis will be on examining and interpreting the structural conditions engendering the text. Felstehausen says classic theories often portray communication as analogous to an electrical system with transmitters, receivers, circuits and feedback loops.

The analogy is deeply suggestive, but as with most analogies, it is also limiting and sometimes misleading. For one thing, investigators tend to place primary attention on senders and receivers and the links between them rather than focus on social structure and message structure. A focus on communicators and channels subsequently influences the way communication models are applied. (Felstehausen, 1983, p. 47.)

This study will examine and utilise communication models, but will not focus on the models to the exclusion of 'social structure and message structure', or the conditions of the text. For this writer there is no inconsistency between positing a theoretical analysis that delves into social structure and message structure, and formulating these in diagrammatic form. While acknowledging the fact that models are inevitably incomplete, oversimplified and involve some concealed assumptions, and that no model is suitable for all levels of analysis (McQuail and Windahl, 1981, p. 2), this study places emphasis on the organising function of the models. Models are able to order and relate systems to each other, to provide in a simplified way, information which would otherwise be complicated or ambiguous, and to make it possible to predict the outcome or course of events.

It will be noted that the models the study employs are mechanistic rather than psychological, pragmatic or interactional. There are two reasons for this. The first is that none of the current paradigms of development communication are within the broad framework of behaviouristic psychology. Nor are there current paradigms in the practice and research of development communication that follow the interactional perspective, with its assertion that every social interaction begins and ends with a consideration of the human self, or the pragmatic perspective, with its abstract general systems approach. As has been mentioned before, the intention of this study is not to evolve new development communication paradigms, but to utilise current perspectives and relate them to theatre-for-development.

The second reason is that this study is not concerned with a psychological explication of theatrical communication. While acknowledging that social psychology has had a great influence in the study of communication (it has had little or no influence in the study of development communication), this writer postulates that since a behaviouristic conceptualisation of communication places the locus of communication within the individual, it therefore places the locus of change with the individual. It views communication as a stimulus–response phenomenon, and its emphasis is on attitude and behavioural change. My argument is that the locus for change is not set within the individual, and problems of underdevelopment do not lie with villagers as individuals who are ignorant and traditional, and who must therefore be stimulated into action. Failed development lies within larger political and economic structures.

It is for this reason that I examine communication in the context of these structures. This is not to negate the importance of change at an individual level, nor the importance of information in achieving it, but it is in line with current thinking in development communication that places change within a larger context of social structures — some of which are restrictive to change at the individual level. This study will therefore not examine how theatre functions psychologically. It will not delve into the internal cognitive and affective make-up of the theatre practitioner and the villager, nor the internal mechanisms of perception and information processing. Rather, it will examine how theatre-for-development functions in the context of social and political structures.

I hope that this will have practical application in assisting theatre-for-development practitioners to design programmes that will be more effective in their communication aspects, and also in guiding development planners on the strength and limitations of theatre-for-development in relation to other media at their disposal.

2. Perspectives

Before discussing how theatre functions as communication, we must first examine various perspectives on theatre-for-development and on development communication. This will be done by reviewing crucial literature in these areas. The literature selected has particular relevance, in that while it treats current perspectives in these disciplines, it gives an historical account of theatre in Africa, and of theatre-for-development in particular. It also gives an account of the various perspectives and orthodoxies in the history of mass communication in general, and of development communication in particular. We shall also define some of the basic concepts used in the study.

An overview of some of the crucial literature on theatre-for-development indicates that there have been various theatre-for-development or popular theatre experiments in Africa, and these have differed in objective and methodology. The general notion, however, is that of taking theatre to the people, and using theatre not only to reflect and interpret society, but to transform it. First, let us examine an historical perspective.

The development of theatre in Africa

Kamlongera (1989), in a major study, describes the development of theatre in Africa from a medium of entertainment for the colonial elite to a post-independence African theatre. Various approaches to using theatre as a medium of education and development are discussed. The study is by far the most important work to come out of Africa on this subject, because it is much more detailed than previous studies, and has a wider scope.

Before dealing with theatre-for-development, Kamlongera begins by examining colonial education and drama. The colonialists' intention of promoting drama among Africans was geared towards weaning them from their 'pagan' and 'uncivilised' ways. It was suggested that an evolving African drama must be based on dance, must be childlike and simple in form, must have music, must involve story-telling, and must have drumming. This drama did not take into account traditional African forms, for the missionaries had already decided they were going to accept only those 'native' practices that suited their civilising mission. They therefore decided to introduce European drama into Africa instead of understanding precolonial African theatre forms. In order to make the work appealing to Africans, some token attention was paid to African ways of enjoying and producing entertainment.

> The drama that was being created emphasised 'noise' and what was being considered the strongest asset in African performance, 'spectacle'. Attempts to create anything thought-provoking were de-emphasised. Folklore provided character traits that were to be used in propaganda plays. For instance the clever hare was synonymous to the clever character in a drama. Cleverness being the same as readiness to adopt western ideas. (Kamlongera, 1989, p. 9.)

Open propaganda was therefore the main objective behind efforts to create drama among Africans. It will be noted that open propaganda remains the intention in many contemporary theatre-for-development programmes, and that the semblance of Africanness given to such works prevails.

Indigenous African drama, the author argues, exists in context, and by context he means 'the situation in which particular "human intention and action" take place' (Kamlongera 1989, p. 15). Such a situation will be created by a specific community or society with its own conventions, established by the community itself and not by any outside force. The method of creativity is pegged to the nature of the function that drama is supposed to fulfil in a ceremony. Ceremonies themselves are loaded with ritual significance, and this is what has been studied most in this area. The stress has been on ceremonies, festivals and rites and how drama functions in them, rather than on performance. The aesthetic qualities embedded in the ceremonies is not fully recognised, in spite of the acknowledgement that most of the action of these ceremonies is performed through song, dance, mime and even dialogue. What Kamlongera argues, therefore, is that these ceremonies have both ritual and theatre.

> Ritual elements are summed up in the overall intentions of those who initiate the ceremonies in an attempt to reconcile man and his environment. Theatre surfaces as part of the fulfilment of these intentions. In this respect ritual is bigger than theatre. But these two are not exclusive of each other. (Kamlongera 1989, p. 26.)

Theatre was part of a people's life. The contemporary African theatre practitioner is aware of the need to evolve an authentic African theatre that will be relevant to the community, and also be part of the people's life. This awareness manifests itself by debates and creative works that try to marry indigenous performance modes with Western styles.

The travelling theatre concept

After examining the function of theatre in society in Africa from pre-colonial times, through the colonial era and the period of the 'struggle' for independence, to the post-independence period, where a major concern of African literature in general, and theatre in particular, was total disillusionment with the political situation, and a realignment with the 'masses' in their struggle for better living conditions, Kamlongera deals with the concept of 'travelling theatre' or taking theatre to the people. He says that the idea of a touring theatre company, or a travelling theatre, stems from the attempt to pattern modern theatre on traditional modes. From time immemorial, traditional artists travelled from village to village performing their arts. This they did on their own initiative, or at the invitation of important personages in host villages, and their performance was composed of dance, story-telling and drumming. An example of such a group of artists are the *Alarinjo* performers of Nigeria, an indigenous traditional travelling theatre that was recreational and at the same time ceremonial.

In more recent times popular groups emerged, in West Africa and South Africa, that travel from city to city, and sometimes from country to country, performing theatre. These are mostly commercial groups. Examples are the Ghanaian Concert Party, the Nigerian Opera and the South African musical theatre of such practitioners as Gibson Kente. There is also the syncretic theatre, such as the *Malipenga* dance-drama, which travels from village to village in Malawi at the invitation of other similar groups. 'Syncretic' suggests that this is a theatre that has emerged out of bringing together foreign elements of performance with indigenous ones.

The concept of a travelling theatre was later taken up by university drama groups like those from Ibadan (Nigeria), Makerere (Uganda), Chikwakwa (Zambia) and Chancellor College (Malawi). This came as a result of some university dons wishing to tour their productions among the people outside the campuses. They set out to teach the people about the phenomena of theatre as they understood it in the classroom. Gradually however, they learnt a few lessons about theatre in society from the people. Initially they took European plays to bemused rural audiences, and later embarked on presenting African adaptations of established plays or locally written plays. In their discussion of the stages of development of popular theatre, Crow and Etherton (1982) see this stage of the 'well-made' play as the beginning, chronologically, of popular theatre in East Africa. But according to Kamlongera popular theatre has existed from time immemorial among the people. When university travelling groups went to the village, the people already had a notion of theatre, although these touring groups considered the audiences to be devoid of theatre experience. 'The theatre artists in these shows were coming down from some ivory tower to show the poor illiterate rural mases something they were missing in their lives' (Kamlongera, 1989, p. 70). These plays were presented in the villages, but rarely did they address themselves to the question of their audiences' reaction to this whole exercise. Even when the emphasis had shifted to presenting plays on local issues, the format was still the one learnt in schools from Western sources. No attempt was made to incorporate or learn from the people's own performance modes. It is only in recent years that such an attempt has been made.

Creating theatre for the people

Kamlongera writes that some practitioners trying to establish a truly African theatre have resorted to adopting ancient legends, myths, and rituals, and presenting these in the context of, and within the understanding of, Western theatre. He says the search for relevant theatre does not necessarily take us along this path, but rather along the path of dealing with contemporary political, social and economic experience.

Efforts to present theatre for the people failed also because the people themselves rejected it.

> Creating theatre for the people is not sufficient by itself. In fact it is not very different from simply touring foreign plays among the people. Whilst the plays may veer towards African experience there has to be sufficient effort to identify an appropriate way of presenting it. (Kamlongera, 1989, p. 70.)

Creating theatre for the people assumes that the people are devoid of any theatre experience. The latest stage now is to try to identify an African aesthetic by creating theatre *with* the people. Theatre practitioners have come to realise that it is fundamental to the development of a people's culture to be with the people in creating theatre.

We note here that Kamlongera's primary concern in creating theatre with the people is that of identifying a truly African aesthetic, and of cultural development. Other studies that will be examined have a different concern in their advocacy for creating theatre with the people. People must be active participants in the creation of theatre, they say, but with the objective of turning theatre into a much more effective medium of adult education.

On identifying a truly African theatre

Kamlongera feels that the developments in recent years indicate that a way has been found of identifying a truly African theatre. This came about when practitioners shifted from the practice of treating the audience as separate from performers. Practitioners are now creating theatre with the people, as exemplified by the work of Laedza Batanani in Botswana, Kamiriithu in Kenya, and that of university travelling theatres in Tanzania, Malawi, Nigeria (Amadu Bello), and Zambia. The work of these groups suffered from myopia for a long time until they started relating it to the needs of the common people in the villages and urban slums. It is adult educators, rather than professional theatre practitioners, who were the forerunners of this movement.

The basis of the work of adult educators such as Paulo Freire, Augusto Boal, Ross Kidd and Michael Etherton lies in participatory research, conscientisation, and development. While these people seem not to be interested in theatre *per se* 'what they aim for ties in very well with the goals of developing theatre or a culture (if we put it in more general terms)' (Kamlongera, 1989, p. 83). By living and creating with the community, a new and genuine theatre language is being evolved. Although this new theatre continues to use the same age-old proverbs and riddles, songs and dances, these forms are not imposed on the people by outside forces who think that is how African theatre should be. Rather the people themselves decide to use the cultural forms they have at their disposal.

Kamlongera feels that theatre-for-development continues the functional nature of indigenous theatre into our modern age.

> It is not a cliche to say indigenous performances in Africa contain within them some functional element. In most cases this takes the form of a didactic statement. Whilst performers might engage in doing spectacular movements and dances, they might also carry within the performances special messages or lessons to some members of their audience. Some work in Theatre for Development is a direct result of recognising this characteristic in indigenous African performances. (Kamlongera, 1989, p. 88.)

It is important to note this because there might be a mistaken conception from what has been said before, that Freire and Boal originated the idea of using theatre to serve a particular function in society. Indeed, Freire's work does not deal with theatre at all. But Boal and other adult educators, such as Ross Kidd and Martin Byram, and theatre practitioners and scholars such as Christopher Kamlongera, Stephen Chifunyise (1985) and David Kerr (1981), saw that theatre can provide a method of implementing Freire's ideas on raising the critical awareness of the disadvantaged people in society so that they will be able to identify their problems as consequences of a particular social order.

A factor contributing to the resurgence of theatre in its current role emerged from the search for ways of supplementing the mass media which, 'have been shown to be incapable of affecting change on their own without some intermediary process' (Kidd 1979, p. 3). This is a view which is supported by Kerr, who says theatre is being encouraged as a tool for adult education because 'of deficiencies in existing educational institutions and communications media which stem from elitism of colonial education and its irrelevancy to the goals of national development' (Kerr 1981, p. 145). Kerr and Kidd both relate popular theatre to adult education, and share one philosophical basis derived from the ideas of Paulo Freire.

Kamlongera's study (1989) notes that in almost all cases where theatre-for-development exists, it is led by a team of theatre experts who work with various types of development or extension workers. These theatre practitioners help the extension workers to create theatre that will carry messages on such themes as nutrition, literacy, health and agriculture around the villages. The theatre varies from straight drama to songs, dance and puppetry. The songs are usually simple, catchy tunes with a clear message, composed and sung by the extension workers together with the audience. Sometimes these songs are recorded and broadcast by radio. The dances employed in this kind of theatre are those with mimetic elements. What takes place could be termed dance-drama. Puppetry, on the other hand, is losing its grip on adult audiences, in spite of its popularity among practitioners. Adults find it too childish, and in some areas it is found to be culturally unacceptable. Drama is the most extensively used.

Government agents and autonomous practitioners
After presenting specific examples and case studies of projects in Malawi and Zambia, Kamlongera concludes his study by analysing the work described in the case studies.

Theatre-for-development workers, he says, fall into two groups: govern-- ment agents and autonomous practitioners. The failure of the former to produce results in adult education gave rise to autonomous groups of which Chancellor College Travelling Theatre (Mbalachanda, Malawi) is an example. Government agents depend on government salaries for their survival. Within Malawian society these belong to the *petite bourgeoisie*. The farmers to whom the messages are directed, on the other hand, form the peasantry or proletariat of the society. They depend for their living on what they grow and sell to the government at prices determined by the latter.

The relationship between the groups will reflect the contradictions between them. Even if the government servants carry no particular doctrines when they go out to the farmers, they still display certain values and ideas, most of which have been inherited from colonial days. The tendency is for them to assume that all native practices must be replaced by modern ones from Europe, and therefore go out to teach villagers, who are treated as passive recipients of information. This is reflected in the kind of theatre they do, which does not expect the villagers to question or complain about anything.

Although some adult educators in the projects that he studied use puppet theatre, Kamlongera dismisses this because it is not built on indigenous modes of entertainment. It fails to respect audience responses, engages in manipulative work, and does not encourage a critical spirit among those it reaches. The messages are taken for granted.

> Puppetry is not an indigenous theatre tradition in Malawi. So any critical appreciation of such work by Malawians cannot go beyond simply an expression of 'escapist' fun. They cannot say whether the puppet operator was making a mistake or not. They might comment on the music and the words in the recording because they are recognizable from their own lives, but not on the puppets except where they are rejected totally on cultural grounds. (Kamlongera 1989, p. 227.)

Puppet theatre in Malawi cannot, therefore, be called popular theatre, since it ignores indigenous aesthetics. Its practitioners, of course, do not claim to propagate popular theatre.

The work of the other projects that Kamlongera examines, such as the Chancellor College Travelling Theatre at Mbalachanda, and the Zambian International Theatre Institute, is based on Paulo Freire's (1972) ideas.

Kamlongera says that development and theatre practitioners in Malawi and Zambia have greatly reduced the potential impact of their work among the people by choosing to work within their countries' existing political structures.

> In countries where the masses have been heavily politicised through the efficiency of one-party state systems, like in Malawi and Zambia, any work with the masses must respect the local party hierarchy. This is so even if the government gives approval to work aimed at the masses — as it happened in the Mbalachanda workshop in Malawi. Work carried out amongst the masses enjoys success or failure depending on which side of the party it is. (Kamlongera 1989, p. 240.)

When practitioners have to go through the party in order to carry out their work, they inevitably lose some autonomy. Any attempt to invoke critical awareness among the disadvantaged outside party structures and policy 'may infringe upon a set-up which has its own procedures for doing so' (Kamlongera 1989, p. 240). Theatre-for-development in this context will deal with development as identified by government planners and politicians, rather than by communities themselves through a process of critically analysing their objective situation.

The anomaly of community participation

Another anomaly is that although the practitioners talk of community participation in planning and running popular theatre, 'the theatre genre being talked about does not (as an idea) come from them' (Kamlongera 1989, p. 241). Even though the theatre may use modes borrowed from the people's own modes of performance, such as songs and dances, the process of theatre production as creation is imposed in a benevolent style from outside the community. The community does not decide to use theatre in the first instance, but only participates when outside forces have decided on this particular medium. 'Participation in Freire's terms means total involvement even at the level of conceptualising the vehicle of articulation' (Kamlongera 1989, p. 241). This means that theatre-for-development as practised in the rest of Africa is incompatible with the ideas of Freire, since the educator, according to him, must be a co-worker and not an applier of formulas. Theatre practitioners are now seeking to join the rural communities as co-workers in the process of creating a theatre that will be more relevant, and this process involves:

> marrying what is good from international theatre practice and the people's own indigenous forms and ways of articulating them without necessarily revoking exoticism possible around cither form. Communication is the kingpin of this marriage. (Kamlongera 1989, p. 246.)

The Laedza Batanani experience

Kidd and Byram (1981) have written a case study of Laedza Batanani (loosely translated as 'Community Awakening'), a non-formal education project in Botswana, which also attempted to follow a Freirian model. This project used popular theatre as a medium of encouraging participation, raising community issues, fostering discussion, and promoting collective action.

Laedza Batanani is the most documented of such projects in Africa. It was founded in 1974 in the Bokalaka area of northern Botswana by a community leader and two adult educators. Its basic goal was to find a way of motivating people to participate in development, and hence overcome the problem of indifference to government development efforts in the area. There was an assumption by the initiators of the project that:

> a major constraint on development was people's apathy and indifference; what was needed was a means of 'sparking' people's interest and involvement. This mobilizational, educational and collective action process required a new approach to non-formal education. The

organizers rejected the existing approach of merely providing services and information; they felt this reinforced dependence and individualism rather than encouraging self-reliant collective action. (Kidd and Byram 1981, p. 1.)

This project involved annual tours of the six major villages in the area, in which a team of extension workers and community leaders presented a programme of popular theatre performances and community discussions. Before the tours there were community planning workshops in which traditional leaders, village development committee members, extension workers, and leaders of other community organisations discussed a list of community problems, selected one or two of those they thought were the most important and soluble, and then improvised a short skit to reflect the problems.

Actors' workshops followed, in which a smaller group of extension workers and community leaders created a much more polished performance from the skit, using puppetry, songs and dances. This group toured the villages, where performances were held at the *kgotla* (village meeting place). After the performances, audiences were divided into small groups and each group discussed the problems presented in the performance, and possible solutions to these problems. These discussions were led by the actors. Afterwards the audience reassembled, and each group gave its report. The audience then tried to reach a consensus on the action to be taken.

The next stage was a follow-up action, where extension workers from various departments assisted the community members in the implementation of their resolutions. For instance, if the villagers decided that a particular nutrition problem could be solved by growing more vegetables, agricultural demonstrators ran a number of vegetable gardening courses and issued seeds to families who wanted to set up vegetable gardens.

While Laedza Batanani was meant to be a programme to increase participation of rural villagers, deepen their critical awareness, and mobilise community members for community action, Kidd and Byram have noted in their assessment of the project that these objectives were not attained because of problems of interpretation of such concepts as 'participation', 'critical analysis' and 'action'. Although the villagers participated in performances at the *kgotla* and in the discussions that followed, they had no say in the selection of the campaign issues, and in structuring how they were to be presented for discussion. They did not control the education process, since this was controlled by the more powerful members of the community — the government workers and community leaders. These people made the theatre reflect the views and interests of dominant groups in the society.

Participation as mere performance is no guarantee of progressive change; unless rural villagers control the popular theatre process they may be used as mere mouthpieces of ideas produced by others which mystify their reality and condition them to accept a passive, dependent, uncritical role in an inequitable social structure. (Kidd and Byram 1981, p. 12.)

Participation was not only a method of theatre; it was the goal. This goal was to overcome low participation in development programmes on the part of rural communities by motivating them out of their apathy and indifference through theatre. When apathy and indifference were cited as a constraint on development, they were presented as self-inflicted characteristics of rural villagers; no account was given of why villagers refused to attend development meetings or participate in communal projects. Apathy and indifference simply became an explanatory cause of poverty and under-development, 'rather than being understood as a symptom of, or a response to, an inequitable social structure. In this way the Freirian concept of "culture of silence" is converted into the "blaming the victim" ideology of conventional development work' (Kidd and Byram 1981, p. 16).

Laedza Batanani tried to reach the avowed goal of raising critical consciousness by first finding out the concerns of the community, and then involving the community in workshops and post-performance discussions. In reality, however, the focus was more on technical solutions than on the examination of historical, economic and political factors to explain rural problems. For example, in the performances on sexually transmitted diseases, the plays were limited to the explication of symptoms, causes, cure and prevention, but nothing was said about how the diseases were socially produced. Thus only a partial solution to the problem was presented.

Secondly, problems were not analysed in terms of the different perspectives of different social classes in the community, and the different class interests they represented. Problems were identified and treated in isolation, without analysing their common roots in the political and economic structure. The emphasis was on a technical solution to individual problems rather than on understanding why the problems existed in the first place. The analysis was limited to the village as if it were an autonomous unit independent of larger social structures, thus shifting attention away from what the dominant class in the sub-continent is doing, to what the villagers themselves are doing to create and perpetuate their own poverty.

Kidd and Byram further note that, for Friere, authentic dialogue must lead to action. However, in Laedza Batanani the performances and discussions led to very little action. There was limited follow-up action of a collective nature, and no continuing organisational process. Community action was expected somehow to follow from the heightened interest generated by the performances, an unrealistic view of the power of popular theatre.

The authors conclude that there is a need to reassess popular theatre. A realignment with the original goals would require a shift away from the undifferentiated community approach, in which the more powerful community members dominate, to a genuine popular participation approach involving the most oppressed sectors of the community, and assuring participant control over the programme. The prominent role given to popular theatre in non-formal education must be de-emphasised, and more attention paid to a sustained progamme of group organisation, education and action. And, finally, 'a critical assessment of the social and political context and a more strategic sense of the possibilities and constraints of change' is required (Kidd and Byram 1981, p. 27).

The concerns that Kidd and Byram articulate in their study are valid. Many theatre-for-development projects in Africa, including the Marotholi Travelling Theatre, whose work is examined in greater detail in this study, have shifted from the original goals of genuine community participation, critical awareness, and collective action. When only lip service is paid to community participation, and all the programme planning is done by community leaders and extension workers, who in many cases are government servants or work for parastatal organisations such as universities, critical awareness will not result. The theatre will examine the issues from the perspective of the dominant classes in society. The poorest sectors in the community, who should be the priority target group in any community development programme, remain passive consumers of the ideas and values of these powerful classes.

Censorship and self-censorship
One major problem that Kidd and Byram do not examine in their study is the role that censorship and self-censorship might have played in the project's failure to achieve its goals. An examination of this nature is incomplete without a discussion of the social and political constraints under which this kind of theatre operates. For instance, to what extent was it possible for community development workers, extension workers and community leaders working within government structures, to encourage a critical analysis that would finally lead to action that in any way deviated from current government policy? Horn (1980) has noted, in his study of censorship in African theatre, that there is great sensitivity on the part of the ruling classes in Africa to theatre that reflects popular social and political attitudes. Governments are rarely distressed by social commentary offered in university theatres, or in playhouses that are patronised by national elites in the cities. But when plays which might agitate the disadvantaged are performed directly to or by the people in the villages and township slums, censorship is swiftly imposed.

An often-cited case is that of Ngugi wa Thiong'o and Nugugi wa Mirii, who were both detained and later exiled from Kenya after creating and producing a play which examined the plight of the peasants and industrial labourers of rural Limuru, as part of the Kamiriithu Community Education and Cultural Centre's adult literacy project. The play was performed by the labourers and peasants themselves. Throughout Africa, however, there have been many instances of censorship, and some of these are documented in Horn's study.

Fear of censure and censorship make it possible for extension workers and theatre practitioners employed by government or parastatal agencies to exercise some self-censorship in the very act of composition. In this case, theatre becomes a medium that merely disseminates information on development programmes. It does not go beyond that.

The crucial problem of form and ideology

In their excellent treatment of popular drama and popular analysis in Africa, Crow and Etherton (1982) focus on the crucial problem of form and ideology. They write that the process of taking theatre to the people began when established plays, developed according to the criteria of the 'well-made play', toured communities. In many cases these plays were not suitable for the audiences, since they dealt with situations far removed from the world of the rural communities. The Makerere University Travelling Theatre, which toured Ugandan villages in the mid-1960s, is given as an example of this. A stage followed when bureaucratically inspired plays, on such themes as family planning, health education and building pit latrines, were performed to rural and urban communities. Some of these plays were sponsored by international agencies, such as UNESCO and the International Planned Parenthood Federation, and governments of all political hues eager to promote their own programmes and implement their social policies through theatre. The objective here was social change.

Another stage — and these did not necessarily happen chronologically — placed its emphasis on the art of the theatre rather than on social change or state propaganda. Drama practitioners and intellectuals held workshops in target communities where community members created plays. These were performed to provide entertainment for the community. Beyond this there was no specific political objective. The Chikwakwa (grass-roots) travelling theatre in Zambia was an example of this, although it eventually moved to touring ready-made productions in rural communities.

In the fourth stage, villagers make plays about their problems. Here the emphasis is on the people's participation in solving community problems. Development and extension workers are used as actors, performers and animators. They research specific problems of the target community before plays are devised. There is therefore contact between performers and potential audiences before plays are performed.

The audiences also complete plays that are deliberately left unfinished, either through lengthy discussion between the theatre activists and audience members who have been divided into several small groups, or by audience members acting out solutions, or both. At this stage, what are known as folk media (story-telling, songs, dance, etc.) are used.

To Paulo Freire, Crow and Etherton add Augusto Boal, another writer who has greatly influenced the development of radical popular theatre. Boal, like Freire, did his work in Latin America. In his book, *Theatre of the Oppressed* (Boal 1979), he carries the meaning of popular theatre in the direction of making the people not just the audiences, but also the actors and creators of the drama. He says that theatre can be utilised by all people, whether they have artistic talent or not. Therefore the means of production of theatre should be transferred to the people so that they can use it.

Popular theatre and the 'well-made' play

Popular theatre, therefore, indicates a wide, contradictory range of theatrical activities and different types of drama. Crow and Etherton's own definition is that it is a theatre

> through which intellectuals try to communicate with the people most disadvantaged in their society, either by presenting plays to them in which problems of society are articulated from the point of view of the people, or by getting them to present plays to themselves which increasingly help them to analyze their society. (Crow and Etherton 1982, p. 574.)

The term 'intellectual', as used here, signifies educated persons actively working for social change.

The weakness that the authors see in the 'well-made' play is that spectators become passive consumers of a finished product. On the other hand there are problems in abandoning 'well-made' plays as part of an effort to demystify the art of the theatre, and to get those interested confident enough to involve themselves in acting through improvisation. Abandoning an established form forces one to substitute a new form. The experience of the authors is that people in rural African communities, with no previous experience of contemporary theatre and little formal artistic education, who are interested in using drama, need more than anything else the skills of drama. According to the authors, these skills can be attained through the 'established form' of what they call the 'well-made' play.

Limitations of propagandist theatre

State-run and propagandist theatre has the limitation of naïveté in assessing problems of social development, and advocates short-term solutions within the context of political pragmatism. This is similar to the short-term technical solution problem observed by Kidd and Byram (1981) in the work of Laedza Batanani. International funding agencies such as UNESCO also tend to act as agents of the government in the countries where they operate, rather than of the people whose suffering the funding is supposed to alleviate. Such programmes tend to concentrate on those problems that can be solved locally, and leave aside the structural causes of these problems. This kind of theatre is unable to awaken consciousness concerning wider problems.

> Indeed, this sort of 'conscientization' of the masses is seen even by socialist governments as a rival to its own programmes and perspectives. It might not be allowed to function beyond its self-imposed local limitations; and even then the dramatic skills and techniques may as well be used for reactionary and ultimately repressive policies. (Crow and Etherton 1982, p. 577.)

Efficacy of drama in raising consciousness

Drama can raise consciousness because it is a mode of communication that has a life of its own, argue the authors. As a form of skilfully contrived escapism it allows the audience to take collective imaginative refuge in a more pleasurable realm of existence than their everyday one. It engages them in a dramatic fiction that has a connection to their everyday reality.

The potency of drama as communication in the context of rural development lies in the fact that adult educators and community development workers are able to explain the benefits of social phenomena outside the peasants' own experience. The authors give an example of a literacy programme where drama can depict the advantages of literacy. They write that the peasants' collective imagination can be focused on the possibility of a better life based on literacy skills, which in turn would infuse them with the desire to be literate. A more desirable reality is enacted, and the strategies for achieving it explored. Such a play might emanate from discussion with the community, or from observing their lives.

The role of catalysts

Catalysts — a term the authors use to signify those outsiders with specialist skills in theatre and in community development who work as organised groups in communities — must have a higher level of social consciousness than the villagers, based on their education and general social experience. An adventurous catalyst group may use elements of Boal's 'rehearsal

theatre' (Boal 1979, pp. 120–55). This is designed to transform the spectators into actors by having them complete plays deliberately left unfinished by the performers.

A truly popular theatre is one where people initiate and develop theatrical explorations of their problems and so engage in a continuous process of self-education. Catalysts should increasingly involve the spectators both in creating and performing the play, until such time as the catalyst is no longer necessary, since the spectators have themselves become actors. To reach this ideal, a catalyst group should not only be able to raise the consciousness of its target audience, but also to impart theatre skills, and an understanding of the relation between drama and problem-exploration. The community members would then be able to initiate and sustain dramatic activity in their communities. For catalysts to do this, they must have a higher level of critical awareness in terms of political and social issues. They must be critically vigilant of their own ideological proclivities, and must be prepared to test them against experience. The individual members of the catalyst group each have their personal ideology, and if they are all from a similar social and educational background, their personal ideologies will to some extent coincide. The inevitable temptation will be for them to believe that raising the consciousness of the disadvantaged is the same as getting people to see things from the perspective of their (catalysts') common, 'correct', ideology.

> Clearly, the catalyst group's unconscious or uncritical commitment to an ideology militates against the development of open-ended, collaborative forms of community drama. (This would still be the case even if the ideology were 'correct'.) It hinders the group from being receptive to the views expressed by members of the target audience; and while their own shared beliefs and prejudices remain unconscious or uncritically accepted they are unlikely to be able to articulate dramatically the full extent and implications of a social contradiction. (Crow and Etherton 1982, p. 585.)

In the authors' experience this leads to the catalysts tending either to be inhibited by their ideological proclivities and therefore say less in their plays than they are capable of, or consciously to tailor their statements to fit their ideology. The authors emphasise that there cannot be any prescriptive solution to this problem. However, for catalyst groups to bring and keep their own consciousness at an adequate level they must actively involve themselves in the practical lives of their target audiences by living with the target communities over a period of time. They must participate in the villagers' social and economic lives, not just as detached, albeit sympathetic, observers of their daily lives and problems. They will then be able to embody

in a dramatic form ideological conflicts and the circumstances from which they have arisen.

Practical problems of devising plays

The authors state that there are practical problems in devising, through improvisation, the basic working outline or scenario of a play. In most cases catalysts are adult educators and community development officers without any professional skills or expertise as actors and writers, who have nonetheless discovered the potency of drama as a medium of communication. There is the problem of educating these educators at a technical theatrical level. Seeking assistance from theatre professionals, who are likely not to have a thorough understanding of the theatrical and practical problems involved in popular theatre, may be counter-productive. Theatre professionals are likely to impart skills associated with the creation of conventional, 'well-made' plays, rather than the formally open plays that are effective in involving audiences, and in developing their consciousness. These professionals will also be subject to the social, ideological and formal problems specific to this kind of project.

Problems in operating within communities

The authors further state that although the catalyst group can function effectively only if they experience some of a community's problems at first hand by participating in the social and economic lives of the target audience, there are difficulties in achieving this. The first is that it is not easy for a group of outsiders to insert themselves into a community that is likely to be close-knit. Another might arise from the question of whose auspices the catalyst group works under, to which the answer is likely to be a government agency or a parastatal body such as a university. There might well be ideological opposition to a venture of this nature from government officials and other decision-makers in the country. In countries which merely pay lip-service to the idea of improving rural conditions, the idea of an ideologically committed catalyst group living and working at length with a community may not be acceptable. In countries where there is strong class conflict between the peasantry and proletariat on one hand, and the middle class bureaucracy on the other, the catalyst group may find itself embroiled in class warfare — a situation which will be dangerous for them.

Finally, to illustrate the need for the prolonged participation of catalysts in the lives of the target community, in order to bring about a higher level of consciousness, the authors conclude their study by analysing the process of playmaking. They illustrate, by way of example, how one play can lead to another, the first crystallising social problems and inspiring a new one to be written incorporating social contradictions manifested by and in the first. In this way drama becomes a continuous process of consciousness-raising for both the target audience and the catalyst group. Effective popular theatre can only be achieved when the community itself assumes the function of catalysts. When that happens, theatre will have been socialised enough for it to be generally available as a method of self-education for the community.

Theatre, drama and the 'well-made' play

A number of the theoretical positions taken by Crow and Etherton will be addressed in this book, against the background of the Lesotho experience of theatre-for-development. But there are some points that need to be considered before other relevant literature can be discussed. The first is that the authors tend to use the terms 'theatre' and 'drama' interchangeably. It will therefore be necessary to define these terms in order to show why this study prefers the term 'theatre' to 'drama'. The second point is that Crow and Etherton correctly stress the need to demystify the art of acting and to get interested community members involved in performing plays. However, the authors think, incorrectly, that theatre skills can be acquired only through what they call the 'well-made' play, a work scripted in accordance with the conventions of drama. Experience has shown, as will be illustrated in this study, that the skills of acting can be learnt through improvisation. Indeed the narrative itself can be structured through improvisation. People need to learn the skills in order to create theatre on their own in their communities when the professionals have returned to base, so as to have a continuous community dialogue through theatre, but the path to this goal is not through scripted plays.

Follow-up action

Kidd and Byram (1981) have illustrated the need for a follow-up action, where solutions reached through the theatrical dialogue are actually implemented. This does not seem to play a role in Crow and Etherton's process of conscientisation. Although they explicate with clarity the process of transforming spectators into dramatic actors, it is not clear how they will then be transformed into social actors. Without a follow-up action theatre becomes an end in itself.

A brief assessment

What clearly emerges in the literature surveyed in this chapter is that theatre practitioners and adult educators utilise theatre with the objective of fulfilling the following functions:

- Development communication;
- motivating communities into initiating and/or participating in developmental activities;

- raising critical awareness/consciousness.

As a medium of development communication, theatre should not be used merely as a tool for disseminating developmental messages — a channel in the communication process — but as a medium for subjecting policies and programmes formulated by government planners to a critique. However, since in many cases it operates within government structures, it is unable to attain this goal. As a vehicle for motivating communities into initiating and participating in developmental activities, it would have impact only if the root cause of a people's 'apathy' is critically examined, not just within the confines of local structures, but in terms of wider historical, social, political and economic forces at play at national and, sometimes, international level. Apathy should not be presented as 'a self-inflicted characteristic of rural villagers' (Kidd and Byram 1981, p. 16), but as a consequence of years of oppression by the colonialist, and later by the neo-colonialist, classes in post-independence Africa. For theatre to act as a vehicle for raising critical awareness, or conscientisation, the target communities should be active participants not only in the performance of the plays, but in the actual planning of the programme, the selection of the content, and, Kamlongera (1989) goes further to say, even in the choice of the medium of articulation. The follow-up stage is crucial, for without it the performance and the community dialogue emanating from it become an end in themselves. Knowledge, by itself, does not necessarily lead to change.

Restated, what all this means is that theatre-for-development must, first and foremost, help people to identify the sources of poverty and underdevelopment, and, secondly, explore ways and means of how such causes may be eradicated. Follow-up action should be the actual application of strategies to eradicate such causes. Theatre should stimulate a continuing dialogue towards solving the problems of the community.

A question yet to be resolved pertains to the practicability and cost-effectiveness of theatre-for-development, particularly in its conscientising function rather than in its role as a medium merely for disseminating developmental messages. It is clear that for theatre to be effective in raising critical awareness, the catalysts must live with the target communities for some time. Catalysts, as has already been stated, are outsiders with specialist skills in theatre and in community development, who work in organised groups in communities. In practice, they are extension workers and theatre practitioners employed by such governmental agencies as the Ministries of Agriculture and Health, or non-governmental and parastatal organisations such as universities, and it is not possible to send catalysts into each rural community for a long time, to enable them to participate fully in the life of the community. This means that in any one year catalysts would be able to conscientise only a few pilot villages, and the greater part of the country would remain neglected. In a country like Lesotho, the vast majority of the most disadvantaged people live in small villages spread throughout the mountain areas. It would be neither practicable nor cost-effective to have catalysts in all these areas, and therefore the vast majority of the rural population will remain unconscientised through this medium. This is the majority currently neglected by national development programmes, which are concentrated in urban areas and in those rural areas easily accessible to government officials. This aspect necessitates a study of the cost-effectiveness of theatre-for-development in comparison with other media, but it is not within the scope of this book to examine this issue.

Crow and Etherton (1982) talk of the potency of drama as *communication*, and Kamlongera (1989) writes that '*communication* is the kingpin' of a marriage between what is good from international theatre practice and people's own indigenous forms. These writers acknowledge the communicative aspects of theatre, but none of them, and no other writers in this field, examines how popular theatre, or theatre-for-development, functions as communication.

Development communication models

Many orthodoxies in the history of mass communication theory have been either discarded or modified, but continue to bear relevance in today's debates, particularly in development communication studies. The earliest of such orthodoxies is the Lasswell Formula (formulated by American political scientist Harold D. Lasswell in 1948), which can be transformed into the basic model shown in Figure 2.1.

Figure 2.1
The Lasswell Formula

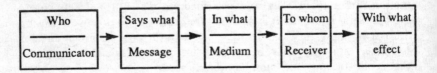

Because of its simplicity, this formula continues to be used to give structure to discussions on communication. Each element of the formula is used to represent a distinct type of communication research: who — control studies; says what — content analysis; in which channel — media analysis; to whom — audience analysis; with what effect — effect analysis. Its weakness lies in that it takes for granted that the communicator intends to influence the receiver, and that the message will always have an effect on the receiver. It takes communication as being a predominantly persuasive process. When the model was formulated, the consensus was that mass media exercised a powerful and persuasive influence on audiences. This is referred to as the 'bullet theory' since it assumed that the audiences were passive victims and easily penetrated by messages from the media.

> Underlying this consensus was (1) the creation of mass audiences on a scale that was unprecedented through the application of new technology — the rotary press, film and radio — to the mass production of communication; (2) a fashionable though not unchallenged view, that urbanization and industrialization had created a society that was volatile, unstable, rootless, alienated and inherently susceptible to manipulation; (3) linked to a view of urbanized man as being relatively defenceless, an easy prey to mass communication since he was no longer anchored in the network of social relations and stable, inherited values that characterized settled, rural communities; (4) anecdotal but seemingly persuasive evidence that the mass media had brainwashed people during World War 1, and engineered the rise of fascism in Europe between the wars. (Curran *et al*, 1982, p. 11.)

According to the model, then, the media have great impact, and, through modern scientific techniques, the extent, depth and size, of penetration can be measured. The premises of this model are based on industrialised and technological Western countries, where the majority no longer lives in rural areas. It will be noted that the 'most powerful effects' orthodoxy is currently adhered to by African governments and their development planners. In spite of the fact that African societies are still 'anchored in the network of social relations and stable, inherited values that characterise settled, rural communities', communication planners in Lesotho, for example, continue to transmit messages through the radio to widely dispersed rural villages in the hope that the messages will have impact. There is usually very little or no feedback.

Figure 2.2
The Shannon-Weaver linear one-way model (1949)

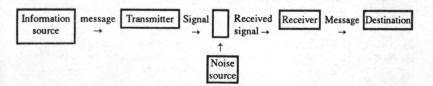

Kasoma (1983), writing on participatory communication and development, discusses the concept of one-way communication and attempts to show how this model has influenced most government development planning in developing countries. A one-way communication system is represented by the Shannon–Weaver model (Figure 2.2). The model accounts for a top-down, one-way communication process, where development planners send messages to villages, usually through a mass medium such as radio. There is no way that the sender of the message can get immediate feedback from the villager. No attempt is made to involve the villagers by consulting them before the plans are formulated. Such plans

Figure 2.3
The MacLean–Westley Model

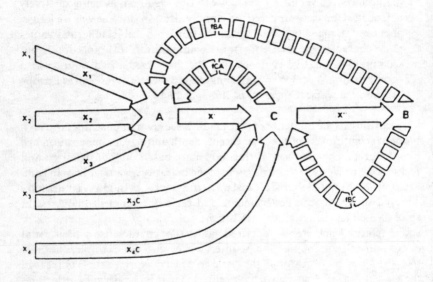

(Source: McQuail and Windahl, 1981)

Note: In mass communication A is described as an 'advocate' and refers to the position of individuals or organisations which have something to say about X's to the public as a whole. They might be politicians or advertisers, or news sources. The assumption built into the term 'advocate' is that A's are purposive communicators. C is the media organisation or the individual within it, who selects among the A's for access to the channel reaching the audience, according to criteria of perceived relevance to audience interests and needs. They may also select among the X's for communicating to B. An implied aspect of the C role is that it serves as an agent of the needs of B, as well as for A. Essentially this role is non-purposive, there is no communicative purpose except to satisfy the needs of B. (See McQuail and Windahl 1981, p. 26.)

carry a high risk of failure since they do not take into account how the people's needs can be assessed, how best development messages can be disseminated, and how the people's views can be gauged. The planner functions under the presumption that his messages do reach the target audience, and do have powerful effects.

Effective communication bridges the gap between planner and rural community. The effectiveness of communication, however, lies not only in the dissemination of developmental messages from the government to the people, but in the people's involvement in assessing and prioritising their needs. In participatory communication there is an exchange of information between the parties concerned so that they understand one another's point of view. Kasoma finds the Maclean–Westley model (Figure 2.3) most illustrative of a two-way communication system. Developmental messages are sent to the people from the government A; the medium used is the extension officer C, who processes the information and passes it to the people at B. The people react to the message, and there is feedback at fBA, fBC and fCA. fBA is direct feedback from the people to the government, and it can happen only if the people have direct access to government institutions which formulate development policy. In fBC people express their views to the extension workers, and in fCA the extension worker reports the people's views to the government. X stands for development issues about which communication takes place, and X' is the choice made by the communicator on the issues to be transmitted. X" is the message as modified to suit the audience, and transmitted to them. X_3C and X_4C are observations about developmental issues made directly by the extension worker.

Kasoma notes that the Maclean–Westley model is idealistic because it does not explain what happens in real life. Villagers do not normally have direct access to government ministries, which are usually located in the capital city or in district headquarters. Government ministers and senior government officials rarely go out to the villages; when they do, they go to address public meetings which themselves lack feedback. However, Kasoma's adaptation of this model has more problems than the one he has pointed out.

The Maclean–Westley model was developed in 1957 with the intention of providing a systematic treatment most appropriate for mass communication research. It is basically a conceptual model of mass communication, in which the possibilities for feedback are minimised or delayed.

Kasoma's adaptation explains an interpersonal communication relationship, in which there is immediate feedback, since C is not a media organisation but an individual who serves as an agent for A to meet the needs of B. Except for responding to messages from A, there are no messages that originate from B. This then becomes the typical situation in today's development communication, where outside planners formulate development programmes and impose them on rural communities. Contrary to what Kasoma says, this model does not represent ideal participatory communication. In participatory communication, rural communities create their own messages, based on their own needs, which are best known to them, and these are transmitted to the government and to other developmental agencies. This means that the rural communities not only send messages in the form of feedback, but also initiate the process of communication.

The model in its original function attempts to explain a system of relationship which is mutually beneficial to senders and receivers, and balances their interests. The assumption is that the relationship is only a communicative one. In practice, however, the relationship is also political between A and C, and therefore between C and B. A may have power over C, and C nearly always depends on A for information, without which he may not operate. Kasoma's adaptation suffers from the same problems as the original model, since it assumes that the relationship among the three main participants is balanced and mutually beneficial. The extension worker, however, is an employee of the government, and is dependent on it. The government has political power over him, and over the target audience, and the monopoly to create messages and disseminate them through the agency of the extension worker. These messages may or may not be beneficial to the target audience.

From a one-step model to multi-step model
The use of models generally designed for highly technological and urbanised societies is problematic in explaining communication processes in rural societies in the developing world. Indeed, some of these models are no longer adequate to explain communication processes in the society in which they were formulated. From the orthodoxies of 'the bullet theory' (sometimes referred to as the 'hypodermic needle model'), essentially a one-step flow model postulating that the mass media have direct, immediate and powerful effects on a passive audience, the paradigms on the power of the media have shifted. A reassessment of impact studies led to a new orthodoxy of limited effects. This entailed selective exposure, selective perception, and selective retention. Selective exposure is the tendency of individual members of the audience to attend to communication messages that are consistent with their existing attitudes and beliefs. Selective perception is the tendency to interpret communication messages in terms of one's existing attitude and beliefs, and selective retention is the tendency to remember messages that are consistent with one's existing attitudes and beliefs (see Klapper 1960). The limited effects model was reinforced by uses and gratification studies which argued that audiences were active rather

than passive. But some scholars (McLeod and Becker 1974) felt that the limited effects model, by making the audience member so active and selective that any effect could be obtained from any message, came close to substituting the fable of the omniscient audience for the myth of the omnipotent media.

The uses and gratification research tradition was a reaction to the simplicity of the hypodermic model and its overstatement of media effects. Research into the effects of mass communication had neglected the role of audience motivation in the effects process. The uses and gratification model suggests that the individual uses of media content act as an intervening variable — mitigating or enhancing the effects of a message. The presumption of media power had been based on the mass society thesis. The conclusion about the lack of media influence was a repudiation of this thesis.

> The view of society as being composed of isolated and anomic individuals gave way to a view of society as a honeycomb of small groups bound by a rich web of personal ties and dependences. Stable group pressure, it was concluded, helped to shield the individual from media influence. (Curran *et al*, 1982, p. 12.)

The *one-step flow* model was a refinement of the hypodermic needle model, and stated that mass media channels communicate directly to the mass audience, but do not reach the audience equally, nor do they have the same impact on each of them. According to Rogers (1973), the one-step model recognises that the media are not all-powerful. The screening aspects of selective exposure, perception and retention affect media impact, and differing effects occur for various members of the receiving audience.

The *two-step flow* model was, on the other hand, a decisive discarding of the hypodermic needle model, for it introduced the role of interpersonal communication in mass media, through the concept of opinion leaders. It involves the assumption that individuals are not social isolates, but members of social groups in interaction with other people. These social relationships mediated the audiences' response and reaction to media messages. Messages are transferred in the first instance from the media to opinion leaders. This step is merely a transfer of information. From opinion leaders messages are transferred to their followers who are fellow-members of the society. This step involves not only the transfer of information, but the spread of influence as well. Figure 2.4 shows how the two-step flow model compares with the one-step flow model (Katz and Lazarsfeld, 1955).

Although the two-step flow model is an improvement on the one-step flow model, it still postulates a passive audience, for it implies that the only individuals active in seeking information were opinion leaders. A more

Figure 2.4
The one-step flow model and the two-step flow model

One-step flow model

Two-step flow model

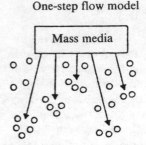

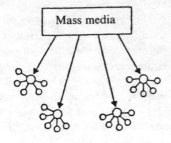

    o Isolated individuals
       constituting a mass

O = Opinion leader

⭗ Individuals in social
    contact with an opinion
    leader

(Source: McQuail and Windahl, 1981.)

accurate reflection of reality is that some individuals can be followers on some subjects and leaders on others. Indeed the term 'opinion leader' as used here is misleading, since it does not identify those who originate ideas. The model does not take into account those who neither attend to mass media nor discuss the messages with those who do. This is a third category of non-participants; those who are not leaders are not necessarily followers.

The model does not consider the possibility of direct influence from the media to the individual without passing through opinion leaders, nor does it consider that change may occur in several stages, as later indicated by the multi-step flow model, which is based on a sequential relaying function without specifying the number of steps nor that the message must emanate from a source via mass media channels. A criticism of the two-step model is that the model is appropriate only to a developed world situation. In less technological and less urbanised countries opinion leaders may obtain messages from channels other than mass media. Community leaders in villages where very few mass media are available depend for their information mostly on interpersonal channels, such as conversations with extension workers, personal visits to the towns, and attending public meetings. In these circumstances there is a longer relay of contact for passing information and influence from one person to another.

The diffusion of innovations paradigm

A paradigm that has had the most influence in a great deal of development communication planning is that of *diffusion of innovations*, and this is technologically based. Indeed the exponents of this paradigm define development communication as the study of how to apply various kinds of communication technology and techniques to different social problems in developing countries (McAnary 1980, p. xii). This definition illustrates the reliance on technological solutions in the attempt to reach and improve the lot of the rural poor. In this paradigm there is an interaction of interpersonal and mass communication in the process of encouraging the adoption of innovations — new ideas and practices such as farming methods that will increase productivity, or certain health practices that can reduce illness.

According to McQuail and Windahl (1981), the target for most efforts in innovation diffusion have been farmers and members of rural populations. These are now a feature of most programmes for development in Third World countries, and relate not only to the diffusion of agriculture and health innovations, but to issues that concern social and political life. Emphasis is given here to non-media sources (neighbours, extension workers, etc.), and the existence of a campaign in which behavioural changes are sought by giving information and trying to influence motivations and attitudes.

Rogers and Shoemaker (1973) have summarised a large amount of empirical research on diffusion, and what emerges from their work is that this model is much tested in many situations in the Third World. The model, illustrated in Figure 2.5, is based on the assumption that there are four distinct steps in the innovation diffusion process:

- Knowledge: the individual gains an awareness of the existence of an innovation, and how it functions.
- Persuasion: the individual forms a favourable or unfavourable attitude towards the innovation.
- Decision: the individual engages in activities that lead to a choice whether to adopt or reject the innovation.
- Confirmation: the individual seeks reinforcement about the innovation decision. He may reverse his decision if exposed to conflicting messages about the innovation.

Analysing this model, McQuail and Windahl (1981) say that it distinguishes the three main stages of the whole event into antecedents, process and consequence. *Antecedents* refer to those circumstances of the event, or characteristics of the people involved, which make it more or less likely that an individual will either be exposed to information about an innovation or will experience needs to which the information is relevant.

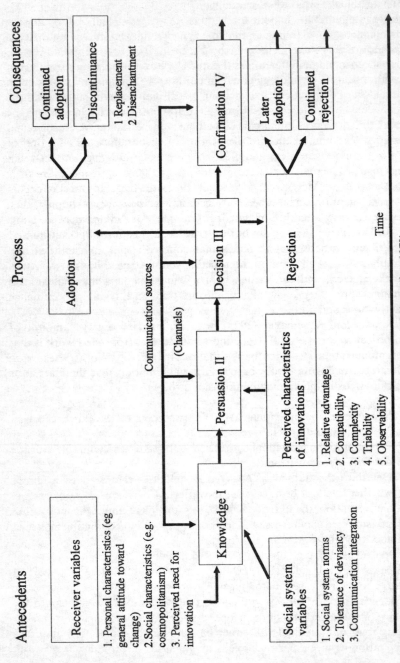

Figure 2.5: Paradigm of the innovation-diffusion process. (Rogers and Shoemaker, 1973)

The *process* involves learning, attitude change and decision. The *consequences* stage refers to the later history of use or disuse, if adoption takes place at all. Diffusion of innovation will normally involve different communication channels. Mass media channels are primarily knowledge creators, while the interpersonal channels feature more in persuading the individual to form or change his or her attitude. McQuail and Windahl's criticism of this model is that it is too prescriptive in many respects, since it involves a number of assumptions about an ideal way of proceeding which may not fit in with the actual conditions. One of the two authors of this model has himself described the outmodedness of the paradigm (Rogers 1976), and his criticism is consistent with McQuail and Windahl's. The major criticism is that the model is designed from the perspective of an external or superior agent of change who, on technical grounds, decides what is beneficial to the target audience, and proceeds to use his resources to promote it. The change does not occur from below, originated by those who need it, but is imposed upon them by outside forces who have already determined what kind of change it should be. The process then becomes a manipulative one. The model does not allow for the randomness of real-life decision-making situations. It is possible for an innovation to be adopted with little knowledge, or for prestige, or in imitation of others. Finally, the model lacks the necessary feedback loops from later to earlier steps, and so becomes a one-way channel.

We shall see that the diffusionist model is dominant in development communication in Lesotho, and that a lot of theatre-for-development created there today follows this paradigm. Innovations being diffused originate from highly technological Western countries, and in many cases are not only inappropriate for conditions in Third World countries, but reinforce dependency, and therefore perpetuate underdevelopment.

The Marxist critical tradition and the liberal–pluralist view

The Marxist critical tradition is gaining an increasing influence on mass communication research (Curran *et al*, 1982). Its tendency is to dismiss empirical communication research as being disabled in its theoretical approach, since it does not take into account that the media are ideological agencies that play a central role in maintaining class domination. In Gurevitch *et al* (1982) the division and opposition between the empiricist (referred to as liberal–pluralist) and Marxist views of the media are drawn as follows:

Marxist
1. Capitalist society is one of class domination.
2. Various class views are fought in the media within the context of domination by certain classes.

3. Ultimate media control is concentrated in monopoly capital.
4. Autonomy of media professionals is illusory since they are socialised into the norms of the dominant classes, and have internalised them.
5. The media therefore relay interpretive frameworks consonant with the interests of the dominant classes.
6. While media audiences may negotiate and contest these frameworks, they lack access to alternative meaning systems and are therefore unable to reject definitions offered by the media in favour of oppositional definitions.

Liberal–pluralist
1. Society is a complex of competing groups and interests, none of which are predominant all of the time.
2. Media organisations are bounded organisational systems enjoying autonomy from state, political parties and interest groups.
3. Media control is in the hands of an autonomous managerial elite who have given flexibility and independence to media professionals.
4. The relationship between media institutions and their audiences is entered into voluntarily on equal terms.
5. Audiences are able to manipulate media in a variety of ways to suit their own needs and dispositions.

The distinctions between liberal–pluralist and Marxist approaches are often conceived of as distinctions between empiricism and theory. The exclusively theoretical Marxist critical perspective is that mass media are powerful agencies. The analysis is that of social and political structures, rather than an empirical examination of the presence or absence of effects on individuals. Classical empirical research on the other hand has through the years shifted from the 'most-powerful' effects bullet theories to a view of the mass media as having only limited influence.

However, according to Curran *et al* (1982), the two positions are not as irreconcilable as they may appear. The classical empirical studies, they say, did not demonstrate that the mass media had very little influence, but rather revealed the central role of the media in consolidating and reinforcing the values and attitudes of audience members. Marxists have also argued that the mass media play a crucial role in reinforcing dominant social norms and values that legitimise the social system. There is therefore no inconsistency in the two approaches.

The alleged dichotomy between the 'grand-theoretical' and the 'atheoretical' approaches to media study represented by the two opposed traditions of Marxism and liberalism is also a little misleading. The liberal tradition in mass communication research has been characterized by a greater attention to empirical investigation. But it does not constitute an 'atheoretical' approach: on the contrary, empirical communications research is based upon theoretical models of society even if these are often unexamined and unstated. (Curran *et al*, 1982, p. 15.)

From these debates it can be observed that a consensus must exist between the two traditions that mass media are powerful agencies in reinforcing dominant social norms and values. However, the dichotomy continues to exist in other areas. For instance, the liberal–pluralist view is that media structures (in the capitalist world) are autonomous from the state, political parties and interest groups, whereas Marxists argue that the autonomy is illusory since media control is concentrated in monopoly capital, and therefore serves the interests of the dominant class in society. Debates within Marxism have consistently revolved around the problems associated with economic determinism. The media are locked into the power structure, and consequently act largely in tandem with the dominant institutions in society. The media thus 'reproduce the view points of dominant institutions not as one among a number of alternative perspectives, but as the central and "obvious" or "natural" perspective' (Curran *et al*, 1982).

Liberal–pluralist influences on development communication
Development communication practice in most of the Third World, and in Lesotho in particular, is informed by and draws from the work of the liberal–pluralist tradition. However, it is interesting to note that Western researchers and development experts who do their work in Third World countries continue to believe that the mass media will play an important role in national development, not only in the dissemination of information, but by having powerful effects on attitude change. This is in spite of an established view in the liberal–pluralist tradition of the developed world that the media performs a mainly reinforcing role with respect to attitude.

Although the orthodoxy that mass media have powerful effects on attitude and behavioural change has shifted, and has been replaced by a limited effects paradigm in the Western world, communication programmes are planned and conducted as though mass media messages will have such great impact that attitudes and behaviour of rural communities will suddenly change. Messages flow from broadcasting stations in capital cities to villages in the periphery. Communication flows in a single direction and feedback is limited. The content of the programmes is decided centrally, based on the opinions of the development communication experts as to what rural communities need and want to know. In these cases the emphasis is on telling and teaching rather than the centre and outlying areas exchanging ideas (Berrigan 1979). The stress is on finding ways to stimulate, induce, or even coerce villagers to change their attitudes and behaviour, and to pattern these along the lines of the behaviour of industrialised Western nations (Felstehausen 1973). This application of mass media for develop-ment in underdeveloped countries is based on assumptions, as has already been argued, that are rooted in a conception of social change founded on the experiences of the Western industrialised countries. These assumptions have, however, been reformulated over the past two decades, and according to Shore (1980), current thinking is that communication is not a simple independent variable, but is in fact both a dependent and independent variable in a complex set of relationships with social, economic, and political structures and processes.

Communication is an auxiliary variable subject to the constraints of the rest of the social system. This does not necessarily negate the importance of change at the individual level, nor the importance of information in achieving it, but rather places it within a larger context of social structures, some of which are restrictive to change at the individual level. The question is not only that of defining what communication can accomplish under present restrictive conditions, but also the need to discover how communication can be used to change these conditions (Shore 1980, p. 21). This is a shift away from the idea that the locus for change is within the individual, and the problems of underdevelopment lie with the villager who is ignorant and traditional; it rather locates the reasons for failed development within the larger political and economic structures of the particular country. This reformulation takes into account the external and internal structures of domination, and the structural constraints on the potential of information.

Current emphasis in development communication

The current emphasis in development communication is not only on access to communication media, but participation in media programming. The assumption is that participation in media production leads to participation in community development. This is a shift from the marketing approach, known as 'persuasive communications', to a participatory approach. Whereas in persuasive communication mass media are used to beam messages or directives encouraging people to support development projects, and to highlight benefits that may follow from these projects, in participatory communication the message can emanate from any point, and be added to, questioned, responded to, from any other point. The needs of rural communities are thereby taken into account, since the communities can initiate the process of communication, and do not merely consume and respond to messages that come from 'above'. Some African governments do recognise the need for a participatory process, although the means for achieving it remain elusive. In his keynote address at a national development seminar, the Lesotho Minister of Agriculture, Cooperatives and Marketing said:

> It is against the background of mutual trust and respect that I appeal to everyone to make a constructive contribution in identifying appropriate practical approaches that the Ministry should adopt in implementing its declared national policy of attaining food self-sufficiency and self-reliance in development. If development activities are *initiated and conceived by the people they are more likely to correspond to their needs and desires*. They are founded primarily on self-help, on manpower and resources from within the community. Such a community can be transformed into a self-developing organism with impressive capacities, pulling itself forward across a very broad front. (Phororo 1988, p. 4.) [emphasis mine]

Elsewhere in the same paper the minister says:

> Control and real *participation* of local communities in their development is a precondition of success. Most of our agricultural projects rarely involve farmer participation in design, hence a high rate of failure. (Phororo 1988, p. 6.)

It is explicit government policy in Lesotho that communities should participate in the very planning of their own development. But an examination of the communication structures in the country will show that they do not reflect the situation outlined by the minister. The radio is the major medium of development communication, and most villagers have access to it (LDTC 1987). But this access is limited to the reception of messages, and does not extend to the production and distribution of messages. The question now should be to find a way to draw rural communities into participatory communication rather than the purely information-giving or transfer-of-content model currently used. The Marotholi Travelling Theatre recognised this fact when they wrote, 'For communication to be complete and effective it must be two-way instead of a top-down, one-way flow of information. However for communication to be two-way there must be communication among community members themselves' (MIT Report 1987 p.1).

Community members can only produce and distribute messages if there is dialogue within the community itself. They should be able to analyse their objective situation critically, and assess their needs in the context of structural factors that contribute to their underdevelopment. This means that they must have a critical awareness of those factors, hence the search for a model of communication that will not only disseminate messages on development, but will bring about that critical awareness. Like the theatre scholars mentioned earlier in this chapter, development communication scholars such as Berrigan (1979), Hedebro (1982) and Felstehausen (1973) find the ideas of Paulo Freire (1970, 1972 and 1974) particularly useful in analysing a process that leads to critical awareness. As an adult educator, Freire's practice is based on the idea that education is a process of conscientisation in which the community is helped to articulate its problems, then to provide solutions to those problems. This means that education must give people tools by which they can understand and change society. This applies to communication as well. Freire characterises the communication process as transformational, by which he means communication transforms knowledge and ideas, and consequently reality itself. Since knowledge and ideas as concepts influence how people perceive and act upon nature, communication unveils and transforms the social environment (Felstehausen 1973, p. 48). Freire believes that the average rural community member is not an empty vessel into which facts can be poured, but a knowing being. The task of the communicator is to activate the community to express its needs, to formulate solutions, and to organise politically to achieve its goals. Participation therefore becomes an essential element of liberation.

Berrigan (1979) writes that while people can gain information from non-personal sources such as radio, television and the press, research has shown that such information leads only a few to change behaviour. People learn best from interpersonal contact. It is for this reason that development workers, in their search for an appropriate interpersonal communication medium, view theatre as a medium that can have an impact.

> The need for a democratic vehicle to facilitate dialogue at community level gave birth to the use of theatre as an appropriate medium that can be used for both mass and interpersonal communication. (*MTT Report* 1987, p. 1.)

It is debatable if live theatre can be referred to as mass communication. This is treated in Chapter 5. When theatre is canned and broadcast over the radio or television, it becomes a message packaged for mass communication.

The reasons for the belief in the effectiveness of theatre are stated by Kamlongera (1989), when he writes that, as entertainment, theatre is able to hold the attention of many people, and as a dramatic way of presenting problems it makes the audience and the catalysts themselves see these problems in a fresh and critical way. There is discussion during the creation of the play and after the performance, through which people analyse their problems and work out solutions. Kidd and Byram (1981) refer to theatre-for-development as both method and goal. As a method it mediates development messages; as a goal, its very creation involves the community members in a process that is central to active participation in development.

Definition of basic concepts

In this section the following key terms, as used in this study, are defined: development, communication, information, message, feedback, conscientisation, theatre, drama, popular theatre, agitprop, participatory theatre and theatre-for-conscientisation.

Development: Development is usually defined as both a process and a goal in bringing about social change in order to improve the living standards of the people. However, there is no single accepted interpretation of what social change entails, nor is there a generally accepted standard to measure improved living standards. For most governments in Africa, development means economic growth and technological advancement. The stress is on increased economic productivity, and the Gross National Product (GNP) is the most widely accepted measure of the standard of living. This is an inaccurate indicator because it does not take into account the distribution of economic growth within the country. Peasants may increase productivity, and therefore raise the GNP and the per capita income of the country, while they continue to be impoverished and the national elites get wealthier. Commenting on this phenomenon, which views the Western road of social change, explicitly or implicitly, as synonymous with development, Hedebro writes:

> The road to being a highly developed nation goes through free enterprise and private ownership, and the stress is on rapid economic growth via industrialization and urbanization. Very little is said, however, about the distribution of the economic growth. The notion is that all citizens will benefit through some trickle-down mechanisms. Exactly how this is going to happen is not made clear, however. (Hedebro 1982, p. 19.)

Ake is another scholar who comments on the confusion of development with economic growth, and the 'indifference to the causes of economic backwardness which are rooted in the integration of their [African] economy into the Western capitalist system' (Ake 1981, p. 143). Clearly, the Western notion of development prevails in Africa today, and for many African leaders the quest for development has become the same thing as wanting to be like the West. Hence Africa is faced with a situation where citizens aspire to lifestyles typical of the Western middle-class, and this promotes consumerism. A situation of this nature perpetuates the dependency of African nations upon the West.

The notion of technological advancement also perpetuates dependency, because all advanced technology in Africa is imported from the developed world, mostly the West. Transfer of technology does not break the bonds of underdevelopment in the village, which is where the vast majority of the population in all African countries lives, but reinforces and promotes skewed development characterised by a distribution of wealth that favours the national elites at the expense of the rural poor.

The need for an alternative perspective of development was recognised by Marotholi Travelling Theatre.

> We discovered that development should indeed be a process of social transformation. However many cases of social change in the developing world, and in the industrialized part of the world as well, do not lead to a better quality of life. Social change could also be anti-developmental. We therefore searched for an alternative perspective of development and settled for a definition which stressed that through development a society should achieve a greater control of its social, economic and political destiny. This of course means that the individual members of the community should have increased control of their institutions. (*MTT Report* 1987, p. 9.)

This is greatly influenced by the work of Inayatullah (1967), who stressed the need for a perspective that reflects the search for ways of life where the goals are not simply to catch up with cultures that measure standards of living along a few dimensions only. In this perspective the transfer of products, ideas and technology from the West to developing or Third World countries cannot be considered equivalent to legitimate development. The perspective contends that development must imply liberation — a freeing from all forms of domination, from dependence and oppression. Africa should learn to view development as a process of liberation, for, in spite of political independence, dependency relations still exist not only with the former colonial powers, but with the developed world in general. The emphasis should be on three dimensions: self-reliance; participation; equity in distribution. Another scholar who sees development as a process of liberation writes:

> Developmental progress cannot be measured with but one or a few indicators, such as GNP, GNP/capita or degree of industrialisation. Rather, development in this perspective implies a process whereby the overall personalities of the people of the Third World are rehabilitated and strengthened after years of dehumanisation. It is just as much a

development of humankind as it is a development of material living conditions. (Hedebro 1982, p. 103.)

Viewing development as a process of liberation is contradictory to Western notions of development that have been greatly influenced by Rostow's (1960) view of the world, which was in turn rooted in the economics of the 1920s and 1930s. Rostow proposed that there are various stages of development which are brought about by social factors. In the first phase there are traditional economies that have not reached the take-off stage. Power is decentralised, and formal education (in the Western sense) is low since it serves no useful function. As a result literacy is at a low level. There is subsistence agriculture, and no cash economy since there is a reliance on barter. What large cities there are tend to be trade rather than industrial centres. During this phase communication is by word of mouth, and language specificity confines communication to small groups.

It was predicted that radio would be an important medium of communication at the take-off stage. In the next phase there is more reliance on a cash economy, as people start business activity from their own homes. This is known as the transitional economy, characterised by social dislocation and tremendous change in social patterns. Traditional ties of local character disintegrate as nationalism grows. Communication requirements change, and literacy gains in importance, as does general education. There is a change in the approach to economic support, with subsistence agriculture being replaced by more sophisticated means of transporting goods from one place to another. There is a dependence on finished goods created by means other than handicraft; it therefore becomes important to locate production facilities in a centre that is accessible. The demise of subsistence agriculture results in part of the agricultural workforce moving to the cities to seek employment. Further social dislocation is created when more people are willing to work than there are work opportunities. Wages, as a result, are very low, and goods are produced more cheaply.

Since there is limited literacy, communication on the two-step model (opinion leaders receive information from various media and transmit it to other members of the society through interpersonal communication) is deemed essential. Broadcast and print media begin to assume importance, and advertising begins to feature. Growing industrialisation makes it easier to deliver media.

The next phase is that of a mature or developed economy. During this phase the economy is industralised, diversified and socially integrated. There is both heavy and light industry and the country produces most of its needs. The society is highly mobile, and shares common values. Education reaches everyone, and literacy is an essential requirement for social participation. There is even greater urbanisation, and individuals depend on the mass media to survey the world and to participate socially. Media themselves are at national level with national distribution, and are viably supported by advertising. There is, however, individual interaction with the media, so that both print and broadcast media become specialised. This phase witnesses, for example, the rise of the special interest magazine and the death of the general interest magazine.

The West has made a great effort to force Third World nations to develop according to this model, with media geared towards enhancing this process — that is, attempting to utilise communication to accelerate development from 'take-off' through to mature economy. But this has not materialised in many countries. One weakness of the model is that it presumed that capitalist structures would dominate, and there would not be any controlled or mixed economies. The only path to development is assumed to be through capitalism. Another weakness is that development is equated to industrialisation, with the assumption that all basic requirements for industrialisation are available. The major weakness, however, is that the model does not take into account the distribution of wealth in a country, so although growth did take place according to this model in many cases, the wealth was not equitably distributed. As stated before, in many African countries today the national elites are getting wealthier, while the peasants in the villages and the workers in the urban slums get poorer. In these countries a small section of the population is highly 'developed' and enjoys a First World lifestyle and consumption habits, while the vast majority of the population remains impoverished and underdeveloped. Dependency and oppression prevail.

A new perspective reached by Marotholi Travelling Theatre is that development is a process through which a society achieves greater control of its social, economic and political destiny. The process allows the individual members of society to have control of their institutions, which leads to a liberation from all forms of domination and dependency. This is a perspective shared by this study.

Communication and information: Communication has been defined as a situation where messages flow between institutions, people, and media, with or without feedback, whereas 'information' is used mainly to denote the contents of a message (Hedebro 1982, p. 5). This means that through communication, individuals and institutions exchange meaning through a common system of symbols. Communication is therefore social interaction through messages. Fiske writes that all communication involves signs and codes that are transmitted and made available to others, and that transmitting and receiving signs and codes is the practice of social relationships. Signs are 'artefacts or acts that refer to something other than themselves, that is they are signifying constructs' (Fiske 1982, p. 2). Codes, on the other hand, are a system into which signs are organised in a text. Fiske further contends that communication is central to the life of any culture, and without it culture would die. The study of communication therefore involves the study of the culture of which it is an integral part.

A distinction is made between mass and interpersonal communication. In communication, a message is sent to the receiver, who may or may not respond. In mass communication, the channel through which the message is conveyed involves a mechanism that reaches a wide and often non-contiguous audience. Newspapers, radio, television, film and magazines are all mass media channels, able to transmit messages to large and widely dispersed audiences. In these media there tends to be a one-way flow of information. Hedebro notes the following characteristics in the mass media:

• Directed in one way with little or no possibility for the receivers to respond to the senders/media.
• Impersonal: the messages are explicitly formulated to suit a mass of people, not a single one.
• Simultaneous: a large number of people receive a message at the same time.
• Public (Hedebro 1982, p. 4.)

In mass communication the initiative and the ability to transmit messages lies mostly with the sender, whereas in interpersonal communication the individual through whom the message is flowing is the channel, and since communication is unmediated and face-to-face (or mediated if a channel like the telephone is used, but direct and open) it tends to be two-way. A situation where the audiences are not merely recipients and consumers of messages, but can initiate, create and transmit messages to one another is sometimes referred to as *participatory communication*. This happens in an interpersonal communication situation, although there is currently a movement to adapt some of the mass media into participatory communication channels. The dichotomy between mass and interpersonal communication will be discussed further in the context of theatre in Chapter 5.

Development communication: Development communication is the utilisation of the media, both mass and interpersonal, to initiate and advance the process of development. This study takes the position that in the Third World, and in Lesotho in particular, this process should involve not merely the transmission of messages on developmental issues, such as the adoption of better agricultural methods, rural sanitation, and primary health care, to the target audiences — the process should also empower the disadvantaged in the rural areas and the urban slums to have a greater control of their social, political and economic institutions. This in turn will lead to their liberation from all forms of political domination and economic dependency. Development communication cannot but be a political action.

Message: Message is broadly conceived as any form of decoded or interpreted information. It is that which an act of communication is about. It draws its initial shape or purpose from the sender or communicator.

According to Watson and Hill, messages are influenced by the nature of the medium in which the message is sent — by language and gesture; in the case of radio, by the fact that it is exclusively an aural channel; in television, both visual and aural. They further state that the meaningfulness of a message depends, at a basic, instrumental level, on the weight it carries in competition with other messages. It depends equally upon the significance attached to it by receivers.

Messages derive meaning from their context, 'and a crucial part of that context is how other people view and regard the same messages and how our perceptions of those messages are mediated by others' (Watson and Hill 1984, p. 105).

Feedback: Feedback is the regenerative circuit of communication. It can be broadly conceived as the return message transmitted from receiver to sender. It is the response of the receiver to the sender's original message. The distinction between one-way and two-way communication is that the former lacks feedback.

Central to the purpose of feedback is *control*; that is, feedback enables the communicator to adjust his/her message, or response, to that of the sender, and to the context in which the communicative activity takes place. At the interpersonal level feedback is transmitted by voice, expression, gesture, sight, hearing, touch, smell etc. The greater the distance between communicators, the fewer the 'senses' being employed to 'read' and return feedback, the more difficult it is to arrange and control, and the more difficult it is to assess its nature and meaning. (Watson and Hill 1984, p. 71.)

Conscientisation: According to Bryam and Moitse, the development of 'popular theatre' has been strongly influenced by Paulo Freire's concept of conscientisation.

This conscientisation is realised through a process that helps people to identify and understand their problems within the context of a particular social order. Popular theatre provides a means of codifying that social reality. The codification — the theatrical performance — becomes a mirror through which the people can see themselves, their social situation, and the problems they encounter, in a fresh and stimulating way. (Byram and Moitse 1985, p. 81.)

Conscientisation, a methodology of subverting what Freire calls a 'Culture of Silence' through cultural action, is deeply rooted in his philosophy. He advances a formula of dialogue in which teachers and students may collaborate in exploring together new questions, and new alternatives, rather than a situation in which the teacher as 'narrator' encourages a one-way dependence of the student upon the teacher. In a situation where the learner is defined as a passive object, the learner is robbed of the opportunity of becoming creative, and is trapped in a culture of silence, since he is perceived as mute in the face of superior knowledge and power.

The learner is unable to have an authentic voice of his own, since he is a passive receiver of the ideas of others, owing to the fact that teaching and learning are not a shared experience. Conscientisation therefore is a process of dialogue which enables the individual to transform himself in relation to his fellows and to act critically towards himself and society. It is a process of 'learning to perceive social, political, and economic contradictions, and to take action againt the oppressive elements of reality' (Freire 1972, p. 15).

The process of conscientisation, therefore, involves the active participation of the people in transforming themselves by engaging in a dialogue through which they identify their problems, reflect on why the problems exist, and then take action to solve the problems.

Theatre and **drama:** 'Theatre' and 'drama' are often treated interchangeably, although they are two distinct types of dramatic expression. Drama is a literary composition, while theatre is actual performance that may or may not emanate from literary composition. Theatre involves live performance that has action planned to create a coherent and significant dramatic impression. Although a literary composition may constitute the basic element of a theatrical performance, theatre is not primarily a literary art but uses elements of other arts such as song, dance, and mime, in addition to dialogue and spectacle.

It is such an amalgam of other arts that it may include even visual and plastic arts, not only in the technical aspects of the production but in the performance itself. The failure to recognise this distinction is due to the fact that drama is not a self-sustaining literary form, but reaches its full being when it is interpreted into theatre by actors (though a literary form known as 'closet drama' uses some of the same devices associated with drama for non-theatrical purposes). Without actors there is no theatrical performance.

The same can be said of the audience, who can be thought of as a creative part of a theatrical production. Elam recognises the dissimilarity between the textual material produced *in* the theatre (performance text) and *for* the theatre (dramatic text).

> 'Theatre' is taken to refer here to the complex of phenomena associated with the performer–audience transaction: that, with the production and communication of meaning in the performance itself and with the system underlying it. By 'drama', on the other hand, is meant that mode of fiction designed for stage representation and constructed according to particular ('dramatic') conventions. The epithet 'theatrical' then, is limited to what takes place between and among performers and spectators, while the epithet 'dramatic' indicates the network of factors relating to the represented fiction. (Elam 1984, p. 2.)

The two concepts are dissimilar but intimately correlated, and it is not my intention to make absolute differentiations between them. Although it is now common to refer to theatre as drama, for the purpose of this study it is useful to make the distinction because theatre-for-development rarely emanates from works that began their life as literary composition, and the use of the term 'drama' may give an incorrect impression that theatre-for-development relies on scripted works.

Popular theatre: Laedza Batanani (1974) write that popular theatre includes performances of drama, puppetry, singing, and dancing; and that these performances are called popular because they are aimed at the whole community, not just those who are educated. They involve local people as performers, use local languages, are performed free of charge in public places, and deal with local problems and situations with which everyone can identify. But this definition is inadequate since it does not clearly differentiate between, on the one hand, theatre that may be performed by the people in their own languages, but is imported from outside, using forms that are alien to the local culture, and, on the other hand, a theatre that utilises local performance modes. Both these types of theatre can deal with local problems and situations. But not all of them will examine the issues from the perspective of the people, using their aesthetic codes.

Leis (1979) writes that 'popular' means that a work is comprehensible both for the people as a whole and for the individual; it enriches and expands the people's own forms of expression; it adopts and strengthens the point of view of the most progressive section of the people; and it roots itself in tradition and develops this in a positive manner. This study adopts Leis' definition. Kerr (1982) formulates the following determinants on the material mode of popular theatre production:

Literary Theatre	Popular Theatre
Individual author	Collective creation
Script	Improvisation
Structured stage	Arena trouvé
Charged admission	Free performance
Actor's 'magic'	Actor's self-criticism
Audience applause	Audience participation
Post-performance contemplation	Post-performance analysis (and possible action)

It has already been stated that in pre-colonial Africa, art both functioned and communicated. This was an epoch before the commodification of art, and creators of art were not solely artists, but community members who engaged in the creation of artistic products among other activities. There was little, and in some instances no, differentiation between producers and consumers of art. Artistic products were not owned by any particular individual, and were available to all members of the community at no cost. Some of these elements of folk culture survived colonialism and the new order that came with it, and exist today in Africa's rural villages. A great number of them have evolved in various syncretic forms into a popular culture as defined above. The determinants formulated by Kerr illustrate a situation that exists today in popular performance, not an attempt at retrieving and reconstructing pre-colonial modes that have no relevance in present-day Africa. Adopting and enriching the people's own forms of expression is not, as it may be mistakenly thought, the revival of the great African myths and long-forgotten rituals.

It is under this mistaken impression that Griswold (1982) writes that, in its attempts to preserve folkways and wisdom and to 'reinvent culture', the utilisation of popular theatre in development and education is reactionary and conservative rather than revolutionary and progressive. She sees the argument that indigenous cultural vehicles are the most effective carriers of political and social messages as an attempt to look for new content in old forms, and to claim a pre-colonial authenticity that is lost. Theatre-for-development work in Africa illustrates that practitioners of popular theatre do not believe that transformation involves 'excavating the original primordial essence of a society', nor is it a reinvention of a buried pre-colonial national identity.

The work that will be examined in this study will illustrate that rather than retrieving and reconstructing the forms that pre-colonial folk and popular theatre took, popular theatre practitioners and advocates of theatre-for-development use the people's own performance modes as they are practised today. African societies do not live in a cultural vacuum. It is not possible not to have culture, nor is it possible simply to take one culture off and put another on. Culture itself is dynamic, and in its evolution it gathers new concepts in response to prevailing social circumstances. Throughout African villages and cities people have their own modes of performance that are popular. Using popular theatre is therefore not an attempt to look for new content in old forms, but new content in current popular forms, some of which have evolved or have been syncretised from old forms. These cultural vehicles are the most effective carriers of political and social messages simply because they are forms of artistic expression with which the people are most familiar, since they are part of their everyday experience.

Popular theatre or **theatre-for-development?** This study examines theatre-for-development rather than popular theatre. Popular theatre is examined only when it features in the context of theatre-for-development. The dichotomy here is a simple one and lies in the fact that theatre-for-development may not necessarily utilise popular theatre. For instance, Kamlongera (1989) has noted that a government-sponsored project in Malawi uses forms that are alien to people's own modes of artistic expression, such as puppetry. So did Laedza Batanani in Botswana, and a theatre-for-development project which evolved into Marotholi Travelling Theatre in Lesotho. At times, scripted plays are performed to live audience or broadcast over the radio. At others, small-format film and videos are used. All these lack the elements necessary to make popular theatre, such as people's participation in the creation and performance. They are not rooted in tradition, nor do they always enrich and expand the people's own forms of expression. However, in so far as they are modes of theatre whose objective is to disseminate developmental messages, or to conscientise communities about their objective social, political and economic situation, they are modes of theatre-for-development. So not all theatre-for-development is popular theatre, and vice-versa. However, theatre-for-development is most effective when it *is* popular theatre.

A distinction is often made between popular theatre and art theatre. Etherton (1982) writes that art theatre as a category approaches theatre from the side of the artistic product, and focuses on the process of creativity, whereas popular theatre approaches theatre from the side of the audience and focuses on the process of consumption. However, he makes it clear that the categories are not mutually exclusive, although they can be seen to exist primarily in opposition to each other. Theatre-for-development, even that which is not popular theatre, approaches theatre from the side of the audience, and consumption is the major concern. Use of the term 'art theatre', to describe the kind of theatre that is creator-orientated, has complexity in form and criteria for appreciation, and is consumed by the highly educated elites in society, is misleading, for it suggests that popular theatre is lacking in art.

Why should 'art' as in 'art theatre' be used to distinguish between that kind of theatre that is composed in the theatrical codes of national elites, and uses techniques that are appreciated only by them and are beyond the comprehension of the rest of the society, from the theatre that has a broad appeal within the society and is rooted in the community? Popularity does not make a work inartistic. It merely means the artist as an encoder has utilised codes that are shared by the whole of the community. Codes here are systems into which signs are organised in a text (the text being the performance from which meaning is read). These systems are governed by rules consented to by all members of the community using that code.

Art is found not only in the plush theatres of the urban Third World and metropolitan countries. It is found in the black ghettos of South Africa, where a popular theatre of resistance is performed, and in the villages of Zambia where the Chewa perform the Nyau dance to celebrate rites of passages. It is found in the SISTREN theatre of Jamaica, where working class women use art to explore the mechanisms that oppress women and other powerless groups in the society; in Lesotho, where women perform a theatre of re-birth known as Pitiki; on Likoma island, in Malawi, where peasants perform the militaristic Malipenga mime; in the Kalankuwa role-play performances of the Hausa; and in the story-telling performances of the Akan of Ghana known as Anansesem. Throughout the Third World, in rural and urban areas, peasants and workers are engaged in highly artistic performance modes whose social function — be it social control, domestication or liberation — cannot be divorced from their aesthetic.

Agitprop, participatory theatre and **theatre-for-conscientisation:** Lambert (1982) observes three methods in the use of popular theatre for non-formal education. He says organisers of popular theatre events in this field can be essentially theatre professionals (rather than developmentalists), whose primary interest is the quality of the spectacle and the size of the audience. Such dramatists usually produce didactic (Brechtian) theatre of the *agitprop* type.

The term 'agitprop' originated in 1920 with the formation of the Department of Agitation and Propaganda, a section of the Central Committee of the Communist Party of the Soviet Union. The function of the department was to give ideological direction to the population through all media of communication, such as radio, the press, film, television, theatre, literature and art. The term has come to be used to describe any overt political propagandising in communication media. In theatre-for-development, the meaning of the term has been extended to describe not only those plays that have a political content, but all plays used as development communication, that are message-oriented and exhortatory, rather than focusing on a process of community analysis and community decision-making.

Agitprop is a variety of theatre that has been found to have a strong rallying potential for people to organise and challenge the established system, although in the hands of 'ideologues' it can be a channel capable of communicating an ideology and can turn agitation into a sloganising propaganda exercise.

Table 2.1
Three methods of popular theatre in non-formal education (NFE)

Factor	Agitprop	Participatory	Conscientisation
Play, spectacle, production	Produced by professional group and orientated towards the people	Produced by and for the people *with* spectators	Produced by and for the people *without* spectators
Improvisation level	Actors themselves respond to the local situation	Within the specific parameters of the themes	Throughout; direction never planned
Consciousness (C) or awareness	C. raised from outside on specific themes, eg hygiene, human rights, nutrition, family planning	C. raised from inside on specific themes, eg social disputes, youth delinquency, VD, migration	C. raised from inside as group analysis of social reality/power relations eg landlessness, poverty, corruption
Action ensuing	Informal post-performance discussion may lead to individual action in short-term	Organised post-performance discussion groups may lead to short or medium term group action	Continuing dialogue may lead to long-term organised collective action
View of development (D)	D = planned by individuals and families through NFE	D = planned change by transfer of knowledge and skills by NFE and follow up	D = structural change that can disrupt the status quo
Particpation and continuity	No participation; spectacle as finished product; actors committed but art comes before development	Participation = co-operation on cue; no grassroots control; scant explanation of problems' macro-origin; psuedo-conscientisation	Participation and control increase as catalysts pull out; spectator becomes dramatic actor, then social actor

Another method used by organisers of popular theatre is *participatory theatre*. This is the method most preferred by developmentalists (as opposed to dramatists or theatre professionals) who advocate a community theatre capable of becoming a two-way channel of communication (i.e. including from the bottom up) rather than a one-way, top-down one.

Some 'developmentalists' are government extension agents and officials on the one hand, who use theatre as an effective auxiliary educational tool, but tend to use the form as a vain search for solutions to complex problems of poverty and oppression. (Lambert 1982, p. 242.)

Other developmentalists, on the other hand, go further by using a method of popular theatre that is capable of being a dialectical tool for attaining a critical analysis of reality through a Freirian process of conscientisation. Table 2.1 illustrates what Lambert says are the relative merits of *theatre-for-conscientisation* as contrasted with agitprop and participatory theatre methodologies.

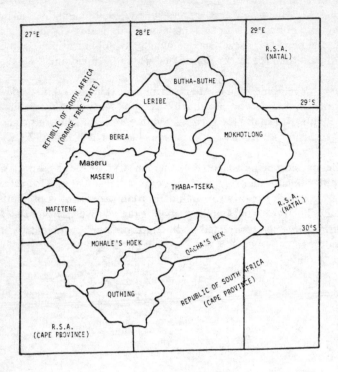

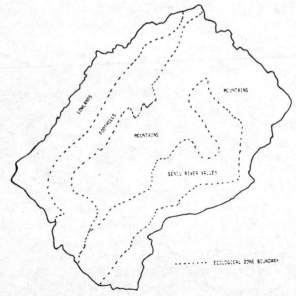

------- ECOLOGICAL ZONE BOUNDARY

3. Lesotho: A Case Study

This book deals with development communication, and essays a structural examination of the context of theatre-for-development. We will now introduce the reader to the conditions that engender the theatre analysed in the subsequent chapters. We give an account of the communication environment in the country, and a brief history of Marotholi Travelling Theatre, which operates within this communication environment.

The problems of underdevelopment

Lesotho (see map) is a small, mountainous country, enclosed on all sides by the Republic of South Africa, which dominates its economy in terms of trade, employment and income. According to the Central Planning and Development Office (1986), the natural endowment of Lesotho is poor, and its economy highly vulnerable to external factors beyond its control. With a *per capita* income of 578 Maloti in 1989 (US$1 = 3 Maloti), Lesotho is designated by the United Nations as one of the 28 least developed countries in the world. About 85 per cent of the population lives in the rural areas and depends on subsistence agriculture or on workers' remittances from abroad for livelihood. About 40 per cent of the male labour force works in the mines and other industries in the Republic of South Africa; their remittances constitute 52 per cent of Lesotho's GNP.

The 1986 census results reported that Lesotho has a population of 1,332,853 resident in the country. An additional 133,653 Basotho (Lesotho citizens) work as migrants in South Africa. In 1986 there were 760,477 males and 817,064 females in the overall population. [The source does not explain the discrepancy of the internally inconsistent statistics]. In the country as a whole, which has an area of 30,350 square kilometres, there are 51 people per square kilometre. Since only a small portion of Lesotho is arable, there are 559 people per square kilometre of arable land (LDTC, 1987). Lesotho can be divided into four ecological and topographical regions, according to vegetation and agricultural activity. The zones are: the lowlands, all territory up to 1,985 metres above sea level; the foothills, land 1,985–2,290 metres above sea level; the mountains, all altitudes above 2,290 metres; the Senqu river valley, geographically within the mountain zone, but distinguished from it by an 'imaginary line above which no winter wheat is grown' (Central Planning and Development Office, 1986).

About 70 per cent of the population lives in the lowlands and foothills, whereas the mountains, the largest zone, are relatively sparsely populated (Murray 1981). According to the Central Planning and Development Office (1986), income in Lesotho is unequally distributed between urban and rural areas, and within the urban and the rural communities. Socially deprived groups include:

- 60 per cent of the population living below the Poverty Datum Line;
- an estimated 48 per cent who are beneficiaries of food aid from international donors;
- 20 per cent of the rural population who are landless;
- 60 per cent of rural households headed or managed by women;
- about 50 per cent of small rural households with no migrant worker or access to remittances;
- 48 per cent of the rural adult population who are illiterate;
- 43 per cent of the labour force who are unemployed;
- 67 per cent of the population not served by potable water supply;
- 49 per cent of mothers delivering outside health institutions;
- 52 per cent of eligible children not attending primary school.

In addition there is the problem of a high infant mortality rate due to malnutrition, and the fact that a large number of children are not fully immunised against infant diseases.

These statistics clearly indicate that Lesotho is an impoverished labour reserve. But only last century it was described as 'a granary of the Free State and the [Cape] Colony' (Murray 1981). This was in 1863, before Lesotho became a British Protectorate. Through the colonial and the post-independence periods there was a transformation from granary to labour reserve. The country is now highly dependent on foreign aid for the people's survival. A report based on the findings of the Marakabei Conference on Successful Small Rural Development Projects (Transformation Resource Centre 1988) gives an account of the problems of foreign aid in relation to underdevelopment. In its earliest form, foreign aid began after the British government accepted Lesotho as a protectorate. Systematic underdevelopment was begun by the undermining of Lesotho's prosperity in the 1860s and 1870s. Taxes were imposed in order to encourage men to work on the newly opened mines of Kimberley and the Witwatersrand.

In addition, the British helped the South Africans to import cheap wheat from Australia and America in order to eliminate Basotho competition. The growing domestic body of independent entrepreneurs was in this way undercut in order to promote an international army of wage labourers. The same thing happened in Lesotho as happened in South Africa. Black people were discouraged from developing the authentic local small-scale capitalism that had been emerging during the mid- and late nineteenth century, and were made dependent on low-paid jobs to feed the very large-scale capitalism that was getting under way in South Africa.

In the first half of the twentieth century, consistent with British colonial policies throughout Africa, Lesotho was subject to benign neglect, because there was no profit to be gained from Lesotho except for her migrant labour. There were some efforts to produce a small educated class, as well as to control soil erosion. Little else was done to change the pattern of a labour-exporting country.

After independence, development aid in the modern sense began to flow into Lesotho. At first, it was primarily British aid, supplemented by South African assistance to the military and to the government in power. But none of this has moved Lesotho at all towards the self-sufficiency she once enjoyed. The reasons for this failure lie in the policies implicit in foreign aid projects. In many of the projects imposed on Lesotho, people did not work together, but instead worked for the aid agency or government ministry as day labourers, paid either with food or with cash. Development was intended for the rural areas, but in fact the substantive aid went to the towns, where offices and houses and infrastructure suited to the needs of donor and local bureaucracies were built, where machines were stored and repaired, and where shops, banks and post offices provided additional support for the elite. Plans for these projects were prepared by government officials in foreign capitals and were tailored to the specific needs of the Lesotho government by local bureaucrats.

As a result, decisions were made for the people, and in the discussions of foreign aid personnel the recipients of the schemes were treated like immature children. Decentralisation was often mentioned, but the juggernaut of bureaucracy consolidated its grip on Maseru (the capital city), to the extent that any official assigned to a district headquarters, or, even worse, to a rural village, felt that he or she had been sent into exile. National development plans were never shown to rural people, much less prepared by them. In all instances communication between the bureaucrats and the rural population was top-down and one-way, following the Lasswellian formula, or the simple Shannon–Weaver linear paradigm. Marotholi Travelling Theatre observed:

> When we examine various development projects in Lesotho we find that in many cases communication is top-down. In other words, planners from outside the community decide what is good for the community and impose projects without finding out from the 'beneficiaries' what their needs are. More often than not such projects fail to realise their objectives because people lack the motivation to participate in the projects of which they feel they are not part. In our tours of the villages we have in fact discovered that the general attitude is that the responsibility of failure or success of such projects rests with the 'government' (by which is meant any development agency — be it government or non-governmental). People feel that things are being done for them, and it is up to the 'benefactor' to see to it that they succeed. They see themselves as mere recipients — an attitude which reinforces dependency. (*MTT Report* 1987, p. 1.)

Even representatives coming from the villages and elected by the villagers rarely consulted those villagers, but sat in Maseru to decide how best to benefit themselves, or talked to their fellows in the elite, and only secondarily thought how to assist the intended beneficiaries. Food-aid dependency has increased every year since independence. Each year there are discussions of how to reduce it, but nothing follows. Villagers who have now internalised dependency ask how they are going to be paid when they do village development work, even on their own land. If there is no cash or food aid, they resist being involved.

Massive foreign aid schemes have piled up debt without producing substantive results. Economic uplift does not happen, because the money earned by migrant labourers goes back to the source in South Africa, as their families spend it on consumer goods imported from that country, rather than investing it in the Lesotho economy. Self-reliance, self-employment, income-generation and employment in the rural sector are not a reality as yet, because of this increased dependency on aid programmes and South African consumer goods. Lesotho is an integral part of the Southern African Customs Union, and thus has little real incentive to produce its own goods for its own people. Tractors, for example, continue to be brought in from foreign countries; there is thus little pressure on the owners of the hundreds of derelict tractors around the country to get them working again (Transformation Resource Centre 1988, pp. 4–5).

This situation of underdevelopment can be explained in terms of the formulations of centre–periphery theorists (also known as the dependency theorists). These formulations were evolved as a primarily economic theory, which postulates that colonialism created an order where colonised nations produced raw materials, and colonial powers finished products. This established an economic order that is difficult to break even long after the colonies regain their political independence. Galtung (1971), a dependency theorist, views the world as divided into centre and periphery nations, which are themselves divided into centres and peripheries. He conceives of imperialism as a dominance relation between the centre (industrialised) and the periphery (underdeveloped) nations, where the centre (the elite) of the periphery nations form a bridgehead for the centre nation. Periphery nations like Lesotho continue to export raw materials in the form of labour, wool and mohair, and import finished products from a centre nation like South Africa. Lesotho then becomes dependent on the centre, and cannot develop its own industrial base. The centre–periphery model has three levels:

i   Global: a dominance–dependence relationship between nations;
ii national: a dominance–dependence relationship between urban and rural areas within a country;
iii community: a dominance–dependence relationship between rich and poor in a community.

This means that the rural areas in Lesotho are the periphery of a periphery nation whose centre is the capital, Maseru, where the national elite lives. Within the periphery of the periphery nation there is the centre composed of the wealthy community members, with the poor as the periphery of the periphery of the periphery. Centre nations themselves have their own peripheries at national and community level. For example, in the United States, often considered the most highly developed nation of all, large groups live under conditions that cannot be more adequately described than as underdeveloped (Hedebro 1982, p. 10).

The highly developed sections of periphery societies compose the centre of the periphery nations. Some groups in Lesotho are not underdeveloped, since they are in a position to enjoy the results of the dependency relationship with the centre nations, which continue to give aid, which perpetuates such a relationship. This is aid intended for the rural areas, but it ends up further developing the centre. The dependency relations are thus beneficial and profitable to the centre of the periphery nations. An empirical test of Galtung's (1971) theory of imperialism confirms that while the dependency relations produce a disharmony of interest, evidenced by a widening gap in living conditions, between the nations as a whole, 'there is nevertheless a harmony of interest between the centre of the periphery nation and the centre of the centre nation' (Gidengil 1978). Lesotho's centre continues to prosper in this way while the periphery spirals downwards.

> The high rate of exploitation in the periphery enables local ruling classes and allied elites to live on a level comparable to that of the bourgeoisies of the centre, while at the same time making possible a massive flow of monetized surplus product (in the form of profits, interests, rents, royalties, etc.) from periphery to centre. (Sweezy 1981, p. 76.)

Communication is essential for the perpetuation of this system. Information tends to flow from the centre to the periphery, and very seldom the other way round. The information flows are vehicles for values and ideology from the centre to the periphery. If peripheries developed their own set of values, they would not be dependent on the centre. Mass communication as it exists in periphery nations reinforces dependency, contrary to Rostow's (1960) proposition that mass communication is an important tool in development.

The forces that have shaped this situation will continue to work, and it is unlikely that they can be stopped or controlled by national governments, until such time that the periphery of the periphery nation is empowered to create its own messages expressing its needs, and its own solutions to the problems of its underdevelopment. But the periphery will not be able to create such messages if it has no critical consciousness to analyse the structural causes of its underdevelopment.

An unconscientised periphery may merely create messages that serve to perpetuate current dependency relations, rather than those that will overthrow the exploitative structure. Effective development communication cannot but be a political action for liberation. This applies to theatre-for-development. Even when messages are not overtly political, they may contribute to the process of liberation. For example, if a literacy campaign results in the people not only acquiring writing and reading skills, but raising their critical awareness, it becomes a process of liberation. Villagers will be able to identify the sources of poverty, and devise ways of eradicating them. A health education campaign, if it does not deal merely with causes, prevention and cure of the diseases, nor concentrate on technical solutions, but examines the structural (social and political) causes of disease, is a process of liberation.

The communication environment

Communication structures
The communication structures used for development communication in Lesotho do not reflect a desire to break away from the dependency relations

explicated above. As in most developing countries, there was a rapid diffusion of mass media in Lesotho during the 1970s and 1980s. Radio is the most widespread mass medium in the rural areas (LDTC 1986), and therefore the most frequently used for development communication. Radio is a comparatively inexpensive medium, able to reach the widespread villages without a costly transmitter–receiver system. Other advantages are that it overlaps literacy, and can be used in areas with no electricity. The disadvantage is that it has no instant feedback. Delayed feedback, through letters, is sparse and unreliable as a reflection of the responses of the total audience. Also, the periphery is unable to use it to create its own messages.

Judging from the way radio programmes are designed, the Lesotho broadcaster seems to operate under concepts of mass media that conceive of the audience as passive collections of individuals directly and strongly influenced by the mass media. Radio Lesotho's relationship with its audience can be illustrated by the dominance model in Figure 3.1. In this dominance model the contact is one-directional; there is no feedback from audience to communicator. The physical facilities for production and distribution are located in Maseru, and are inaccessible to most members of the public. The mass communicator defines the audience according to his purposes, and the relationship is within his control. The intention is to reach and influence as many people as possible in a pre defined public. The audience is an object of mass persuasion.

Figure 3.1

A dominance model of the communicator-audience relationship

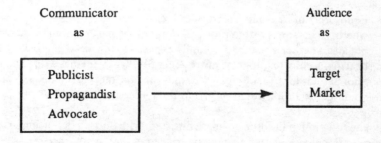

Lesotho has a number of institutions, public and private, involved in development communication. The most significant are the Health Education Division of the Ministry of Health, the Lesotho Distance Teaching Centre of the Ministry of Education, the Institute of Extra-Mural Studies of the National University of Lesotho, the Ministry of Information and Broadcasting (with its radio, television, press and news agency sections), the information sectors of various government ministeries, privately owned and operated newspapers and magazines, various projects supported by international organisations such as UNICEF and World Health Organisation, projects supported by foreign governments such as the United States Agency for International Development, projects supported by non-governmental organisations such as German Agro-Action, and also private hospitals and clinics that have social mobilisation programmes in their health service areas. Women's organisations, trade unions, associations of artists and intellectuals, and other formal and informal groups at all levels play a role in disseminating developmental messages, particularly in their areas of interest.

In the private sector Lesotho publishes five weekly newspapers, one fortnightly, and one quarterly. There are also six magazines. There are no daily newspapers, and thus a heavy dependence on foreign print media, mostly from South Africa.

Access and exposure

Access is a necessary, but not sufficient, condition for exposure. *Access* generally refers to the essential physical potential for exposure — the situation where there is a newspaper, radio, television, or other mass medium within reasonable range of the potential audience. In some cases in rural areas, this might be an individual's access to a private radio, but it can also be a situation of a shared radio or a newspaper read by a number of people. In most rural areas, access is primarily to radio and print. (Shore 1980, p. 25.)

Exposure is more complicated than access because it deals not only with whether a person is within physical range of the particular mass medium but also whether a person is actually exposed to the message. *Exposure* is hearing, seeing, reading, or, more generally, experiencing, with at least a minimal amount of interest, the mass media message. This exposure might occur at individual or group level. (Shore 1980, p. 26.)

The situation in Lesotho is quite consistent with Shore's definition in that rural areas have access primarily to radio and print media such as newspapers, posters, and calendars. A survey by the Lesotho Distance Teaching Centre (LDTC, 1987) indicated that 62.2 per cent of the people in Lesotho own radio sets. Eighty per cent of people who have radios said that their radio sets were in good working condition. About half of the people who either do not own radios or do not repair their broken sets have access to a radio at a friend's or relative's house.

The survey measured not only access, but, by examining such questions as most liked programme by ecological zone, time favoured for radio listenership by zone, frequency of listenership by education level, and most liked radio stations, exposure was also measured. The finding was that a majority of the people has not only access to a radio, but exposure as well. The survey further indicated that Radio Lesotho is the most popular station in all the ecological regions; with 83.7 per cent of those who have access to radio sets tuning to the station. The survey found that the national papers do not enjoy a wide readership in rural Lesotho. Only 21 per cent of rural people can be reached through newspapers. Television reaches the least number of people since the signal covers only a few lowland towns, and only the well-off can afford to purchase the expensive sets.

Shore says that it is important to consider a broader view of access, to include access to the production and distribution of messages. None of the mass media institutions have a system whereby the public, particularly the rural poor, can produce and distribute messages, except for a few letters to the editor or postcards to request programmes on Radio Lesotho. Access in Lesotho is defined purely in terms of physical access to the reception of mass media. Another problem is that most of the mass media resources and facilities are located in the capital, and try to reach all parts of the country from there. There are, for example, no community newspapers based in the rural areas to articulate the aspirations of the local communities. Newspapers in church centres outside the capital (Morija and Mazened) have national character and distribution.

Contradictions of policy and practice

It must be noted that it is not government policy to have top-down planning of development programmes in Lesotho, but it is the actual practice of government officials. The government recognises that development is ineffective if it becomes solely a top-down process, with decisions made in Maseru alone.

> Mass participation and support are critical for the success of most programmes, particularly those in the rural sector. Such support can only be generated if the people are able to actively participate in the decision-making process. Government is implementing a policy of decentralisation to facilitate participation. (Central Planning and Development Office 1986, p. 25.)

In pursuance of this policy, the government's objective is to devise a system of bottom-up, involving local communities and field workers, with emphasis on the mountains and the southern districts, and to improve the efficiency and performance of the chiefs as agents of development in the villages.

Government ministries have long had extension workers who are either based in the villages, or visit rural areas frequently, to provide those communities with technical advice and social services. The Ministry of Health, for instance, has devised a village health worker system, where some community members volunteer to be trained in primary health practices. They in turn tend the sick in their communities, and refer serious cases to nurse clinicians, qualified nurses trained to diagnose and treat some diseases, also based in the villages. This system has successfully brought health services closer to the rural communities.

The Ministry of the Interior also sends extension workers out to the villages, to assist in the provision of potable water for rural communities. The Ministry of Agriculture has a large network of extension workers whose main function is to give people information on better farming methods; this is in addition to the Agricultural Information Service, whose objective is to broadcast and publish information concerning agriculture. This service uses radio, pamphlets, and agricultural campaigns. Its programmes are broadcast over Radio Lesotho, and the pamphlets are distributed free of charge to villagers by mail, and by hand during the campaigns. In the campaigns, audio and video tapes, pamphlets and posters are used. Although the initiative, in this example, is taken by the government — messages are pre-recorded on small-format audio-visual media by subject matter specialists — at least here an attempt is made to involve people in a discussion. There is instant feedback. But the villagers do not create the messages; they merely react to messages pre-determined and pre-packaged by bureaucrats at the head office.

These programmes work according to a diffusion of innovations model, and this applies to other ministries as well. Both mass and interpersonal channels are used to influence attitude and behaviour, and encourage an adoption of new methods in agriculture, health practices, and village water supply. The extension worker is a superior external agent representing the government who, usually on technical grounds, decides what is beneficial for the rural communities, and proceeds to promote it by mobilising government resources. Although the interpersonal elements have positive aspects since there is an instant feedback, the people are not involved in the formulation of the plans, but react to plans formulated by outsiders. The introduction of an interpersonal element in a mass communication situation does not of itself bring about social change, hence the failure of communication systems in Lesotho. Genuine, rather than lip-service, participation of rural communities in their own development can be achieved only if villagers create their own messages.

Absence of articulated communication policies

A major problem in the failure of communications systems in Lesotho to be effective in development communication is that the country has no explicit, integrated communication policies. According to Lee (1976), communication policies are sets of principles and norms established to guide the behaviour of communication systems. Although Lesotho's communication policies are not explicit in legislation or in a constitution, it would be incorrect to say there are none at all since no state can exist without them. In the case of Lesotho, these can be deduced from rules and procedures, or are implicit in accepted practices at national, institutional, and professional levels. They are, however, latent, fragmented, and uncoordinated, rather than clearly articulated and harmonised. It is implicit in the practice of such national agencies as Radio Lesotho, Health Education Division, the Lesotho Distance Teaching Centre, and the government newspapers, that one of the major objectives is to use the mass communication systems to reach all the people in Lesotho, with a special emphasis on those who live in rural areas. However, the work seems to be uncoordinated among various agencies involved. Effective planning for effective communication can only take place within the context of communication policies. Such policies may be very general — in the nature of desirable goals and principles — or may be more specific and practically binding. They may have worldwide, regional, national or sub-national dimensions.

Traditional modes in the rural areas
The communication environment of rural Lesotho includes modes that have been inherited from pre-colonial, traditional systems. In Lesotho's traditional societies, the transmission of messages was not mediated or interposed, as in today's mass media, but depended on interpersonal channels. The *khotla*, besides being a court of law, was a place where men gathered to discuss the affairs of the village. Visitors from other areas were much valued at the *khotla*, for they brought news of events and occurrences outside the community. Some of the information transmitted through the *khotla* emanated from women at home, and there was a network of transmission channels through the extended family, friends and neighbours. Women had their own groups, such as communal work parties, and their own rituals and games. These also acted as transmission channels. A major transmission channel in the village was the *pitso*, a public gathering of the adults in the community. The *pitso* was not a top-down communication process where the leadership addressed the people. The leadership did not go to the *pitso* to give directives, but to get the views of the people, on which decisions would be based.

At the national and international levels, agents of transmission of news and other messages were *lititimi*. These were runners placed at intervals throughout the country, whose function was to relay urgent messages, usually of an emergency nature, fast. *Lititimi* would run day and night, relaying messages from one to another until the message reached its destination.

Children in Lesotho had a great deal of general knowledge of their own world, which they gained through folklore, oral literature, and various ceremonies and rituals. Literature such as *litsomo* (folk tales), *lipale* (stories), *lilotho* (riddles), and *maele* (proverbs) was highly imaginative and educational. Songs (*lipina*) and poems (*lithoko le lithothokiso*) preserved the history of the people, and their values, and these were transmitted from one generation to another. Women played a vital role in this transmission, especially the grandmothers, who spent a lot of time with children, imparting to them traditional values through the channels of folklore. Various performance modes, such as the *mohobelo* dance for men, and *mokhibo* for women, were popular. Girls sang *lipina-tsa-mokopu*, which always carried social commentary on the life of the community. Another mode which emerged later, as men began to work as migrant labourers in the mines of South Africa, is *lifela*, a form of poetry which is also a vehicle for social commentary.

As traditional values changed with modernisation, agents and channels of transmission of messages changed as well. New technologies brought about interposed or mediated media which created the concept of a mass audience. Channels that permitted a source to reach a large and often widely dispersed audience were introduced, and there was less dependence on interpersonal communication.

Although news agencies and correspondents replaced *lititimi*, other interpersonal channels survived modernisation, and continue to be utilised by rural communities throughout Lesotho. One such channel is the *pitso*, which was adopted by the colonial administrator and continues to be used in the post-independence era. Its nature and its function, however, have changed. Whereas in pre-colonial Lesotho the *pitso* was a forum for the discussion of issues in a two-way communication process where everyone participated, today's *pitso* is a top-down, one-way process. This negative change happened as a result of colonialism, since colonial administrators gave only directives that had to be followed without any argument. Today's political leaders have inherited this situation, and utilise the *pitso* as the colonialist did before. Other interpersonal channels still popular in the rural areas are performance modes such as *mohobelo*, *mokhibo*, *pina-tsa-mokopu*, and *lifela*. These modes exist in their original form alongside other, syncretic, modes that have emerged from them. *Litsomo*, *lipale*, *lilotho*, *maele*, *lithoko* and *lithothokiso* are other interpersonal forms of communication that rural people use to receive and give information. These have even been incorporated into the school curriculum. It may be noted here that when art forms such as *lithoko* are adapted into an education curriculum they become a different kind of a product, reproduced and consumed in a different and quite specialised way.

Marotholi Travelling Theatre

Marotholi Travelling Theatre functions within the communication environment outlined above. The company's objective is to use theatre as a medium for development communication. Their theatre involves the use of traditional or indigenous performance modes with which the rural communities are familiar, and in which they will fully participate. Their work is not an attempt to retrieve and reconstruct the forms that pre-colonial popular theatre took, or an inherently conservative act, as Griswold (1982) puts it, of 'reinventing a buried precolonial national identity', or a reinvention of culture, but a utilisation of indigenous modes of cultural expression currently popular throughout the rural areas of Lesotho.

A brief history

The Theatre-for-Development Project was established in 1982 by a joint working party of the English Department and the Institute of Extra Mural Studies of the National University of Lesotho. Its goal was to initiate and support community development and self-help programmes through the use of theatre. The target areas were the rural communities in the Roma Valley, where the university is located, and the Lesotho Institute of Correction — the prison service.

In 1984 the Project, for the first time, received funding from the Ford Foundation, which enabled it to improve programme flexibility and increase the number of target areas. Prior to funding, the Project's activities were limited because it operated without a budget and within the confines of a semester course on practical theatre offered by the English department. Between 1982 and 1985 the Project produced a number of plays dealing with such themes as reforestation, migrant labour, cooperative societies, and rehabilitation of prisoners. These plays were performed in target areas, and some of them were broadcast over Radio Lesotho for a wider audience.

In 1986 the performing group of the Theatre-for-Development Project adopted the name Marotholi (from *marotholi-a-pula* which means rain-drops) Travelling Theatre, and became a permanent theatre company based at the university. It continued to take trained performers from those who had successfully completed a one-semester practical theatre course offered by the English department, but operated throughout the year outside the confines of the course. In 1988 Marotholi became autonomous from the Theatre-for-Development Project. It was registered as a non-profit society, based outside the university, composed not only of university students but also of teachers in rural schools, civil servants, adult educators who worked for agencies other than the university, and community-based groups such as village health workers and women's organisations.

It must be noted that the work discussed in this study under Marotholi includes work produced by the Theatre-for-Development Project prior to the formal establishment of Marotholi.

Until 1986 Marotholi used the agitprop method of theatre. They toured with pre-packaged productions which they created after going through a five-step process: information-gathering in the target communities, information analysis, story improvisation, rehearsal, community performances. In this method the only community participation was in group discussions that took place after performances. In 1986 Marotholi changed from agitprop to participatory theatre and theatre-for-conscientisation. Participatory theatre (comgen theatre) is produced by and for the people with the help of catalysts. Plays are improvised within the specific parameters of the themes. The difference between this method and agitprop is that members of the community themselves are the performers, rather than a group from outside.

Theatre-for-conscientisation is a higher stage of participatory theatre. The main difference between the two is that in theatre-for-conscientisation the spectacle is produced by and for the people without spectators, since those who may initially be spectators later become actors. Improvisation happens throughout the life of the production, and the direction the play takes at each performance is never pre-planned. Here too catalysts are necessary because the performers must be made to acquire the essential skills to mount an effective production.

Boal (1979) has developed a method in two parts, both of which are designed to transform spectators into actors. The two stages are known as *simultaneous dramaturgy* and *forum theatre*. In simultaneous dramaturgy, catalysts perform a short scene suggested by a local person, halt the action at a crisis point, and ask the audience to offer solutions. The actors become like puppets, and perform the actions strictly on the spectators' orders. The 'best' solution is arrived at by trial, error, discussion, then audience consensus. Thus the action ceases to be deterministic; everything is subject to criticism and rectification. Everything can be changed by any spectator at a moment's notice without censorship. The actor does not cease his role as interpreter.

In forum theatre actors and spectators converge. The participants tell a story with some social problem, then improvise, rehearse, and present it to the rest of the group as a skit. The audience members are asked if they agree with the solution. Any spectator is invited to replace any actor and lead the action in the direction that seems most appropriate to him or her. He or she must not make speeches, but must act to evoke responses from the others on the performance space.

This goes much further than simultaneous dramaturgy since the spectators lose their safe seats, as the line of demarcation between actor and audience diminishes. It has been argued (see Lambert 1982) that such theatre offers the means whereby all possible paths may be examined. The emphasis is self-education. Consciousness is raised from inside as the group analyse social reality and power relations. When the spectators themselves become actors the catalyst group is no longer necessary. At this stage, community participation and control increase.

Marotholi have sometimes modified this method. The group is often engaged to participate in the communication campaigns of governmental and non-governmental development agencies such as UNICEF, Rural Sanitation Project of the Ministry of Heath, and Welthungerhilfe (German Agro-Action). The themes that they treat on these occasions are those that promote the services of these agencies. It therefore becomes necessary for the catalysts to select the theme of the play. In this case the play does not begin with a short scene suggested by a local person. The catalysts themselves improvise and rehearse the scene. Right from the beginning the audience is invited to participate. Boal's two stages have been combined. The spectators are free to comment or come to the stage and act. Throughout the play there is discussion and debate on the issues raised. At any moment, when the catalysts or the spectators think it necessary, the action of the play stops, and there is discussion on the issues raised in the play. In most cases audience discussion and the action of the play flow into one another, as members of the audience tend to shuttle in the discussion of the issues between the world of the play and the world of the community. In this way the theatrical performance becomes a vehicle for discussion and social analysis. Post-performance discussion, as in the case of agitprop, becomes unnecessary.

Marotholi travel throughout the country performing their plays in villages. Some of the villages they visit are inaccessible by road, and therefore neglected by development agencies. Their plays deal with such themes as community self-reliance, trade unionism among the migrant workers, primary health care, and rural sanitation. Some performances are sponsored by development agencies that have related programmes in Lesotho. International donors, such as the Ford Foundation, Welthunger-hilfe, and the Canada Fund for Local Initiatives, have funded the collective. The collective also generates its own funds by producing educational videos on behalf of such clients as the TB Control Unit and the AIDS Control Programme, both of the Ministry of Health. It is with such funding that the collective is able to create plays that emanate from the community, rather than those whose themes and content have been suggested by the development agencies.

Information-gathering methods

The information-gathering stage is crucial since it is at this point that the catalysts get into initial contact with the target community, and assess their needs. At a workshop held in Kumba in Cameroon (see Eyoh 1987), the participants experimented with various methods of information-gathering, the results of which gave a coherent structure to the methods previously used by practitioners in various permutations. The workshop itself was of significance, since it made a positive contribution to the search for effective methodologies in the practice of theatre-for-development. Among its objectives were to initiate theatre practitioners, development cadres and villagers in the use of theatre-for-conscientisation and for mobilisation, to demonstrate the process of theatre-for-development with the view to enabling the Cameroonian authorities to assess its potential as a development tool, and to assess the effectiveness of the methodology, both in its immediate feasibility and long term impact. The various methods of information-gathering with which the workshop participants experimented were as follows:

- The *flooding method*, whereby a whole group would flood the village, meeting the villagers wherever they were and holding informal discussions with them;
- the *homestead technique*, which involved living with a family and trying to pick up as much information as possible through discussion and observation;
- the *interview method*, through which formal interviews would be held with designated people in the villages;
- the *performance method*, which involved improvisation through which both participants and villagers would obtain a deeper understanding of issues, with the improvisation changing as such understanding grew;
- the *official eye technique*, which simply meant obtaining information from official sources;
- the *hierarchical method*, whereby the participants talked with the village chief and councillors. (Eyoh 1987, p. 8.)

At the workshop, all these methods were used in varying permutations. Marotholi Travelling Theatre have also used all these methods of data collection, although it shall be observed that some methods tend to be dominant in their work. In 1982 the Theatre-for-Development Project of the National University of Lesotho used two methods, one of which was not explored by the Kumba workshop. This is the *public meeting method*. According to Andrew Horn, the director of the project:

The team, composed of seventeen undergraduates, most of whom were mature age students with previous experience of either primary-level teaching or the Civil Service, and their instructor visited Ha Libopuoa where the local chieftainess had called a *pitso*, an open village meeting, at which villagers could freely air their grievances on a host of subjects suggested by themselves. An extensive list of problems was assembled, including poor road access, inadequate medical facilities, insufficient expert agricultural guidance, party political tension, drunkenness and the contamination of freshwater streams by human effluent. (Horn 1984, p. 46.)

Besides gathering information in a public meeting situation, the group also used the official eye technique and the hierarchical method by talking with the chiefs and the village development committees. At the International Conference on Theatre-for-Development held in Maseru, Lesotho,* in 1985, Horn said, 'Because of the constraints of time we cannot go for more than a day to investigate the problems. We usually have a big meeting with the Development Committee comprising fifteen to thirty people.' The method currently preferred by Marotholi is the flooding method, although a permutation of other methods may from time to time feature very strongly. They have found the flooding method much more effective than the public meeting method because of the strong element of discontinuous discourse in it, rather than the continuous discourse of a public meeting. (For treatment of the continuous discourse/discontinuous discourse dichotomy, see Chapter 5.) The interpersonal interaction in the flooding method is such that neither the villager nor the data collector control the effects of the communication, as they both become sources and receivers. In the public meeting method, the source is distinguishable from the receiver. The data collector is the source who will have a continuous discourse with the gathered villagers by explaining to them the purpose of the visit and eliciting from them their problems. In the form of feedback the villagers will then express their problems and their needs. As in any public meeting, there will be those eloquent and influential members of the community who will dominate the feedback session. At the end of the day the issues are examined from the perspective of the dominant members of the community, and the theatre fails to be the democratic vehicle it seeks to be.

Although, for the reasons stated above, Marotholi find the flooding method more effective than the public meeting method, there is a movement in their work towards the homestead technique and the performance method, which they feel are even more effective. However, the constraints of time that Horn spoke about still exist, and only on rare occasions are they able to stay in a village for a number of days on end. The fact of living in the village facilitates information gathering, as the Kumba workshop also

* All the citations from the 1985 Maseru conference are from personal notes taken by the author during the proceedings.

discovered. Eyoh writes that staying with the villagers helped the participants 'to gain a deeper understanding of the reality of rural existence rather than the superficial knowledge often gathered through cursory visits to the villages' (Eyoh 1987, p. 6).

Information-analysis is usually done by the members of Marotholi when they return to base. During this stage they prioritise the issues and work out a drama based on the problems identified. Reporting on a workshop held in Zimbabwe to orient development cadres and consolidate their ideas in the field of theatre-for-development, Kidd writes of the limitation of this process as experienced by the participants of the workshop:

> The process worked well as a means of putting across information and development messages but it had a number of limitations as a process of popular education or conscientization. Notably, it left the villagers out of the key stages of the process — *analysis of the initial data* and dramatization — and forced the villagers into the relatively passive role of being objects of an externally-controlled research process, and an audience for messages and analyses produced by outsiders (rather than doing their own critical thinking). (Kidd 1985, p. 180.) [Emphasis mine]

He recommends that instead of retreating to base after collecting the data, the outsider team should remain in the village and develop the analysis and the dramatisation with the villagers. In this way the resulting performance will achieve what a resource person at the Zimbabwe workshop called the 'theatre-for-development process', which he summarised as follows:

a)   Building a relationship with members of the community and motivating them to participate;

b)   working with them to study their situation and identify issues for in-depth analysis;

c)   learning the indigenous forms of cultural expression of the area, and utilising them for the theatre-for-development activity;

d)   exploring through drama, dance, mime, and song (coupled with discussion) ways of deepening the understanding of the issues and looking for solutions;

e)   organising a performance as a way of bringing the community together and agreeing on solutions and action;

f)   discussing with the villagers ways in which this short-term activity could be continued by the villagers on their own (follow up);

g)   evaluating the whole experience and drawing out the lessons learned. (Kidd 1985, p. 182.)

After the data has been analysed, a story is created through improvisation and rehearsed. Generally the plays are unscripted as authorship is communal. These steps vary widely depending on the methodology of the theatre used. They will therefore be discussed in greater detail when the plays are analysed.

4. Traditional and Popular Media in Lesotho

In the discussion in Chapter 3 on the communication environment of Lesotho, it was noted that the rural areas have a variety of vibrant traditional communication systems, most of which are steeped in performance. These are not dead modes that belong to the annals of history or anthropology; they continue to serve society as tools of communication.

The work of Marotholi Travelling Theatre in using traditional and popular media has positively answered the question: 'can traditional media carry modern messages, and if they can, should they; if they cannot, should they be modified so that they can?' (Lent 1982, p. 9). The question presumes that traditional media do not carry modern messages, as though culture in the developing world is static and preoccupied with the past. The traditional performance modes in Lesotho carried modern messages long before Marotholi utilised them to ensure the participation of the people in development communication. As communication researchers in this area, Marotholi are looking at various strategies for using indigenous communication systems, which Wang and Dissanayake say have the following characteristics:

(a) They can be readily adapted to new themes, with a varying degree of flexibility.
(b) They are directed towards a homogeneous ethnolinguistic audience rather than an audience consisting of a variety of social groups.
(c) They are consistent with the oral traditions in developing regions, where audience participation is not only common, but important.
(d) The credibility of the information or messages transmitted through the channels of the indigenous communication system is usually higher than that of the mass communication system since the former is a known entity of proved reliability.
(e) Messages and information that are transmitted through the indigenous communication system are usually more effective in promoting changes in beliefs and attitudes because they are characterised by emotions,

feelings, values and social experiences shared by members of the culture.

(f) Smaller cost is involved in the use of indigenous communication system as compared with modern technology-based media. (Wang and Dissanayake 1982.)

It is clear, therefore, that rural communities have a well-tried framework of communication and learning. Marotholi Travelling Theatre's objective is to show how, with a few modifications, these popular structures can be strengthened as a vehicle of both community dialogue and community decision-making.

Not all indigenous performance modes lend themselves to being used, either in the context of, or as theatre-for-development. In *Kopano ke Matla!* (analysed in Chapter 6), the celebratory *monyanyako* was used to punctuate the scenes, and to show a passage of time. Songs of this nature lend themselves well for this purpose because they are generally all-purpose songs performed at any happy occasion, and are popular with people — urban and rural — of all ages. However these songs cannot on their own function as a vehicle for community dialogue even though they may carry developmental messages in their lyrics. They can be used in the context of a play (a sign in a macrosign) to reinforce the messages that are being transmitted by the participants among themselves.

Lifela, on the other hand, are much more flexible, owing to their nature as poetic self-definition created from traditional sources to express class consciousness and resistance to the controls of the migrant labour system. Performances of *lifela* are not confined to mine compounds, but are popular in the villages as well, since the cultural impact of the mine is all too great in the village life in Lesotho.

> *Lifela* are heard on mine compounds, at Sesotho beer houses in South African shanty towns and in Lesotho, at labour recruitment centres, in the fields during harvest, along the roads; almost everywhere that *likheleke*, the 'eloquent ones' meet, as well as on Radio Sesotho [the South African Broadcasting Corporation's Sesotho service] and Radio Lesotho. (Coplan 1989, p. 3.)

Lifela are regarded as songs in contrast of the speech of *lithoko* (poetry). They sound to the Western ear 'more like rhythmic declamation or chanting' (Coplan 1989, p. 4), and are performed by both men and women. The male singers are primarily migrant workers in the South African mines originating in Lesotho's rural villages. Female singers on the other hand have a more varied background, and have generally lived for a considerable time in both urban and rural areas of Lesotho, and in the South African

74 When People Play People

townships. Women singers also have another variation of *lifela*, popular in the shebeens, called *seoeleoelele* after the ideophonic sound sung by the women to open and punctuate the *lifela*.

Sometimes there are contests among the performers, a dialogic exchange between a male *kheleke* and a woman singer, or between two men, instead of the usual recitation. At a village in Mafeteng, where the Marotholi had gone to perform one of their plays, there was an impromptu debate in verse between two migrants. As in the *Dondang Sayang* performances in Malaysia (Lent 1982, p. 14), the performers continued their debate until one of them could not think of a response and ran out of 'eloquence'. Throughout the performance the audience listened to the content of *lifela* from both parties, and to the wit and humour. They also listened attentively to make sure that there was no repetition, and that no expressions had been 'stolen' from other known singers of *lifela*. People listen to the meaning of the words, evaluate them and make a critical appreciation of style, diction, and imagery, and react to what is said not only through applause but through their own *lifela*. This is one strong characteristic of the genre which makes it most suited for use in development communication.

Another characteristic is that *lifela* have a story-line. A *sefela* (singular of *lifela*) 'is a series of narrative episodes phrased and connected in an idiom of interlocking metaphoric tropes' (Coplan 1989, p. 26). The themes treated include travelling, social and physical geography, chieftainship, traditional medicine, religion, the mine environment and labour relations, and social relations in the villages. Coplan cites evidence to show that migrants no longer regard the environments of the mines and home villages as two separate social fields — at least as expressed by their *lifela*. (Coplan 1989, p. 26.)

Lifela do sometimes act as a vehicle of protest, and express a sense of deprivation and powerlessness. They reflect upon the people's own experiences. Expressing his dissatisfaction with the collaborative domination of the ruling classes in Lesotho, the mine management and the South African regime, the *kheleke* Makeka Likhojane (Coplan 1989, p. 3) sing:

Li fapana li na le kutse;	They crossed one another, ours and a freight train;
Kutse ena e apere matata;	The freight train wore karosses [skin capes, once a chiefly prerogative]
E nkile likhomo le furu'a lesere;	It carried cattle, feeding on fodder;
Lipholo li tloha ho Verwoerd	Oxen given by Verwoerd
Tse tlang ho Tona-kholo . . .	To the Prime Minister [of Lesotho] . . .

This is only an extract from Likhojane's *sefela*. *Lifela* are much longer, and a good *kheleke* can recite for over an hour.

Commenting on Likhojane's *sefela* Coplan writes:

> Crossing paths with a freight train while on the way to the mines, the poet reflects that the freight, dressed in the cattlehide robes of royalty rather than in the wool blankets of migrants, is a vehicle of social dominance. Cattle are the quintessential social currency of Sotho pastoral life, vehicles of ritual communication, social reproduction, and domestic security through sacrifice, bridewealth, agricultural productivity, capital accumulation, and in this case especially, patron–client relationship. Here Lesotho's prime minister, the late Chief Jonathan, has sent his subjects to labour for his counterpart in South Africa, in return for gifts of cattle. Victims of this exchange, the migrants see themselves as having more in common with the cattle than the chiefly clients. They are a cargo 'driven like oxen' to the mines, rather than followers sharing in the redistributive beneficience of an autonomous stratified state. (Coplan 1989, p. 3.)

This clearly shows that *lifela* in Lesotho, like a lot of oral literature in Africa, carry modern messages that have a high degree of sophistication and relevance in reflecting the people's struggles in dealing with social and economic coercion. A lot of oral literature is already a vehicle of social protest. The role of the theatre-for-development catalyst, as is the case with Marotholi Travelling Theatre, is to build on this characteristic of protest in *lifela*, by introducing elements of critical analysis, so that ways and means of solving problems may be examined, rather than merely reflecting on the problems. This is a movement, put another way, from protest to resistance, since the emphasis now is on those actions that the villagers can take themselves in order to remedy the oppressive situation reflected in their *lifela*. This is, therefore, an extension of Basotho culture into new domains of experience.

Marotholi use *lifela* in the context of a structured play (combining familiar and novel symbols) while they are experimenting with the assistance of various *likheleke* on how *lifela* can be used on their own as a macrosign. An accordion, played by a member of the group who is a professional accordion player at his own shebeen in one of the villages of Roma, is usually used as an accompanist. Accordion and drum (*koriana le meropa*) music is very popular in the rural areas, and is often used to accompany *lifela*, and especially *seoeleoelele*. Today there are famous *lifela* singers such as Tau-ea-Matsekha, Puseletso Seema and Apolo Ntabanyane, and accordionists like Forere Motloheloa, who are recording artists of *lifela* (particularly *seoeleoelele*) and whose records sell in thousands since their music is popular in Lesotho, even among the educated elite, who no longer look down upon it. This music of the recording stars is a further syncretisation of *lifela*, since guitars and other musical instruments have been added.

Marotholi have also used *lipina-tsa-mokopu* (songs of the pumpkin), a song–dance mode performed by girls, and of late, young women, who assemble usually in the evenings to perform. Originally these were performances done at harvest time, but now they are popular throughout the year. Sometimes groups of girls from neighbouring villages challenge one another for a competition of song and dance. Although the function of *pina-tsa-mokopu* is primarily to entertain, they are also a reflection of the world the girls live in, and the social relations in the village. The lyrics of the songs, as the girls dance in a circle, are usually simple and repetitive, such as in the following *mokopu* song:

Sale la ka la ponto	My earring worth a pound
Sale la ka la ponto	My earring worth a pound
La tholoa ke balisana	Was picked up by herdboys
La tholoa ke balisana.	Was picked up by herdboys.

At a point the song stops, and a performer comes centre-stage to recite a short poem in rhythmic speech, while the other singers clap hands, stamp their feet and chant. One such recitation that has been recorded by Radio Lesotho goes as follows:

Hoja kea busa kea laela,	If I were ruling and in command,
Nkabe ke re likomponi li koaloe	I would instruct that all mines be closed.
Li koalloe makako a bashanyana	Be closed for all these haughty boys.
Ba tenne banana ka mafereho:	They have bothered the girls with love proposals:
U tla utloa, 'Nyoe, nyoe	You'll hear them say, 'Nyoe, nyoe
Kea u rata.'	I love you.'
Woza monn'aka!	Come my husband!

Here the other performers respond
Woza mosali oa ka!	Come my wife!

This song is a form of social protest against the eradication of social values brought about by the migrant labour culture. Boys leave their villages to work in the South African mines, and when they return they have undergone a transformation. They are now men, for they have been hardened by their hard labour in the mines. At the same time they have acquired some wealth which, they think, makes them attractive to women. All this is part of gender politics in the villages of Lesotho, while at the same time an indictment of the migrant labour system. The world that these songs reflect is the world of the village as it is today.

A song from the Leribe district carried in it developmental messages on village water supply. Without any external agent suggesting it, the girls of one village who had gone to compete in a neighbouring village observed that their hosts did not have water taps in their village, but drew water from an uncovered well, and composed the following song to ridicule them:

Helang bonang banana	Hey, see the girls
Bonang banana ba Ha Qokolo	See the girls of Qokolo's village.
Ba kha metsi liqanthaneng,	They draw water from dirty ponds,
Ba tsekisana metsi	They fight over water
Le liqanqane.	With frogs.
Helang bonang banana,	Hey, see the girls,
Banana ba Ha Mositi ba iphotlileng;	Girls of Mositi's village who have washed themselves;
Ba kha metsi lipompong.	They draw water from taps,
A lelemela feela lipompong.	The water flows from the taps.
Hela! lipompo . . .	Hela! taps . . .
Lipompo tsa ngoan'a morena.	Taps of the chief's child.
Lipompo!	Taps!
Lipompo li molemo, lipompo!	Taps, are useful, taps!

This song transmits social messages and information in an informal atmosphere of village performance. It is created by the performers without being prompted by developmentalists or catalysts from outside. It indicates that *lipina-tsa-mokopu* are a form that can be exploited not only to disseminate information in an informal manner but to invite critical thinking amoung the young women in the village on those issues that concern them. It confirms the assertion that folk songs 'are usually regarded as an entertainment, but they can be both effective and efficient as a communication medium in a society with a strong oral tradition' (Wang and Dissanayake 1982, p. 6). It is no different in other African countries, as Kabwe Kasoma, a theatre practitioner and scholar from Zambia, indicated at the Maseru conference on Theatre-for-Development. There are songs among the Bemba where people sing and others counteract. 'The in-laws sing and the other side of the in-laws listen attentively to the message of that song so as to be able to counteract.' Kasoma was responding to Andrew Horn's statement that songs on their own 'are unable to communicate content and change people's ideas. They may be good for rallying people, but they are just like slogans. They don't invite critical thinking'.

Marotholi Travelling Theatre have incorporated a number of the people's dances in their theatre, such as *mokhibo*, *mohobelo*, *ndlhamu*, *liphotha*, and other syncretic ones such as gumboot dance (also called *liphotha* by Basotho) in which the performers slap and pound their rubber boots in rhythmic performance. It is popular with mine labourers, but in Marotholi it is performed by both men and women, to the delight of the villagers. *Mokhibo* is the most popular form of dance performed by troupes of girls or women

> . . . who bounce gently to the rhythm of a single *moropa* [drum] from an upright sitting or low kneeling position on the ground, with graceful swaying and shaking movements of the head, shoulders, arms, chest, and hips. (Coplan 1989, p. 19.)

The music is led by a soloist, whose lyrics also reflect the experiences and concerns of the villagers. The chorus sings and clap hands in the background. The following is one such song that was recorded for broadcast on Radio Lesotho:

Ke tla isa lengolo lena Ho mang	To whom am I going to deliver this letter
Ha ho se na morena	When there is no chief
Ka khotla?	At the *khotla*?

The song protests against the irresponsibility of current village traditional leadership, who no longr attend to the affairs of the village. In the past the chief and his councillors sat at the *khotla* to deal with the problems of the village, and to hear cases. Today, however, people go to the *khotla* with their problems only to find that the chief is not there. It must be noted that not all *mokhibo* songs have such overt political messages. However they all reflect the experiences and conerns of the villagers. The same applies to *lipina-tsa-mokopu*.

Mohobelo, *ndhlamu* and *liphotha* are men's dances. *Mohobelo* is a graceful stamping dance performed at ceremonial occasions and for recreation. The song is led by a soloist, known as *sephoko*, and this may at times sound like passages from a *sefela*. The other men, the performers themselves, respond in a chorus, while they stamp their feet in a slow rhythmic movement. *Ndhlamu* is a much faster dance usually performed by younger men. It was originally a Zulu dance learned at the mines by Basotho migrant workers. *Liphotha* is usually performed by a solo dancer while the other people sing and clap hands. Marotholi Travelling Theatre report:

> What is fascinating is that the company did not incorporate 'Liphotha' in a play, but used the art form on its own as children's theatre [a play for

children]. While the children sang, clapped hands and responded to the dancers, the dancers did 'Liphotha' and mimed the role of flies in the transmission of diseases. (Mda 1986, p. 20.)

However, not all traditional performance modes in Lesotho can be used in or as theatre-for-development. There are those modes of performance whose meaning is deeply rooted in the context of a specific ceremony or ritual. For example, during the *pitiki* ceremony which is usually held around the fourth month after the birth of a baby, a 'theatre of rebirth' is performed by women.

[W]omen from the village and nearby villages group themselves into teams and perform a series of song and dance performances called *litolobonya*. As women taking part in this performance are barely dressed, men and children are not allowed to watch. (Moitse 1989, p. 39.)

On this occasion the ritual of 'the child coming into being' is enacted, beginning with its conception by miming the sexual act; then pregnancy, labour pains, and finally the birth itself. Performances of the *pitiki* theatre and its *litolobonya* dances would operate outside their social context in theatre-for-development, and would invoke a hostile response from the audiences, whereas dances like *mokhibo* and *mohobelo* are not out of context at such occasions, since they are celebratory dances, always performed at feasts and social functions.

Marotholi have also avoided using songs that are associated with *lebollo*, the ritual of circumcision and initiation of boys into manhood, although some of these songs, called *mangae*, have been known to express social protest, as Moitse has illustrated with the following song, which she recorded in one village:

He jo khafa, he jo khafa,   Hey oh tax, hey oh tax,
Khafa e koaloe, Ha Ramabanta.   Tax should be abolished at
    Ramabanta.

Luma lumang kaofela Basotho   Protest, protest all of you Basotho
Ke utloa le ntomela lekhonono   I hear you respond reluctantly
Ho Ramabanta.   At Ho Ramabanta.
    (Moitse 1989, p. 14.)

Here the initiate, who probably comes from Ha Ramabanta village, calls upon the people of Lesotho to resist exploitation by the ruling classes. Such *mangae* have the potential of being used for conscientisation. However, since they are associated with a secret ritualistic ceremony that is open only to those who have been initiated into it, Marotholi feel that performing such songs would amount to disrespect for the people's sacred institutions, an act which would alienate them from the theatre — even though the performance of *mangae* by the initiates is not secret, but is done publicly when all members of the community are assembled. Indeed men can sometimes be heard singing *mangae* while working, outside the context of the ritual, and some of these songs have been recorded by Radio Lesotho and are broadcast to listeners throughout the country.

5. Theatre-for-Development as Communication

In this chapter, we shall examine how theatre-for-development functions as communication, and how meaning is negotiated between performer and spectator in that communicative act. The chapter sets a theoretical framework for the analysis of the work of Marotholi Travelling Theatre in the next chapter. The examination, therefore, centres on theatrical communication in theatre-for-development, and the rules underlying it.

Current theatre research suffers from an inadequacy of terminology. There has been, over the years, a tendency for scholars to use literary terminology in the discussion of theatre. As a result, theatre, as a performing art, has been unable to evolve a terminology of its own

> The year 1931 is an important date in the history of theatre studies. Until that time dramatic poetics — the descriptive science of the drama and theatrical performance — has made little substantial progress, since its Aristotelian origins. The drama had become (and largely remains) an annexe of the property of literary critics, while the stage spectacle, considered too ephemeral a phenomenon for systematic study, had been effectively staked off as the happy hunting ground of reviewers, reminiscing actors, historians and prescriptive theorists. (Elam 1980, p. 5.)

The year 1931 is important in that it saw the publication, in Czechoslovakia, of two pioneering studies that laid the foundations for a new direction in theatrical and dramatic theory, by providing a structural method for a scientific analysis of theatre and drama using semiotics or semiology. Semiotics is the science of the production of meaning in society. It is concerned with the processes involved in the generation and exchange of meaning, or of *signification* and *communication*. Semiotics has in recent years emerged with a terminology potentially useful in the furtherance of a universally accepted discussion of theatre. This study has no intention of being a semiological analysis of theatre, mass and interpersonal communication. However, in appropriating some concepts and terminology of semiotics in its explication of the phenomenon of theatre-for-development, it recognises that semiology offers the best method of examining how meaning is negotiated between performer and spectator in theatre. Semiotics recognises one crucial assertion: that the performer–spectator bond is a communication relationship, hence its usefulness in a study that attempts to place theatre in the context of development communication theory.

The point was made in chapter 2 that in development communication not only mass media channels are used, but interpersonal ones as well. The question then is: can theatre be categorised as a mass or an interpersonal medium? In their introduction to the uses and gratifications approach to mass communication research, then new, Katz, *et al* (1979, p. 19) claim that in mid-nineteenth-century Italy opera was a 'mass' medium. Although they do not expand on this assertion, the assumption is that they refer to opera as a mass medium because of the broad appeal this art form had, which cut across the social and class spectrum of Italian society. This was before opera detached itself from the common festival. The picture today is different, since opera is part of expensive elite culture, with highly educated consumers. But even before its appropriation by the national elites and the ruling classes for their sole use, it could not be conceived of as a mass communication medium. Without going into the theories of the rise of the image of mass society — a concept that was of central importance for early thinking about the media — formulated by Comte (1915), and the *gemein-schaft/gesellschaft* formulations of Tönnies (1957), it is adequate for the purposes of this study to point out that our current understanding of mass communication is that the message is mediated and distributed to a widely dispersed audience. What makes film a mass communication medium when mid-nineteenth-century opera or contemporary live theatre are not, is the multipliability factor. Mass media have an ability to multiply a message and make it available in many places. In opera the textual material produced for stage representation is the libretto and its music, in conventional theatre the dramatic text or script. But these forms cannot be duplicated, as each performance, even by the same performers, will be different from every other, with the complexity of audience response heightening this difference. The opera of that period could more accurately be termed a popular form of expression, rather than a mass medium existing before the concepts of a mass society were invented.

Opera is used here as an example of live performance that has been referred to as a mass medium, whereas in fact live performances cannot be defined as mass media. In theatre-for-development there is no dramatic text that acts as a referent for the performance text. Each performance is village-specific in that it deals with problems prevailing in that particular area, from the perspective of the community members themselves. It therefore cannot be duplicated in any other area, at any other performance. It is not mediated by technology, not even of the conventional theatre. Although Marotholi characterised their theatre as being both mass and interpersonal communication, the elements of mass communication are not, in fact, present in it; the work uses solely interpersonal channels.

Table 5.1
Communication situations

Private		Public		
Face-to-face	*Interposed*	*Face-to-face*		*Interposed*
			Assembled	Nonassembled
two women converse at a village well	two people converse on telephone or two-way radio	a *pitso* or a performance a play	cinema audience	Listening to radio or viewing television at home

Table 5.1 shows a simple classification of communication situations, suggested by Deutschmann (1957), with examples added by this writer. In this classification theatre falls into the 'face-to-face public communication' category. Table 5.2, on the other hand, shows Rogers' (1973), distinguishing characteristics of interpersonal and mass media channels.

Table 5.2
Characteristics of communication channels

characteristics	interpersonnel	mass media
Message flow	tends to be two-way	tends to be one-way
Communication context	face-to-face	interposed
Amount of feedback readily available	high	low
Ability to overcome selective processes (primarily selective exposure	high	low
Speed to large audiences	relatively slow	relatively rapid
Possible effect	attitude formation and change	knowledge change

There are many approaches to the study of interpersonal communication, ranging from Goffman's sociological tradition of role theory and his concern with dramatic metaphor (see Deutsch and Krauss 1965), and Burke's (1945) dramatism which consists of five key terms, or 'the pentad', reminiscent of the Lasswellian formula, to model-based analysis of the components of a communication system and their function. In this study, we will examine the nature and effects of interpersonal communication in theatre-for-development.

Interpersonal channels, it has been stated, are not mediated, as they are in print or the electronic media. The word 'channels' refers to the way the signs in a message are made available to an audience. An audience is the receiver of the message, and it is active and selective, rather than passive, and may make a variety of uses of the message. Human communication therefore becomes a 'relationship between two or more active persons, entered into with the aid of shared signs' (Schramm 1973, p. 161). The sign links a material vehicle, or *signifier*, with a mental concept, or *signified*.

In theatre-for-development text, in which the participants interact in order to produce meaning, is a macrosign which can be broken down into smaller units of signs. Through these signs the catalysts and the audiences interact to produce and exchange meaning. Signs are organised into codes, systems governed by rules which are consented to by members of the community using that code. This means that codes and signs operate within a culture, which in turn depends upon the use of these codes and signs for its existence. Theatre is made up of linguistic, spatial, gestural, scenographic, and illuminational codes, among others. Dramatic performance is a set of signs and codes that serve to characterise and to advance dramatic action; for theatre-for-development to be successful in its objectives, it must therefore employ signs and codes that are shared by the catalysts and the audience members. The communication failure that Kamlongera (1989), referred to in the work of the Puppet Theatre of the Extension Services Branch of the Malawian Ministry of Agriculture was largely due to the differences in encoding and decoding between senders and receivers, since puppetry uses a set of codes alien to Malawian culture.

Table 5.2 makes clear that interpersonal channels have an advantage over mass media channels on attitude formation and change. The objective of theatre-for-development is to bring about a change in attitude, rather than merely giving the disadvantaged information that will increase their knowledge for its own sake. The change in attitude is achieved through the audience's active participation in creating the message. If the participants do not share the same code, active participation will not be possible. Conscientisation is a process that comes through active participation, and does involve a change of attitude since one is drawn out of the 'culture of silence' and becomes an activist in the analysis of social problems and in the search for a solution.

A concept relevant to any discussion of theatre as an interpersonal channel of communication for development is that of homophily and heterophily. Homophily denotes the degree to which pairs of individuals who interact through messages have similarities in such attributes as beliefs, values, education, and in ideological outlook determined by class position. Heterophily denotes the degree to which individuals differ in these attributes. The homophily principle suggests that, given a free choice, human beings tend to interact with people most like themselves. When a source can interact with any one of a number of different receivers, the tendency will be to select a receiver who is most like the source. Heterophilous communication is normally ineffective. Effective communication occurs when source and receiver are homophilous, since they share common meanings, attitudes, language and other social and cultural codes. Catalysts, in a theatre-for-development situation are normally heterophilous with their rural audiences, due to their educational, social and economic levels. In Figure 5.1 the source A and the target receiver a are homophilous. Given a choice, the two would be expected to interact with each other, and the interaction would be a successful one. But when source A interacts with receiver b, there is heterophily and the two would not normally seek to communicate with each other. If they do interact through messages the transaction is likely to be ineffective. A development expert sent by a donor country to work with rural people in a developing country is an example of this heterophilous situation. But it is not only the expatriate development experts who are heterophilous. Members of the ruling classes, the national elites, and the bureaucrats of the developing world are heterophilous to rural populations in their countries. A purely homophilous situation is not possible, since no two people are exactly alike, hence we must more accurately talk of the degree of homophily. Also, for any person to want to change the attitude or behaviour of another there must be some heterophily present between the two. Heterophily is therefore essential for any change to be effected. In Figure 5.1, source B has *optimal heterophily* with receiver b, a state that exists when the source has only slightly more of attribute X than does his receiver. The implications of optimal heterophily for interpersonal communication in mass communication are great.

> To establish heterophily, the major change agent normally will be unable to communicate with the ultimate receiver. Rather, he must employ intermediaries to conduct these communication transactions. These intermediaries are those referred to as 'opinion leaders'. Opinion leaders tend to be much like their followers, but usually adopt new ideas somewhat more rapidly. (McCroskey, *et al.* 1973, p. 195.)

The concept of opinion leadership was discussed in our section (see p. 29) dealing with Katz and Lazarfeld's (1955), two-step flow model.

Figure 5.1 Heterophily and Homophily

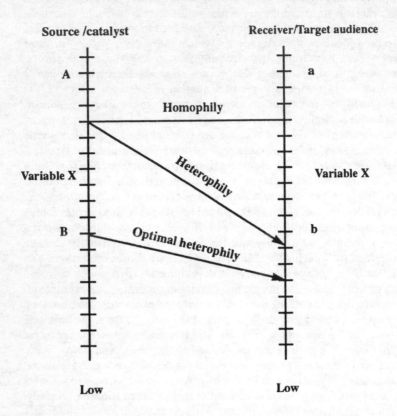

Generally opinion leaders are characterised by more formal education, higher social status, greater readiness to adopt new ideas, more social participation, more media exposure, and greater empathic ability. Although opinion leaders are distinguishable from their followers, the differences are small; they have a lesser degree of heterophily (or a greater degree of homophily) in relation to their followers — hence the state of optimal heterophily. It was noted in our earlier discussion that opinion leaders are not the only members of the community active in information seeking, and that people can be opinion leaders in some subjects and followers in others. The term 'opinion leaders' does not necessarily refer to those who originate ideas, but rather to those who readily adopt them.

A truly popular theatre-for-development is more interested in the most disadvantaged members of a community creating their own messages, than in preparing them readily to adopt innovations introduced by an external agent. The main goal is that the most disadvantaged, who obviously will not fall within the definition posited for opinion leadership, should have the ability to assess innovations in relation to their objective needs, and the political implications involved, before they decide to adopt or not to adopt them. To create messages does not mean merely to respond to messages created by external agents about innovations, but to initiate the process of communication, so that the most disadvantaged members of the community, involved in the culture of silence, can express their political, social and economic needs. In this way, social change will be determined by the community.

Catalysts are themselves heterophilous to villagers. In many cases they are intellectuals from universities alienated from rural society, although some of them may have rural origins. Others are bureaucrats from government ministries who may have adopted the aesthetic and ideological values of the ruling classes, and are likely to purvey these in the name of development. This will be reflected in the kind of theatre they create, which will be diffusionist (based on the diffusion of innovations model), and will not be a vehicle for community dialogue. The example given by Kamlongera (1989), about the Malawian Ministry of Agriculture puppet theatre clearly illustrates this point. The heterophilous communication caused by class-determined ideological differences between the catalysts and the rural community members can be made effective only if the catalysts have a greater level of empathy than the villagers. Empathy is the ability to project oneself into the role of another. Heterophily is an important barrier to effective communication but it may be overcome by source–receiver empathy. To be able to create a critical consciousness among audiences, a catalyst does not need to have a similar class determinant to that of the audience, but does need empathy. The source of empathy is political commitment, brought about by a higher level of critical awareness than that of the community members. This means that catalysts cannot create critical awareness if they themselves do not have a higher level of critical awareness. Their work will merely amount to a dissemination of messages, and their theatre will be diffusionist.

The goal of creating a forum for the most disadvantaged, the most oppressed, members of the rural community does not mean workers in theatre-for-development having no need for opinion leaders. Getting into the village, and bringing the community members together, cannot be done by catalysts on their own, since they are outsiders. The cooperation of opinion leaders, such as chiefs and village elders, is necessary. It must be noted, however, that not in all instances will the village traditional and political leadership be the opinion leadership as well. In some instances chiefs are themselves followers of opinion leaders. For example the village health workers in Lesotho are opinion leaders in the area of primary health care; they act as intermediaries between the community members, on the one hand, and the hospitals and Ministry of Health on the other. When catalysts want to create theatre-for-development on health-related issues, it would be advantageous for them to utilise the Village Health Worker system to get into the villages and to mobilise the community members. When opinion leaders have done their work, the process of turning a performance that merely disseminates messages on how to prepare an oral rehydration solution into a theatre that will conscientise the audience on the social and political causes of disease, and examine self-reliant solutions, happens in the process of creation, rehearsal or performance of the play, depending on the method of theatre used.

Another concept that has relevance in the discussion of theatre-for-development as an interpersonal channel is that of the discontinuous–continuous discourse dichotomy. In discontinuous discourse people speak alternately, and no one person in the group does all the speaking. In this type of discourse all the participants — catalysts and their audiences — become both sources and receivers, with their roles constantly shifting. All members of the group are present while any member of the group speaks, and the communication is face-to-face.

> Because of the interaction during small group communication it is difficult for any single individual to control the effects of the communication. No specific person is the 'source' who can manipulate the effects on the 'receivers'. There is a multiplicity of channels among the various participants, and each of these channels permit influence of one person upon another; however, at the same time each channel potentially serves to inhibit the effects desired by other people. Nevertheless, by virtue of the nature of discontinuous discourse in small group communications, it is possible for an individual member to determine the needs of the other members of the group and to adapt to them in such a way as to achieve his intended effect more easily than in circumstances where the discourse is continuous. In short, the response of person C may cause A to have a different effect on B than intended, but C's response permits A to adapt to C's needs and possibly increase his influence on him. (McCroskey *et al*, 1973, pp. 189–90.)

McCroskey *et al* are writing of interpersonal communication in a small group. This, however, works as well in theatre-for-development situations in which theatre-for-conscientisation is used. In theatre-for-conscientisation, each participant is encouraged to voice his ideas, thus allowing him to bring his influence to bear on the final results.

Continuous discourse is found, as well as in mediated communication, such as print and electronic media, in public address communication. This element has resulted in public address not being recognised as interpersonal communication, although it is face-to-face. In public address the source is distinguishable from the receiver; the source does the talking and all the other people, the audience, are receivers. The *pitso*, described in chapter 3, is an example of continuous discourse. In agitprop, the performers function in a unit as the source, and the audience as receivers. Interaction between the two is severely limited, hence it becomes very important for the source to be able to recognise, interpret, and adapt to audience response or feedback. This means that in the communication process the audience members do not create their messages, but respond to the messages created by the performers, who are external agents. In discontinuous discourse, it is possible for any participant — be it a catalyst or a community member — to begin the transaction without knowing much about the other participants involved, and still be successful. In continuous discourse, prior receiver analysis is required for successful communication. Hence the necessity of the information gathering stage before agitprop practitioners can create their plays, which they will pre-package for an audience of receivers. Some feedback may happen during the performance when audience express their feelings about the events depicted in the play, but most of the feedback is received during the post-performance discussion, in which the discourse becomes discontinuous. In agitprop some adaptation of the message during communication may be possible, depending on the proficiency of the practitioners, but the basic message must be prepared before the transaction begins. If the source incorrectly analyses the receivers and their needs during the information-gathering and date-analysis stages, an inappropriate and thus ineffective message is likely to be developed. It is clear that although agitprop has the essential interpersonal element of face-to-face communication, the performance text is neither mass nor interpersonal communication, but can be accurately categorised as 'public address communication'. Post-performance discussions are interpersonal.

Agitprop as practiced by some practitioners has much greater possibilities of becoming a stimulus–response situation, as in Figure 5.2, where the receiver does not become a source in turn. In a stimulus–response model, the information-giving process is unidirectional and the roles of the participants are fixed. This need not be the case, since it is not necessarily characteristic of agitprop to follow this model. At its best, as has already been argued, it follows the diffusionist model, but at its worst it may follow a stimulus–response model. This happens when performers from outside, using their own theatrical code, present a performance text, with the assumption that it will act as a stimulus to the audiences who will then have specific reactions to it. This principle is outmoded even in mass communication research, since it gave rise to the notion of the mass communication process being merely a process of persuasion. However, it will be illustrated when the work of Marotholi Travelling Theatre is analysed in the next chapter that some practitioners do view theatre-for-development as a process of persuasion.

Figure 5.2
The stimulus-response model

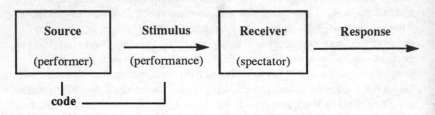

Elam objects to a scheme that views the performer–spectator relationship in theatre (not only in agitprop) along the lines of the stimulus–response model, because in such a scheme the

> actor–audience transaction appears to be based on the weakest forms of bourgeois spectacle where a passive audience may indeed obediently provide predetermined and automatic responses to a predictable set of signals (many a West End or Broadway comedy has operated success-fully on this principle). (Elam 1980, p. 34.)

This has happened a great deal when practitioners have created comedies ridiculing attitudes and behaviour of rural people from the perspective and ideological standpoint of the ruling classes and national elites. In many cases such programmes are classic examples of the 'blaming of the victim' syndrome, where rural communities are blamed as sources of poverty. The normal reaction to the theatrical stimulus is laughter, and nothing ever happens after that. Elam goes further to say that:

> Not only are the audience's signals, in any vital form of theatre, an essential contribution to the formation and reception of the performance text — and indeed various postwar performers and directors such as the Becks and Richard Schechner have extended the bounds of the performance to include the audience explicitly — but the spectator, by virtue of his very patronage of the performance, can be said to *initiate* the communicative circuit (his arrival and readiness being, as it were, the preliminary signals which provoke the performers proper into action . . .). (Elam 1980, p. 34.)

The inclusion of audiences in the performance of theatre-for-development has already been discussed at length in this study. In popular theatre it happens not merely because the director wants to extend the bounds of performance but because it is in the nature of traditional performance modes not to have a performer–audience line of demarcation. Our point of departure, though, lies with the initiation of communication. For Elam, when the audiences arrive for a performance, even if they remain passive receivers of the theatrical message throughout the performance, they have initiated communication, and are therefore active participants in the communication process. Our position is that the performers initiate communication by inviting the prospective audience to attend the performance. When the audience attends, it is responding to, not initiating, the communication process. This study's view of audience participation in the communication process involves an articulated exchange of messages, where all the participants can in turn create their own messages and transmit them to others. Indeed it is when the audience sets the agenda, and creates community dialogue within its own framework, that the process of conscientisation takes place.

It is clear that for communication to happen the receiver must be acquainted with the sender's code, and must be able to decode the message. Formation and understanding of messages involves encoding and decoding. In theatre this is not a linear process as in the Shannon–Weaver one-way model, shown in Figure 2.2 (see p. 25). This model is quite inadequate to explain theatre as communication, the more so because performance brings about a multiplication of communicational factors. (Its inadequacy in explaining mass communication is discussed in chapter 2.)

Of particular interest is Elam's theatrical communication model, shown in Figure 5.3. Elam writes that at each stage in the theatrical communication process there arises, rather than a single element, a complex of potential components. The dramatist may be identified as the source of theatrical information. The dramatic text, where it exists, is both a pretext and a constituent of the performance text. Unlike literary critics, Elam does not assume the priority of the written play over the performance, even though chronologically the writing of the play precedes any given performance of it. It is legitimate, he says, to claim that it is the performance, or at least a possible 'model' performance, that constrains the dramatic text in its very articulation.

What this suggests is that written/performance text relationship is not one of simple priority but a complex of reciprocal constrains constituting a powerful *intertexuality*. Each text bears the other's traces, the performance assimilating those aspects of the written play which the performers choose to transcodify, and the dramatic text being 'spoken' at

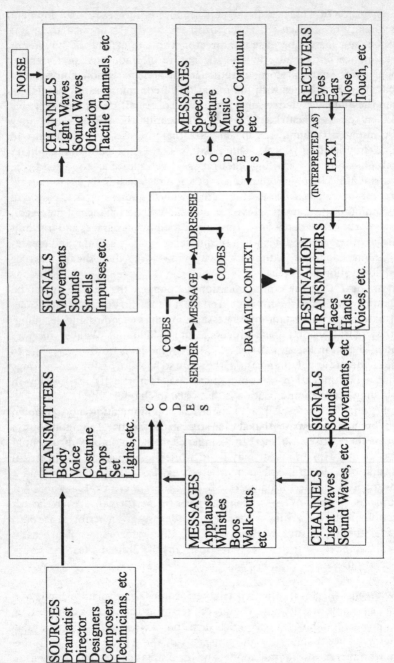

Figure 5.3: Elam's Theatrical Communication Model

every point by the model performance — or the *n* possible performances — that motivate it. This intertexual relationship is problematic rather than automatic and symmetrical. Any given performance is only to a limited degree constrained by the indications of the written text, just as the latter does not usually bear the traces of any *actual* performance. It is a relationship that cannot be accounted for in terms of facile determinism. (Elam 1980, p. 209.)

Another source of theatrical information is the director, whose decisions and instructions determine to a great extent the choice of transmitters. Together with the actors, set designer, composer, stage manager, lighting designer and other technicians, the director decides what form the signals will take, and how the messages will be encoded. With metonymic accessories such as costumes, properties and sets, the voices and bodies of the actors become transmitters. The signals transmitted by these bodies are movement, sound or electrical impulses. The signals are selected and arranged 'syntactically according to a wide range of sign or signalling *systems* and travel through any number of physical channels available for human communication, from light and sound waves to olfactory and tactile means (in modern contact performances smell and touch become significant constraints upon reception of the whole text)' (Elam 1980, p. 37). Because of the multiplication of components and systems, it is impossible to talk of a single theatrical message. The performance is made up of multiple messages transmitted through speech, gesture, lighting and sound effects etc., as an integrated text according to the dramatic, theatrical and cultural codes at his disposal.

On receiving and decoding these signals, the spectator in turn becomes a transmitter of signals to the performers, in the form of laughter, applause, whistles, boos, and so on. These signals are transmitted along visual and acoustic channels, and will be interpreted by the performers and members of the audience as either hostility or approval. There is therefore feedback from spectator to performer. However, one distinguishing feature of theatre is that the performer–audience communication does not take a direct form, unless the actor directly addresses the audience, as is the case in some prologues, epilogues, asides, apostrophes and even whole plays.

[T]he actor–spectator transaction within the *theatrical* context is mediated by the *dramatic* context in which a fictional speaker addresses a fictional listener. It is this dramatic communicational situation which is ostended to the spectator . . . and this peculiar obliqueness of the actor–audience relationship must be accounted for in any model. (Elam 1980, p. 38.)

This indirectness in theatrical communication is a complicating factor in designing a model that will adequately explain theatrical communication. In Figure 5.3, Elam has designed a simplified representation of theatrical communication. He warns that the model is undoubtedly reductive and mechanistic, but it does at least serve as an illustration of the multi-levelled character of the theatrical communicational exchange.

Every communicative act depends upon the information-value of the message. *Semantic* information refers to what is generally understood in colloquial use as the 'intelligence given about some topic'. It is 'the sum of new knowledge given regarding the state of affairs referred to'. In theatrical performance this knowledge is about the fictional dramatic world represented in the performance. In Elam's model it appertains to the 'dramatic context' box. This can be designated *dramatic information*. This dramatic information can be conveyed by any or all of the systems involved in a theatrical production, and can be translated from one kind of message to another, irrespective of the physical qualities of signs or signals used.

To illustrate this point, Elam gives an example of the means through which the information 'night falls' may be conveyed. It may be conveyed by means of a lighting change, a verbal reference or, in Oriental theatre, gesturally. The audience expects to receive a more or less coherent set of signs which they will interpret, and reconstruct the world represented in the performance text. Audiences do not go to the theatre only to be informed about 'other worlds'. The fact that they can go to see the production of plays that they have already seen suggests that there are other informational levels on which theatrical messages work. Elam explains these levels thus:

> In elementary communication, signal-information is purely functional and remains quite distinct from the semantic content assigned to the message. On stage, however, the physical characteristics of the signs and signals are not only ostended for their own sake (the texture of the costumes or the actors' bodies being major sources of pleasure), *but contribute directly to the production of meaning*. Signal-information, that is to say, becomes, in the theatre, a source of semantic information, owing to the ability of the material qualities of the message to connote a range of meanings in their own right. (Elam 1980, p. 41.) [Emphasis mine]

To illustrate this point further, Elam gives an example of two performances of *Agamemnon*. Both of these will give more or less the same dramatic information regarding the state of Greek society, the course of events in the Trojan Wars, the interaction between the characters in the play, and so on, but if one performance is limited to reproducing the main elements of the Greek stage, and the other lavishly modern in its representational means, there will be differences in the audiences' decoding of the two performance texts. One text may be understood, say, in terms of universal metaphysical conflicts, and the other in terms of personal and material conflicts between the individual participants in the performance text. Theatrical information has many levels on which messages work, hence the complexity of any model that attempts to explain the communication aspects of the theatre.

Elam's work is an in-depth study of the semiotics of theatre and drama, and goes further than the analysis of the theatrical models explained above. The interest of this study, however, is not in the semiotics of theatre *per se*, but in how Elam's model can be utilised to explain the phenomenon of theatre-for-development — particularly in its communicative aspects. In Elam's model the dramatist is the source of information. Other sources are the director, the actors (in their capacity as decision-makers, initiative-takers and funds of ideas), and other technical personnel of the theatre. All these people represent significant influence on the performance. Agitprop as theatre-for-development could certainly be explained in a similar manner, since it is a prepackaged production that may be created from a dramatic text composed by a dramatist. In other forms of popular theatre-for-development this would not be the case, since the play is created jointly by the actors and the director (catalysts) on one hand, and the audiences who gradually become actors themselves, on the other. In this situation, the sources of information are both the catalysts and the audience. All of them make decisions on how to encode the message, and what transmitters to use.

When the performance text emerges from their joint efforts, it has not been motivated by a dramatic text. Intertexuality exists, but it is not between the written and the performance texts, but between the social context and the performance text. As in Elam's model, the transmitters are a multiplicator of components such as voices and bodies of the actors (and 'actors' here refers to both catalysts and spectators), musical instruments such as drums and the accordion, and metonymic accessories such as props and sets.

The emphasis, however, in popular theatre-for-development is to minimise some of these components, so as to avoid illusionistic representation as found in 'naturalistic' staging. For this reason there is a movement away from using sets, and the use of props is cut to a bare minimum. Among the sources in this kind of theatre, costume designers, set designers and lighting designers will not be found. Indeed, artificial transmitters can be illusionists, and will influence the spectator's perception and decoding of messages. They may participate as connotative presences in their own right. It is for this reason that Brecht insisted on making the source of light visible in his theatre in order to prevent the element of illusion.

Although Elam does not mention it, elements in the structure of the stage itself, such as the proscenium, play a role in the transmission process. The preference of popular theatre-for-development is the arena *trouvé*. Besides the fact that this is the conventional staging of indigenous performance modes, it also eliminates the line of demarcation between actor and audience that exists in the illusionistic 'fourth-wall' proscenium staging. One objective of popular theatre-for-development is to draw the audience's attention to the sign-vehicle and its social context rather than the signified and its dramatic equivalent. Signifier and signified become one in this process. It is the same objective observed about radical theatre and cinema-verité:

> At a performance of radical theatre, the audience is part of the performance and there is no division between stalls and footlights. Signifier and signified become one. In cinema-verité the characters play themselves and enact their lives before the camera. They create and are created; they all stand in metonymic relation to the completed part. (Van Zyl 1977, p. 39.)

In Elam's model the feedback process happens, as is normally the case in elementary communication, when the spectator receives and decodes the message from the performers on the stage, then in turn becomes a transmitter of signals of approval or hostility to the performer, encoded in forms of laughter, boos, walkouts and whistles. In popular theatre-for-development the audience participates both as source and destination, and so do the performers. Not only are there no divisions between 'stalls and footlights', there are indeed no stalls and footlights. The audience–performer communication takes a direct form at the two levels of the world of the play and the world of the society in which the play is being created and performed. These two worlds constantly shift, and at times merge into each other. At times a fictional speaker addresses a fictional listener, a fictional speaker addresses a real-life listener, and a real-life speaker addresses a real-life listener. The oblique actor–spectator relationship constantly shifts to a direct relationship. All these are complicating factors in the drawing of a model that will explain theatre-for-development. After examining the work of Marotholi Travelling Theatre in the next chapter, it will be the task of this study to examine whether Elam's model can be adapted, or if a new model that will adequately explain theatre-for-development can be created.

It has already been mentioned that theatre-for-development avoids the use of illusionistic elements of the theatre. It was the same with Brecht, whose goal was to purge the stage of everything 'magical' such as sets that convey the flavour of a particular place, lighting effects, and sound effects. Theatre-for-development encourages the metaphoric assertion of the phenomenon of the stage, rather than the impersonation. For instance, an empty stage becomes for the audience a corn field, a government office or an underground mine shaft. The theatrical sign in this situation can be transformed with versatility. For instance in a play on migrant labour performed by Marotholi Travelling Theatre, the miners helmets become at times chairs, at times buckets of water.

The removal of illusion goes further than in Brechtian philosophy, to the actor who must not allow himelf to become completely transformed on the stage into the character he is portraying. He reproduces the dialogue, but he never tries to persuade himself (and thereby others) that this amounts to a complete transformation. The actor avoids living himself into the part. There is also the question of removing 'hypnotic tension' by relaxing the tempo of conversation, and by acting without tautened muscles, and of dropping the fourth wall assumption so that the actor can even talk directly to the audience. All these techniques are found in theatre-for-development. However, on the process of *historicisation*, where actors treat present day events and modes of behaviour with detachment, as an historian treats the past, we must take a new direction. Characters cannot alienate themselves from the events of the play, for these depict their real life situation. They will get emotionally involved, and only later distance themselves emotionally in order to analyse the sources of the problems and to work out solutions. Even Brecht concedes that empathy cannot be removed entirely, that some empathy is necessary.

> The English translation (or Verfremdungseffekt, strange-making effect) into 'alienation effect' is an obvious misnomer since Brecht's entire notion of writing was not based on alienating the spectator — the spectator has already been alienated. The task is to de-alienate him and society. (Gugelberger 1985, p. 10.)

A critical attitude in acting does not necessarily mean that the performers will not be emotionally involved, especially if the performance text relates directly to their lives. In fact, empathy is essential for effective communication.

6. People Play People: The Theatre of Marotholi

Marotholi Travelling Theatre has taken several approaches to theatre-for-development: beginning in the early years with agitprop, and later changing to theatre-for-conscientisation and participatory theatre. On some occasions it has adapted agitprop, by inserting in it elements of theatre-for-conscientisation. In this chapter, we will examine more closely the plays created by the group together with their audiences.

The plays to be examined fall into the categories of agitprop, theatre-for-conscientisation and participatory theatre, as identified by Lambert (1982), who in turn based his analysis on the work of Boal (see Chapter 2). The first play is entitled *Kopano ke Matla!* ('Unity is Strength'), and deals with cooperative societies. The rest of the plays were originally untitled, but for the purpose of this study they will be given titles based on their themes. These are *Rural Sanitation*, *Agro-Action*, *Trade Unions*, and *Alcoholism*. All the plays are in Sesotho, the national language of Lesotho. Lesotho being homogeneous, the language is spoken throughout the country; this makes the work of the theatre practitioner simpler, since participants share common codes as far as language is concerned.

Agitprop: *Kopano ke Matla!*

Brief history of *Kopano ke Matla!*
The following history of the play is recorded in Horn and Davenport (1985).

> Following upon the largely enthusiastic receptions which greeted the Project's first four productions, it was decided to go outside the context of the undergraduate instructional programme for the next phase of activity. [All the previous plays had been performed in the context of a Practical Theatre course offered by the English Department of the National University of Lesotho.] A team of students, all but two of whom had participated in previous productions, were recruited to mount a play

during the university's winter holidays, in May and June 1984. As the Institute of Extra Mural Studies (IEMS) has an active programme of guidance in co-operative education, it seemed appropriate that the project should turn its attention to the problems which beset fledgling producer co-operatives and to recommend possible solutions to these difficulties. For the first time, the cast did not conduct its research at community level but based its work entirely on interviews with IEMS staff directly concerned with co-operative training. From these discussions, the team concluded that the obvious merits of community co-operatives — greater productivity, the reduction of costs through the bulk-buying of fertilizers, the centralized marketing of produce, the possibility of leasing or purchasing tractors and other equipment, and growing of food for family consumption as well as for sale — were offset in the minds of many by a host of apprehensions. These included the fact that migrant workers see South Africa as the place of work, and Lesotho as the place of rest and thus believe investment in economic activities within Lesotho to be unnecessary; the feeling that co-operatives are merely political fronts for the ruling political party; a reluctance to entrust one's money to banks; a concern that committee members would misuse funds and use the purchased farm machinery for personal gain; the fact that some individuals would not have enough money to join, although they had the will and the energy to participate; and the sense that a general torpor in the country, aggravated by excessive alcohol consumption, would make it difficult to get any effective organisation off the ground.

These matters, and others, were each dwelt upon in the play (see Appendix for text). As in the previous plays, the production integrated song and dance into the flow of action, introducing the characters and commenting upon action just concluded or about to occur. Entitled *Kopano ke Matla!*, (Unity is Strength!), it proved to be both the longest of the Project's plays — running to over an hour, when others had lasted for about forty minutes — and the most widely publicized. Graced with a particularly able cast, and carefully paced and larded with a generous quantity of comedy and pathos, the play was performed not only during the original production period, but in three subsequent revivals.

The first performance was at Ha Ratau, at the office of the Chief of Thaba Bosiu, the historical capital of the Basotho people. Comments from the audience, which numbered well over 250, included the observation that beer interfered with the work of the community and that it was hoped members of the audience would heed the lessons of the play. It was also noted, that, like the co-operative in *Kopano ke Matla!*, the co-operatives which had been launched in the area had started off badly and that the advice of IEMS on getting the organizations going again would be welcome. The IEMS staff immediately offered their assistance in this endeavour.

At Ha Mohalenyana, a great deal of direct publicity (a Land Rover carrying an announcer with a megaphone) was needed to muster an audience of just under 200. It was explained to the team that so many political *pitsos* (public meetings) had been called by government of late that people had become jaded and were reluctant to attend any further gatherings, even if they did involve entertainment. Nonetheless, an attractive audience was ultimately recruited and seemed most disturbed by the character of Mokotla, the lazy man who dies after eating stolen vegetables sprayed with insecticide.

The performance at Ha Lethena, at the foot of the towering Mount Machache, was forced indoors by snow and hail. Inside the local primary school (minimally appointed with a mud floor, tin roof, broken windows and form benches), and audience of about 150, including schoolchildren given a morning off from classes and adults from several widely dispersed villages, welcomed the performance with a warm and moving enthusiasm. Points raised during the open discussion included the following:

1. That the play was 'a mirror. We have seen ourselves';
2. that 'everyone, should pay attention to the message of the play,' both young and old, because the youth can no longer be guaranteed employment in South Africa;
3. that, while there is nothing wrong with beer, the day should begin with work and the beer should follow in the evening as a reward;
4. that laziness is a major obstacle to development and can lead to crime and as the play showed, even death;
5. that the miner who has no interest in investing his energies in Lesotho is a familiar figure and can only be eliminated from the society by teaching children at school about co-operatives and the need to develop one's home country; and
6. that the local co-operative does not run effectively and would benefit from the advice of IEMS.

Ha Ramabanta, where the team performed next, is just above the winter snowline and another indoor performance had to be mounted, in a large classroom belonging to a Roman Catholic primary school. This is a strongly anti-government area and, assuming that all public gatherings are organized to bolster support for the ruling party, the community adamantly refused to attend. Nonetheless some seventy-five people were drawn to the venue and joined animatedly in the discussion following the play, bringing up many of the issues raised at Ha Lethena. The chieftainess of the area invited IEMS to offer courses in Ha Ramabanta to enable co-operatives to be established properly, and twenty or more participants for such a course were recruited on the spot by the IEMS organizer.

After recording the play at the Instructional Materials Resource Centre (IMRC) studios, for broadcasting over Radio Lesotho, the play had its final performance of the series at Ha Moitsupeli, to a rather cold and listless audience of about 250 people. It was felt that IEMS should have been a bit more selective in its choice of venues for this phase of the project, as some of the locales chosen were inhospitable to such activities at that time, and that it would have been better to expend the group's efforts in more congenial districts. It should here be noted that the political complexion of the cast itself was, quite pointedly, ecumenical and that not only the country's two major parties, but minor parties as well, were represented in the team.

With the conclusion of the winter production schedule, enthusiasm for *Kopano ke Matla!* did not wane, either among the cast or the general populace. It was therefore decided to revive the play for a special performance to be presented before His Majesty King Moshoeshoe II. Her Majesty Queen Mamohato, invited dignitaries and the wider public at the Royal Village of Matsieng in September 1984. This event was designed primarily to demonstrate to policy-makers in government ministries and aid agencies what had already been amply demonstrated to villagers throughout the Project's catchment area — that theatre is a powerful vehicle for communication of development information and a significant potential motivating force in the generating of debate within communities. The performance, mounted on a natural stage at one end of Matsieng's broad *pitso* ground, attracted well over 1,000 people, including government officials, university staff, journalists, villagers and schoolchildren, and elicited a good deal of popular notice. The play was again revived in early 1985, for a university audience, and in March 1985, for the International Conference on Theatre for Development in Maseru, on which occasion the production was video-taped by IMRC. The play has since been adapted to a comic book format, for distribution by IEMS and the Ministry of Co-operatives and Rural Development, as part of their education programmes. (Horn and Davenport 1985, pp. 17–20.)

Kopano Ke Matla! as conscientisation

1. Naming: *What* are the problems in our present situation?
2. Reflection: *Why* do these problems exist?
3. Action Praxis: *How* can this situation be changed?

Although *Kopano ke Matla!* posed these three questions, there was no participation by the audience at any stage of the creation and presentation of the play. The problems were examined by the theatre practitioners, and the audiences became mere consumers of a finished product.

In the information-gathering stage of the process, which normally would be the 'naming' stage of the conscientisation process, the official eye technique was used. All the information was obtained from official sources: namely, the IEMS staff directly concerned with co-operative training. The villagers were not interviewed, even to get their point of view in relation to the information gathered from official sources. The conclusions that the performers reached — 'the obvious merits of community co-operatives' — were based on their 'superior knowledge' as outside agents, and did not take into consideration the experience of the villagers. For instance, through the official eye technique the theatre group discovered that the migrant workers see South Africa as the place of work and Lesotho as the place for rest, but no attempt was made to examine, with the villagers, why such attitudes exist. Are there perhaps no structural causes that have over the years cultivated these attitudes in the minds of the villagers? The migrants themselves are in the best position to say why they regard Lesotho as the place of rest, and from there dialogue would continue as to whether Lesotho should really be the place for rest, and whether investment in economic activities within Lesotho is necessary or not.

Again the group learnt of the strong feeling in the rural communities that co-operatives are merely political fronts for the ruling political party. If they had gone out to talk with the people, rather than depend on information from bureaucrats, they would have learnt why villagers harbour such feelings against co-operatives. Instead the play dismisses these concerns in a few lines of dialogue between the women from the well, when one says that co-operatives are bad because:

there is a lot of politics there. When you belong to the ruling party you are the king. Another thing is the church. Always you will find that the Catholics are right in front, and the Protestants far behind.

Another woman answers:

The woman I saw from Lintjeng village said there are no political affairs nor church wranglings in the co-operatives. What is there is the unity of the village.

And with this dialogue the concerns of the villagers have been addressed. No attempt has been made to find out from them what their previous experience of co-operatives and similar organisations is, and why they have come to associate them with political parties and church denominations. Who really benefits from such co-operatives? How effective are they in combating the problems of poverty? Are they really to the benefit of the poorest members of the community, those who are in the periphery, or do they, like most development programmes introduced into rural communities, benefit the centre of these periphery communities? Evidence elsewhere (see Hedebro 1982, p. 110) has shown that those with traditionally strong positions in society have been the ones to gain from co-operatives and credit unions. If so, how can this situation be remedied? These are crucial questions, the answers to which would emerge in a process of community dialogue.

In the naming stage, the subject was chosen solely because IEMS had a programme on co-operative training, and was not selected on the basis of the felt needs of the people. The theatre group then created a play, rehearsed it, and took it to the villages for performances after which there was discussion on the issues raised in the play. There was no community participation in the selection of campaign issues, in the planning of the programme, or in the performances. The concentration was on the product — the ready-made play — rather than on the process. The villagers were therefore not involved in a process of critical analysis. The play became the means of merely putting across information on co-operatives, and not a vehicle for a deep-rooted learning process. Its sole concern was to proffer technical solutions rather than to explicate the problems of rural underdevelopment by examining historical, economic and political factors at play in the perpetuation of the condition. Kidd, reporting on the Zimbabwe workshop, observed a similar trend there, with plays that left the villagers out of the key stages of the process of analysis of the initial data and dramatisation.

[T]he plays tended to be didactic, prescribing new skills, attitudes and practices to be adopted by the villagers rather than raising for discussion the socio-political constraints upon them. (Kidd 1985, p. 180.)

On those plays that involved the villagers through all the stages of the process, he observes:

The villagers experienced a much more sustained, participatory and deep-rooted learning process than if they had watched and discussed a ready-made play produced by outsiders. The plays reflected their reality, their perspectives and their drama-making, and their involvement in making and remaking the drama threw up new insights which would not have surfaced otherwise, and produced a much more critical analysis of the problems and possibilities for change. Their participation in the creative aspect of this work also helped to revitalise their own village cultural activity and to boost their confidence. Finally, the sustained participation provided a good basis for the long-term continuity of the work. (Kidd 1985, p. 198.)

The director of *Kopano ke Matla!*, Professor Andrew Horn, gave his reasons for avoiding any active involvement of the villagers in the theatre during the 1985 International Conference on Theatre for Development in Maseru.* The following dialogue took place among David Kerr, Stephen Chifunyise and Andrew Horn:

Kerr: You can have a play with many alternative endings, and the audience debate on them and choose the best.
Chifunyise: The open-ended play does not offer solutions but makes the audience come up with solutions. Then the play will have an ending which has been suggested by the audience, and that becomes the ending of the play.
Horn: There are tremendous political divisions in Lesotho. When you open up the play in that way you are making a political forum.

This, of course, presumes the false line of demarcation between development and politics discussed at length in Chapter 2 (see pp. 15–17). Horn went further to say,

Plays must give the other side of the argument. But we take sides. We provide a solution. We have all positions presented by characters who are not stereotypes — recognizable characters. But in the end we come up with solutions.

As a result the play is, like the simple skits initially used by development workers in the Zimbabwe workshop (Kidd 1985, p. 182), message-oriented and exhortatory rather than focusing on a process of community analysis and decision-making.

At that stage of the work of the Project that created *Kopano ke Matla!* there was strong resistance on the part of the leadership to any movement that would lead to a participatory approach to theatre-for-development by involving the villagers in key stages of data analysis and dramatisation. This resistance was evident in Horn's comments during a debate between him and Dr Victor Mtubani of the University of Botswana at the Maseru Conference:

Mtubani: The whole thing [theatre-for-development process] has to begin from inside. It is a liberal and comfortable view for us theatre people from

* All the citations from the International Conference on Theatre for Development held in Maseru, Lesotho, in 1985, are from personal notes taken by the author during the proceedings of the conference.

outside to go into the village and do the 'good' work of teaching them [the villagers] things. The whole thing must begin from inside.

Horn: I don't think for a doctor to cure gonorrhoea he must have gonorrhoea. I don't think it is solely for the poor to cure poverty. This is not a group [of actors] who have been imported into the community from a foreign land. Some of these university actors have their roots in the rural areas. They are familiar with the problems, and the culture. We don't have to live in the community to help the community.

Mtubani: It would be more profitable if this encouragement involved the local people. The base must be the villagers, so that the institutions we establish must remain, even when we have gone back to the comforts of our middle-class homes.

Horn's medical doctor/gonorrhoea analogy sums up the philosophy behind the work of agitprop practitioners in theatre-for-development, and its undemocratic nature. The practitioner is an external agent with superior knowledge of the ailments of poverty among the peasants, and of the most suitable cures for such ailments.

Students from the university, even if they have rural origins, are by virtue of their educational status heterophilous to the villagers. Their perspective will not necessarily be the same as that of the peasants. They are external agents as well, since external agents do not necessarily have to originate from a foreign country. It is for this reason that *Kopano ke Matla!* tends to be didactic and prescriptive. The villagers were forced to play a passive role, and therefore became objects of their own development process, rather than the subjects — the active participants. As objects they are merely an audience for messages and analyses made by outsiders. As Mtubani rightly pointed out, a situation of this nature will not produce the organisational momentum and thrust that is vital for the community dialogue through theatre to continue even when the catalysts have left the community. This philosophy of treating villagers as objects was also identified by the Community Theatre for Integrated Rural Development Workshop, held at Telu in Sierra Leone (The Telu Workshop) in 1986, as one of the major reasons for failure of development programmes in the rural Third World. Malamah-Thomas, the workshop co-ordinator, writes:

It has now increasingly been realised that only rarely have the poor — *the real experts on poverty* [emphasis mine], the people who experience it day after day — been consulted about what they need and how they want to develop themselves. They have rarely been allowed to participate in decisions which affect their lives in a way that would unleash their creative energies and abilities. Excluded from participation in their own development process, the poor have been treated as 'objects' to receive *development packages* instead of as people who have first-hand knowledge, born out of hard and bitter experience, about how to survive and develop in a harsh and unfriendly environment. The failure of development programmes and the failure to involve the people in their development process are inextricably intertwined. (Malamah-Thomas 1989, p. 8.)

It is possible that, had the villagers been involved in the process of creating *Kopano ke Matla!*, some of the inconsistencies evinced by the play would have been eliminated. The major one is that through the official-eye technique the theatre group observed that there is a general torpor in the country, aggravated by excessive alcohol consumption. Indeed, the problems of alcoholism are of deep concern to the rural community members in Lesotho. This was clearly indicated by an information-gathering expedition by members of this same Project in the rural areas when they were preparing a play on health-related issues. Horn (1984, p. 46) reports that drunkenness was in the list of problems suggested by the villagers at a *pitso*. In later years the problem of drunkenness emerged when catalysts from Marotholi went to create a play with the peasants at Tebellong, in the Qacha's Nek district of Lesotho (the play is discussed later in this chapter). However, in *Kopano ke Matla!* beer drinking plays an important role, and the shebeen is the centre of all activity. When Chifunyise raised this question at the International Conference on Theatre for Development, Horn replied: 'There is a real world out there. So as not to alienate our audience we have to reflect it. Beer drinking is a major activity and shebeens are social centres. If we were to do a play on alcoholism it would be a different play.'

This reflects a compartmentalised vision of development rather than an integrated one. In Horn's view each developmental issue is unrelated to the others, and the dissemination of information on the issues may even strive in opposite directions, towards contradictory objectives. A similar problem is observed on Radio Lesotho where a programme from the Health Education Unit on the dangers of smoking will immediately be followed by an advertisement extolling the virtues of a particular blend of cigarettes. The messages are sponsored by different interest groups, but they are received by the rural audiences from the same channel. Following Horn's reasoning, it would be in order for the Community Alcoholic Rehabilitation Programme, which has over the years been creating and performing plays on alcoholism in the villages and broadcasting them over Radio Lesotho, to create plays that discourage villagers from joining co-operative societies, in the context of a story that aims to promote the rehabilitation of alcoholics. In any case it is incorrect that the lives of the majority of the people in Lesotho revolve around shebeens. The same themes in *Kapona ke Matla!* can be depicted in family situations. There are vibrant family units in Lesotho. There are friends and neighbours. There are other formal and informal institutions where community members interact with one another. That is the real world of the majority of the Basotho. In the villages only a small minority of drinkers will have shebeens as the centre of their world. Only in this play is the shebeen the centre of community life. Even the success which has been brought about by co-operatives is measured by improved drinking conditions. Those community members who were unable to afford drinks now have enough money to buy as much drink as they want. Even the shebeen itself looks better furnished.

The inconsistencies brought about by lack of participation of villagers in a critical analysis of their problems are further illustrated by the conclusion the villagers themselves reached during the post-performance discussions. They identified laziness as the major obstacle to development, which 'can lead to crime and, as the play showed, even death'. The blaming-the-victim syndrome (see chapter 2; also Kidd and Byram, 1981) becomes the 'victims-blaming-themselves' syndrome, without examining the causes of apathy in the rural communities. Are the victims blaming themselves because the play instructs them to do so? Are they telling the outside agent what he wants to hear? Without denying the fact that there are elements like Lazy Man in any society — including any in the developed world — do the villagers mean that the problems of underdevelopment are due to laziness? Are the bulk of the peasants in Lesotho villages lazy? If so, why do they go to the mines in South Africa to work very hard there? Or are they hardworking but still live in poverty? If that be the case, why do they continue to live in poverty? The play did not help the villagers to examine these questions critically, because the villagers were not involved in the whole process of its creation. There is no self-examination on their part, since the outsiders have already decided what the ailment is and how best to cure it.

The dialogue in *Kopano ke Matla!* was created by the actors through improvisation. After each scene had been improvised, the dialogue just composed would be recorded, and the actors would then memorise the lines. In all performances the dialogue would remain the same, with a few changes such as the name of the village to suit the particular performance. This means that there was a script, produced through the joint authorship of the actors and the director. The play was then rehearsed by the actors and the director alone, and performed in a pre-packaged form.

The quality of the spectacle in the play was of major concern, and the performance was proficiently executed. The structure followed the traditional dramatic curve, with the conflict being introduced in the first scene. It undergoes a suspenseful development, with plot points such as the discovery of the missing chicken and eggs, the accusation of the treasurer and his subsequent confession, the death of Lazy Man, and the climactic arrival of the impoverished miner. The denouement is in the debate as to whether he should be admitted into the co-operative or not, and his final admission.

Characterisation was also effective; the characters had strength and presence, a sense of person and credibility. Their actions were consistent with the culture of the play. So was their style of speech, vocabulary and mannerisms. There was adequate motivation in their actions, although sometimes there was no justification. For instance, Lazy Man is lazy because he is a lazy person. He is not a complex individual acting out of the totality of his experience.

The quality of this play was observed by the literary critic and novelist, Njabulo Ndebele, when he wrote:

> The simplicity of the story, however, is deceptive. The richness of the entire theatrical experience is to be found in the range of typical village characters so wonderfully brought alive on stage by competent actors. They were all there: the resourceful shebeen queen, the village grandmother, the school teacher, the village won't-work who pesters everybody for a drink and other kinds of charity, the local beauty who has retured from 'way back in Welkom' [a mining city in South Africa], the ordinary, decent woman with a rather delinquent, mean, and boastful husband, and a typical extension worker from IEMS. The lasting impression I came away with of all these characters as a group was their enduring humanity, their deceptive simplicity, their infinite patience, their sense of justice and compassion, and their ability to understand and overcome human weakness even in themselves. The actors brought out all these human attributes most convincingly through mastery of gesture, confident vocal delivery, and lively dialogue. There was relatively very little action, but there was never a dull moment. (Ndebele 1984, pp. 1–2.)

Ndebele goes further to comment on the enthusiastic reception of the play by the Matsieng audience, and the recognition articulated by one woman during discussion time who said. 'What we have just seen is ourselves; what we have just seen is how we live.' Then he comments on the competence of the individual actors. One displayed a tremendous talent in the use of the apt facial expression to convey various attitudes, and another

> showed himself to be the master of the deliberately exaggerated gesture which, for me, emphasized the essentially ritualistic nature of drama, the impact of which lies in the balance between convincing social representation on the one hand, and on the other hand, that representation itself as demonstration of message. (Ndebele 1984, p. 2.)

Ndebele's comments are those of a reviewer — in the literary tradition — writing a critical appreciation of the play. They clearly show how effective the play was as a stimulating theatrical experience, executed by theatre practitioners who were highly skilled in their art. But they do not tell the reader how effective the play was in fulfilling its primary function — that of being a medium for development communication. They are useful, however, as an illustration in support of Lambert's (1982) assertion that the organisers of agitprop are essentially theatre professionals whose primary interest is the quality of the spectacle.

Use of performance space: In the staging of the play there was a separation of the audience from the performers, with curtains further separating the backstage area. The actors made their entrances and exits as they would in a purpose-built architectural structure with a proscenium stage. This created the distance between the performers and audience that exists between teacher and students in a traditional model of teaching. In this model, the teacher teaches and the students are taught. The teacher knows everything and the students know nothing. The teacher talks all the time (continuous discourse) and the students listen. The teacher chooses what it is the students will learn. In a participatory model, the separation between performers and audience does not exist. Instead the teacher, who now becomes an animator or catalyst, creates an environment in which thinking, active, creative participants can learn from each other. In this model, the catalyst is in the centre, where most of the participation takes place. But some participation happens all around the arena, as the participants' shared experiences are analysed and become part of the material upon which the training and education are based. Participants choose what it is they want to learn.

In theatre-for-development a participatory situation is achieved through theatre-in-the-round, which is the form that the staging of indigenous and popular performance takes in Lesotho. In this form of staging, those illusionistic elements characteristic of most current Western theatre, which, according to Kerr, came as a result of laissez-faire capitalism, are eliminated.

> Laissez-faire capitalism had another powerful impact on Euro-American theatre — the increasing distance from the seventeenth century onwards between the performers and the audience. The elimination of the orchestra in the neoclassic stage and the growing dominance of the proscenium arch were architectural techniques which did for theatre what capitalism was doing for industry — making a clear distinction between producer and consumer. (Kerr 1988, p. 174.)

In *Kopano ke Matla!* the actors were the producers of messages, and the audiences consumers, and the staging technique reinforced that distinction. This increasing distance is alien to the traditional ways of producing and enjoying performance. This was not taken into account by the Project, since the major concern was not that of placing their theatre in the context of popular performance modes, but of creating theatre as it is understood in the West. This is also illustrated by the fact that in their use of acting space they would, whenever the possibility existed, attempt to simulate a purpose-built theatre rather than use space as it is used by peasants in their performance modes. For example, Horn describes the performance site selected during the team's first visit to Ha Libopuoa for another of their plays:

> A gentle slope behind the main village of the ward ended in a crumbling stone wall, some four feet high and 20 feet long. The area around the wall was cleared, an acting space defined, and a backstage established on the valley side of the wall. The grassy slope offered a naturally raked audience precinct, with unobstructed sight-lines and reasonably adequate acoustics, despite the fact that it was all sited on the spine of a sizeable mountain with breezes tending to blow sound into the valley. (Horn 1984, p. 47.)

This is a description of a quest for space that will provide the illusionistic elements of theatre, with its separation of performers from the audiences, its backstages where 'magic' is produced, and its raked seating arrangements, where the audiences will *sit* and *listen* at their designated space. This is different from the use of the acting space that Kerr says is predominant in the Malawian experience of theatre-for-development, where the division between audience and performer is almost completely discarded.

> To start with, there is no 'theatre' as such, in the sense of a specially designed plant cut off from the real world and serving as a dream-place for the creation of illusions . . .
>
> *The backdrop is that of trees, village houses, or maize gardens.* Real life is not something 'out there' beyond the lobbies and magical lights of the theatre: it impinges on the performance itself. (Kerr 1988, p. 178.) [My emphasis]

This is not to suggest that the Project used stage lights and the other paraphernalia of the theatre in the Lesotho village, but to accentuate the variance of their conception of theatre-for-development from that of those practitioners who prefer to create their theatre with the people. It will be noted that in their subsequent plays Marotholi changed from this technique of staging.

Kopano ke Matla! as communication

Although the process of conscientisation treated above involves communication, this section seeks to explicate the play in terms of specific communication theories discussed in the previous chapters, and to examine how it functions as communication.

Persuasive communication: The play was devised as a vehicle for persuading the villagers to join co-operative societies, or to establish them in villages where they did not exist, by highlighting the benefits that may accrue from these projects. The communicator defined his audience according to his own purposes, as in the dominance model of the communicator–audience relationship in Figure 3.1. (see p. 59) The communicator is both a propagandist and an advocate for co-operative societies, and the goal is to 'sell' the services of IEMS to the villagers. The villagers are a target market. The audience is a set of consumers, who are an object of persuasion. The key feature of the dominance model is the intention to impose views and purposes of the sender on the receiver. This view is supported by the director of the play himself, who said, when explaining *Kopano ke Matla!* to the delegates at the International Conference on Theatre for Development, 'It works very much like advertising works on television. It's meant to persuade. Sometimes it succeeds, sometimes it doesn't.' There is no horizontal communication or peer learning. There is instead a top–bottom centre–periphery communication. In the whole process of *Kopana ke Matla!*, at no stage do the villagers initiate communication. They merely respond to messages created by the theatre group and the staff of the Institute of Extra Mural Studies.

Continuous discourse: The villagers' lack of opportunity to initiate communication implies continuous discourse during the period of the transmission of the message. The whole process is public address communication rather than interpersonal. There is a clear distinction between senders and receivers. Among the senders there is simulated discontinuous discourse in that the dialogic interaction among the characters takes the form of interpersonal communication, although the characters are repeating lines they have memorised. The message emanating from this simulated discontinuous discourse is transmitted to the receivers in a continuous discourse manner, during which the audience does not create its own messages that will determine the direction of the discourse. It may transmit feedback in the form of laughter, booing, heckling, and so on, but the actors' continuous discourse continues in its predetermined course to its conclusion. Only then does the audience engage in discontinuous discourse, during the post-performance feedback period.

Diffusion of innovations: *Kopano Ke Matla!* has elements of the diffusion of innovations paradigm discussed in Chapter 2, although in this case the innovation is not technologically based. The theatrical performance itself takes the place of a mass media channel that is primarily a *knowledge* creator, and the interpersonal channels are used to *persuade* the villager to form or change his attitude about co-operative societies. The external or superior agent of change, in the form of the theatre team and the staff of the Institute of Extra Mural Studies, decides what is beneficial to the audiences, and proceeds to promote it through theatre. When the women from the well discuss the wealth of the co-operative society member from the neighbouring village, and when we see the characters' ultimate wealth, brought about by their own co-operative, the play is dealing with the perceived characteristics of the innovation by showing the audiences its relative advantages. *Decision* on whether to join co-operatives or not is usually made during the post-performance discussions. The follow-up action by IEMS staff is the *confirmation* stage, that is meant to encourage the continued adoption of the innovation, and to persuade those who initially rejected it to change their minds, while engaging the villagers in activities — such as holding training courses on co-operatives — that will reinforce the adoption decision. The emphasis throughout this process is on non-media sources such as the extension workers from IEMS. The extension worker is a broker and dispenser of services and information instead of being 'more of an *animateur* and catalyst stimulating a process of conscientisation' (Malamah-Thomas 1989, p. 5). In *Kopano ke Matla!*, as in most diffusionist work, the reliance is on prescribing technical solutions rather than any structural analysis of the problems of poverty. Commenting on the failure of the diffusionist approach, Malamah-Thomas further writes:

> Since the beginning of the United Nations Second Development Decade, it has been realised that most development/poverty focused projects for the rural areas have floundered. One of the main reasons has been that the projects are conceived within government ministries in urban areas where bureaucrats, out of touch with the needs and aspirations, and ignorant of the socio-economic and other realities, of the people, prepare their blueprints. The projects are implemented by extension agents who were trained as 'constructed technocrats' conditioned to analyse problems in a narrowly technical way and to propagate technical solutions which often fail to address the socio-economic parameters which create the problems in the first place or prevent the people from adopting the recommended practices. (Malamah-Thomas 1989, p. 4.)

The practices recommended in the play, through a communication mode that is top-down, directive and authoritarian, are the adoption of co-operatives in order to combat rural poverty and the abandoning of laziness and corruption (misuse of co-op property by the treasurer). The socio-economic factors that prevent the people from adopting these practices are not addressed. An allusion, merely, to some of these factors is made by the characters in the play when one says co-operatives favour those who are members of the ruling party, and the other dismisses this as being untrue.

The actor–spectator transaction: The source of the theatrical information in *Kopano ke Matla!* is the team comprising the actors and the director. Initially there is no dramatic text, but through improvisation one is created and adhered to. The team jointly decides on how to encode its message, and what transmitters to use. The actor–spectator transaction closely follows Elam's theatrical communication model (see Figure 5.3, p. 92). The model illustrates how feedback messages are transmitted from the audience members to the actors using signals that will be interpreted by the performers and members of the audience as either hostility or approval. But this feedback is limited, as has already been illustrated. The play belongs to a theatrical convention that does not permit the wider range of responses that are possible in interpersonal communication. This limitation impels the question:

> How is it possible to reconcile the claims of the democratic character of the theatre with the very limited possibilities of the individual spectator to express his evaluation by means of the conventional forms of response to which he is entitled? (Stefanova 1988, p. 114.)

The question is prompted by the fact that:

> The belief that 'face-to-face' communication is the most efficient way of attaining understanding among people has its deep roots in human practice. The explanation is that the adequate understanding of what has been said by the partner is based on the direct possibility to interrupt the speaker at any moment of the dialogue with the aim of asking his clarification about a newly-introduced word, a word with double meaning or some ambiguity. (Stefanova 1988, pp. 114–15).

Stefanova is expressing the major advantage of discontinuous discourse. The possibility of interruption is non-existent in conventional theatre, as observed in *Kopano ke Matla!*. For example, when one character says — in the Dramatic Context of Elam's model — that co-operatives are bad because they cheat people and there is discrimination on political and religious grounds, there is no opportunity for a member of the audience to interrupt and ask — in a social context — what the basis of that statement is, or to relate a personal experience of such discrimination. The differences between the communicating parties are therefore not overcome, and no agreement or unity of action in the accomplishment of common practical objectives is attained.

In the work of Marotholi Travelling Theatre, there is a movement towards a theatre that aims to encourage the interruption of the message, thus removing the passivity of the spectactor, who can now respond to the actors by means of the theatre itself. This is a movement towards theatre-for-conscientisation, in which the sign complexes of the feedback are not reduced to 'yes' and 'no', as they are in conventional theatre. Theatre-for-conscientisation opens up a new verbal channel of criticism in both the dramatic and social contexts of the play.

Towards a theatre-for-conscientisation

As theatre-for-conscientisation aims at drawing the audience into full participation in the creation and exchange of developmental messages, it is essential that the audience has a functional level of literacy in the medium used. A number of rural audiences in Lesotho are not literate in the conventional theatre of the developed world, and even if they could interpret some of its codes, many do not bother to attend performances. This is a problem that confronted the Project in Lesotho in its earlier years. Explaining their difficulties in audience recruitment to the participants of the International Conference on Theatre for Development, Horn said:

> People are reluctant to come. They assume that the performance is a government organ. Those who are hostile to the government do not attend. Those who are favourable to the government are tired of *pitsos*. Even if it is explained to them that this is not a *pitso* but at *tšoantšiso* [a Sesotho word that means 'to make look like' that has now been adopted by the language to mean 'a stage play' in the absence of an orginal word for that], the word *tšoantšiso* is very ambiguous in Sesotho. Adults might think that it is a thing for the children. You have to teach people first about the medium. Then use the medium to carry the message.

It is the experience of Marotholi that in some mountain areas, when audiences are recruited, men refuse to attend because they feel that plays are for women and children. However, when performance modes with which the people have a high level of medium-literacy were introduced, the whole village gathered and participated. It is for this reason that Marotholi decided to use modes of performance currently popular in the village, together with elements of international theatre practice such as dialogue and structured scenes that function within the dramatic curve. It was not only for reasons of audience recrutiment that popular performance modes were introduced, but to facilitate communication in a participatory environment using codes shared by all the members of the community.

Participatory Agitprop: the *Rural Sanitation Play*

The next play that will be examined attempted to use some of the popular forms outlined in Chapter 4, in Marotholi's search for a theatre-for-conscientisation. Although the play has strong elements of agitprop, a comparison with *Kopano ke Matla!* will indicate that there has been a perceptible move towards a methodology that, to some extent, involves the people, albeit in a pre-packaged product.

Brief history of the *Rural Sanitation Play*

Early in 1986, Marotholi Travelling Theatre was approached by the Rural Sanitation Project (RSP) of the Ministry of Health to create a play to reinforce their campaign in the southern district of Mohale's Hoek. A new type of toilet, the Ventilated Improved Pit (VIP) latrine, was being introduced, and the campaign's main feature was the dissemination of information on how the latrine worked and how to construct one. The RSP trained technical assistants who were stationed in the target villages. Their role was to build toilets for the villagers, and to train other local builders.

Marotholi was required to create a play that dealt with the following issues:

(a) the health and social problems of indiscriminate defecation;
(b) the role of flies in the transmission of diseases;
(c) handwashing and its contribution in the prevention of diseases;
(d) the management of diarrhoea, including the use of oral rehydration therapy (ORT) to prevent or correct dehydration in diarrhoea patients;
(e) the dangers of giving enema to diarrhoea patients;
(f) the role of latrines in the prevention and control of diarrhoeal diseases;
(g) the main features of VIP latrines;
(h) the construction and maintenance of VIP latrines;
(i) how VIP latrines work and their advantages over other traditional types of latrines;
(j) cost cutting strategies during VIP latrine construction.

Information pertaining to these issues was collected by Marotholi through the official-eye technique from the personnel of the RSP at their head office in Maseru, and the interviewing technique by holding formal interviews with RSP extension workers in the villages, RSP technical assistants, health assistants from the Ministry of Health, and village health workers. The flooding method was used to get the villagers' own views on rural sanitation, and their perception of the causes of the periodic outbreaks of diarrhoea that plagued that region. This flooding method was used in only one village, however. In the other villages the play toured as a ready-made production, based on information gathered in that one village.

The play was first performed at Maphutseng for an audience of 120. Of this performance Marotholi give the following account in their annual report:

> First time the company used arena, without sets, using the Theatre-for-Conscientisation methodology. A rousing welcome from the villagers. A lot of smooth audience interaction with the actors. Even village dogs which strayed into the arena were incorporated into the play. Strong conflicting views on the subject of the play among the members of the audience. Audience members felt that the story-line was most appropriate to their village. Six registered their names for the construction of toilets in their yards. Many nurses, health assistants, technical assistants and village health workers participated. (Mda 1986, pp. 21–2.)

The second performance was at Likoeneng Ha Sechele for an audience of 115 people.

> Very passive and reserved audience. It seemed as though the concept of a *pitso* whereby they were called upon to participate in analysing the problems of sanitation, rather than just being instructed to build VIP toilets, did not go well with them. Audience members did not participate much even in singing. The seating arrangement did not help, for it isolated the actors from the audience. The actors themselves did not have the verve and vitality they usually display on the stage. This served as a good lesson for them because after this performance they discussed ways and means of drawing a reserved audience into active participation. The chief [of the village] was very active in organizing the people and running up and down getting chairs for the audience, and props for the actors. (Mda 1986, p. 23.)

Of the third performance at Mpharane Ha Koko, for an audience of 130 people, the account is as follows:

> The town crier almost went from house to house calling people to the performance site — sometimes calling them by name. This was the most "rampageous" (sic) and boisterous audience in the company's experience. Many of them loved the stage, for they from time to time

crossed it, or just stood there. The actors enjoyed the whole thing for they incorporated such people into the play.

'Mé Ntsoaki, the nurses clinician in charge of the village clinic, was very popular. Some members of the audience were more interested in getting her attention than in the play. One old man stood up, stopped the play and addressed her directly among the audience members. 'Thank you for giving me the opportunity to speak. 'Mé Ntsoaki, I am bothered by teeth. I want you to get me doctors from Maseru to extract my teeth.' Another man stood up and boasted that his own daughter-in-law had a VIP toilet. Others felt that the play was trying to refer to them directly [personally] and was therefore mocking them ('lea re kobisa') because in that very village there had earlier been an outbreak of diarrhoea. 'Why don't you just tell us to build toilets and leave, instead of going around in circles with plays?' one man shouted around the second scene. Another responded, 'Yes, they are trying to ridicule us because they are of the new government which overthrew our prime minister.' Mpharane was in ex-Prime Minister Jonathan's constituency.

The audience sang well right from the beginning and participated throughout the play. The two village health workers and the village nutritionist played their roles in the play very well. The technical assistant was very good in explaining the VIP latrine.

This was the only village where the troupe was offered food by the villagers; papa, motoho [hard porridge and soured soft porridge], fish and canned beef. Whilst they were eating inside a rondavel some villagers called their own meeting outside, where they planned to dig pits jointly and contribute money towards building latrines. Previously, just as the play ended, an old man who had been quietly sitting there watching the play stood up brandishing a M20 note and shouted that he wanted to join the Credit Union so that they may build a latrine for him. Members of the Credit Union registered him immediately. (Mda 1986, pp. 23–4.)

At Liphiring there was an audience of 180. The report for this performance is as follows:

There was some audience participation. Village health workers and the technical assistant joined the actors on the stage and gave a lesson on Oral Rehydration Therapy and VIP latrines respectively. The technical assistant was particularly good as an actor, with good voice projection. During the play the villagers mentioned that they already had an association where they paid money to each member-family on a rotating basis at the end of each month. They decided that some of this money would go towards building toilets. At the end of the play the troupe was invited [by the villagers] to go back to Liphiring in 1988 to see for themselves if not every household would be having a VIP toilet. (Mda 1986, p. 25.)

The final performance in the project area in the Mohale's Hoek district was at Ketane Ha Nohana, for a big audience of over a thousand people. This was during a feast organised by RSP to close a training course for builders of VIP toilets. Also present were pupils from local schools, technical officers, village health workers, nurse clinicians, and a video production crew. This is the performance recorded in the Appendix.

There were three other performances of the play in districts that were not the target areas of the RSP, and were therefore not supported by the project. The first one was at Majaheng in the Berea district, at Tebang in the Mafeteng district, and at Marakabei in the mountain district of Thaba Tseka. Besides the big audience of 601 people, what distinguished the Marakabei performance from others was the participation of local *likheleke*.

[W]hen the first actor came singing 'Lifela', some local 'Lifela' champion singers were disgusted at his lack of artistry [bokheleke]. About three of them, including a Lesotho Evangelical Church minister, joined in and sang 'Lifela' to the great delight of the actors and audience (Mda 1986, p. 28.)

Rural Sanitation Play as conscientisation
Like *Kopana Ke Matla!*, this play was created by the actors in the absence of the villagers. After gathering their information from various sources, the actors went back to base to analyse it, and prioritise it from their own perspective. The next step was to work out a basic storyline, and situate it in a scenario. Dialogue was improvised for each scene during a rehearsal, then the play was taken to the rural areas for performance. However, unlike in *Kopano ke Matla!*, the actors did not memorise the lines they had created, so at each performance the dialogue was different, taking into account the specific conditions of that particular area, and responding to audience participation.

The participatory agitprop characteristic: In so far as the *Rural Sanitation Play* is message-oriented and aims to persuade the people in a particular direction that the creators of the play deem is the correct one for a social transformation of the rural people, and in so far as it lacks audience involvement in the data analysis process and the initial dramatisation, the play has strong elements of agitprop theatre. The subject of the play is selected by an outside agent on the basis of the perceived needs of rural people, and a solution to the problem of rural sanitation, and to health problems such as diarrhoea, is prescribed. The solution itself — that of building not just ordinary latrines but the VIP latrine, of washing one's hands when one comes from the toilet, and of mixing and administering the oral rehydration solution as a short-term measure against diarrhoea — is not reached by the audience, but is provided by the play. However, through the technique of throwing questions to the audience, the play was opened up for audience participation. The audiences respond to questions, and articulate approval or disapproval of the issues raised. For example, when it is suggested that faeces could be used as manure, they strongly disapprove, providing reasons for their disapproval. Even if, at the end of the day, they adopt the VIP toilet, they make it clear that they will not use human faeces as manure. There are, therefore, those aspects of the message that they are prepared to adopt, and those that they reject outright. The technique of opening up the play for audience participation in an exhortatory play that is pre-packaged and provides the solution places the *Rural Sanitation Play* at a point between agitprop and theatre-for-conscientisation. Because of the element of audience participation it can be called participatory agitprop.

Immediate follow-up action: Although the theme of rural sanitation was not selected by the community members, but by extension workers of the RSP, whose main intention was to promote the services of their organisation, and by the Ministry of Health personnel who had identified lack of proper sanitation in the villages as the main cause for outbreaks of diarrhoea, the creators of the play used village-based institutions to mobilise the people to the performances. Instead of relying on the chiefs to call *pitsos* or on the publicity that emanates from the RSP head office in Maseru, village health workers who are members of the community were used to rally their fellow villagers. There was immediate follow-up action, in that those who wanted VIP toilets had their names registered, and arrangements were made to have toilets built for them. The performances were held in the context of an on-going campaign, which made follow-up action possible, since all the necessary services were accessible to the target communities.

Absence of a structural analysis: Like *Kopano ke Matla!*, the *Rural Sanitation Play* did not attempt to raise the issues to the level of a structural analysis of the problems besetting the rural communities. The only concern was to advocate a particular course of action, without really examining any reason that may prevent the people from taking that course. The problems of rural poverty, which may prevent those members of the community who are keen to construct the VIP toilets, but cannot afford to purchase the pipes, concrete slabs and toilet seats that are sold in the clinics of the target villages, were merely glanced at when credit unions were mentioned. But to be a member of a credit union one must have the initial funds to join and pay the required subscription.

The political tensions in Lesotho that Horn talked about continued to manifest themselves in the rural sanitation campaign, as shown by the Mpharane performance where the villagers felt the play was trying to ridicule them, and that the performers were agents of a new government that had overthrown their Prime Minister. The villagers were able to use the performance as a forum for articulating even those concerns that were not related to the theme of rural sanitation. They were not pleased with the new government, and the occasion of the play provided an outlet for these sentiments. Tensions within the community itself were articulated, as in the case of the woman who indicated that there was great displeasure with the behaviour of a local village health worker. These concerns, however, were not delved into by the play, but were tactfully brushed aside, since the primary goal of the performers was to get on with the promotion of the VIP toilet and the services of the RSP.

Perspectival problems: The problems ensuing from leaving the audience out of the process of dramatisation were discussed in relation to *Kopana Ke Matla!*. These are observed again in the *Rural Sanitation Play*. The play is created by university students, some of whom have rural origins. In spite of those origins, they now view issues and problems from a different class position — a perspective that will be reflected in their work. The inclusion of the villagers in the dramatisation process then imbues the work with the peasant's own view of the world. An illustration of this is the play's presentation of the diviner in a villainous light; obviously a view of the practice of divinition and traditional medicine held by the elite. If the peasants were involved in the creation of the play, and therefore in determining who the heroes and villains should be, it is doubtful they would have presented a diviner or traditional doctor as a charlatan, because the people in the periphery areas of Lesotho, and indeed a large section of the centre, believe deeply in the power of traditional medicine, and of divination. Because of this strong belief, the Ministry of Health in Lesotho has decided to incorporate traditional medicine practitioners in the health delivery system of the country.

The staging technique: One of the major differences between *Kopano ke Matla!* and the *Rural Sanitation Play* lay in the staging technique (see Figure 6.1). Whereas in the former play there was a deliberate separation of the actors and the audiences, in the latter play the theatre-in-the-round mode was used, which facilitated audience participation. There was no special scenery to create an illusion of the world of the play separate from the world of the community. The village huts, the trees, the kraals, and the fields became the natural backdrop of the play. The selection of performance sites was not determined by considerations of their suitability in offering raked audience precincts and backstage areas, but by their being an integral part of community activities such as public meetings, and other social functions. The impact of the arena *trouvé* over a staging mode that promotes division between audience and performer was clearly illustrated at the Likoeneng Ha Sechele performance, where the audience was 'very passive and reserved'. Marotholi note in their report that they felt isolated from the audiences, and hence could not freely interact with them either physically or with messages. There was therefore no audience participation during the performance. The arena facilitates participation not only because it brings the audience closer to the performers and eliminates any line of demarcation between the two, but also because this is the form that popular performance takes in the rural areas, and is therefore a mode of staging that the rural people are familiar with.

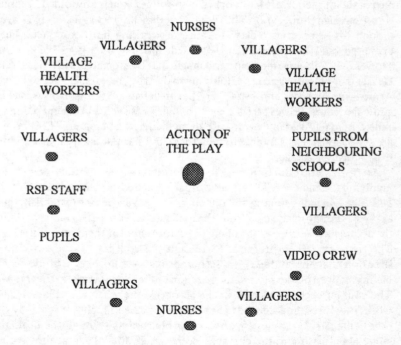

Figure 6.1: Spatial use in the staging of the Rural Sanitation Play
-Ketane Ha Nohana Performance

Utilisation of traditional media: the *Rural Sanitation Play* employed other devices with which the people are familiar in order to facilitate participation. The play opens with a *sefela* performed by one of the main actors, as he walks among the audience members, challenging them to join him. Although some members of the audience at the Marakabei performance felt that he lacked the skills and the eloquence of a true *kheleke*, his *sefela* was usually well received as members of the audience would respond to his singing with *melilietsane* (ululation), and men would jump about doing the *tlala* dance. Both are a spontaneous response of appreciation.

In the manner of *lifela*, the actor begins by praising himself, informing the audience of who he is, where he comes from, and of his greatness. This particular *lifela* singer is boasting about the beauty of his wife, and that many men used to quarrel over her. He then proceeds to tell us about himself, alluding to the fact that he has some skills in the science of traditional medicine. He refers to himself as *Taola*, from *litaola*, which are part of the equipage of those traditional doctors who employ divination as part of their practice. He has worked in the mines, and is now old. The mines won't have anything to do with him now that he 'reeks of old-age', even though his arms grew 'rusty' because of working hard for them. They exploited his labour and then dismissed him. He then goes back to his prowess in traditional medicine and magic that is associated with witchcraft. He can manufacture and send lightning to destroy enemies. He is also brave. Armed with his spear and *knobkierie*, he can defeat anything on his way. The audience learns, however, that even though he is such a brave man, highly skilled in magic and in the practice of medicine, the members of his family are seriously ill. He is unable to help them, but has put his trust in a diviner from a distant village.

After this introduction the play introduces yet another device for involving the audience. The *tlhophe* ritual is enacted, and the members of the audience join in the singing and dancing. This device helps to establish, right at the beginning of the play, that the audience too are performers, and that the actors have come to the village to perform not for them, but with them. The first scene then proceeds to present the conflicts in the story, in a situation that the audience finds humorous — Liloche's attitude to his having stepped on faeces, and the reaction of the other people at the *tlhophe*. The conflict becomes clearer in the second scene when the village health worker features, and her ideas are dismissed as so much nonsense by the other villagers. It develops with various plot points through the dramatic curve, culminating in the climactic scene where the village health worker saves the life of a child through oral rehydration therapy. In this scene the audience is taught how to mix the solution, and what easily accessible containers can be used for the exact measurement of the ingredients.

Rural Sanitation Play as communication

Persuasive communication in participatory agitprop: As in the case of *Kopano ke Matla!*, which was devised as a vehicle for persuasion, participatory agitprop is clearly a vehicle for purposive communication. The *Rural Sanitation Play* is an example of this. The RSP are in an advocacy role as purposive communicators who employ the services of a media organisation, the Marotholi Travelling Theatre, to disseminate messages. Marotholi are not purposive in that they have no communicative purpose of their own, except the general aim of satisfying the perceived needs of the audience. The needs of the RSP are to solve the problems of rural sanitation by marketing the VIP toilet to the villagers and teaching them clean health habits. The perceived needs of the villagers are to find ways of combating outbreaks of diarrhoea and other sanitation-related diseases. Marotholi as a media organisation decides how to package the message in order to serve the needs (perceived needs in the case of the villagers) of both parties effectively.

Community's role in message-creation: The message encourages people to adopt certain practices, and highlights the dangers that may stem from not adopting them. It is a message that emanates from outside agents, and the community members have not played any role in its creation. However in the process of its transmission they are able to transmit their own messages to the communicator. There is some horizontal peer learning. The process is not that of public address, but interpersonal communication. There is discontinuous discourse. Any member of the audience can interrupt, and transmit his own messages in response to what has been said. Sometimes the message transmitted by a member of the audience may not be a response to the communicator's message, but a new message, as illustrated by the man who interrupted the Mpharane performance in order to talk about his teeth. He was more interested in addressing his own concerns than in the issues of rural sanitation. He was saying that if there was going to be any discussion at all on health-related matters, then it must be about lack of dental care in the village. To him rural sanitation was not a priority. Although in this instance his concerns were not addressed by the health authorities, the possibility of creating another play to address them existed. This would have been a play where a community member had initiated the process of communication.

Attaining optimal heterophily: The villagers were not involved in the planning of the programme, nor in selecting the campaign issues. They were merely invited to a *pitso* to see a play brought by Marotholi Travelling Theatre. The troupe itself did not make any attempt to insert itself into the life of the community by participating fully in the economic, social and political life of the villagers. However, the degree of their heterophily was optimalised by their close co-operation with village health workers, who are not external agents in the community. Village health workers are opinion leaders in health-related matters, and as members of the community they have a higher degree of homophily than the personnel of the RSP or members of Marotholi Travelling Theatre. By virtue of the fact that they have been trained in primary health care, their outlook on issues related to the subject is different from that of the ordinary villager, who has had no such training. A combination of these two factors give the village health workers optimal heterophily with the villagers. The village health worker system has been found effective in its intermediary role, not only in Lesotho, but also in Zimbabwe.

> The most successful theatre-for-development projects [in Zimbabwe] have been initiated by extension workers in the Ministry of Health. Using drama, nurses and village health workers have organised basic primary health care campaigns on public health education, nutrition, and child and maternal care. (Chifunyise 1985, p. 6.)

The actor–spectator transaction: Looking at the *Rural Sanitation Play* in terms of Elam's model, it can be concluded that the source of the theatrical information is the combination of the actors and the director. No dramatic text exists as pretext and constituent of the performance text. The source decides on the choice of transmitters, and on how to encode the message using codes shared by both senders and receivers. For instance, one of the decisions is to encode the message into *lifela*, which, to a receiver outside the culture of rural Lesotho, may sound like a series of words, phrases and sentences devoid of meaning, but to members of that culture has profound meaning, since the local villagers are highly literate in that particular mode of communication. In the actor–spectator transaction the theatrical context of the play is mediated by a dramatic context in which a fictional speaker addresses a fictional listener. However unlike in *Kopano ke Matla!*, which closely followed Elam's model, in the *Rural Sanitation Play* there is some interaction between Elam's dramatic context and social context, in that fictional speakers address fictional listeners in a dramatic context, fictional speakers address real-life listeners, and real-life speakers address real-life listeners, all in a social context. The theatrical context is therefore mediated by both dramatic context and social context. At one point the audience–performer communication does not take a direct form but happens through fictional characters (who are senders and receivers in their own context), and at another point there is direct theatrical communication between performer and audience. This adds one more level to the two that Elam's model identifies (theatrical context and dramatic context), that of social context.

Innovation–diffusion: The diffusion of innovations elements observed in *Kopano Ke Matla!* exist in the *Rural Sanitation Play* as well. The innovation is, however, based on an appropriate technology. The reliance on technical solutions that is characteristic of the paradigm is illustrated by the promotion of the VIP toilet, to the exclusion of an examination of any structural factors that contribute to the problems of rural health and sanitation. The superior external agent decides, solely on technical grounds, how best to solve the problems in the villages and devises his own plans to facilitate the solution. No attempt is made to consult the villagers before plans are formulated.

It may be interesting to note that after this innovation had been diffused to rural people in the villages of Lesotho, a debate on its advantages and disadvantages ensued among the superior agents in the centre of the periphery nation, some of whom were from centre nations, sent by their governments or by international agencies as development experts. McCloy, an architect in Lesotho, raised serious doubts — which he backed up by research and technical diagrams — on the value and safety of VIP latrines designed in Lesotho, especially when constructed by non-technical personnel in self-help schemes, as is the case in Lesotho villages. His argument is that every ventilated pit latrine ventilates negatively down the vent pipe and up through the seat instead of the other way round. He writes:

> Negative ventilation defeats the purpose of VIP latrines, because foul odours accumulating in the cabin discourage people from either using and maintaining their latrines. When negative ventilation occurs during the day, the foul air attracts disease-carrying flies and other nasties. These flies feed on the faeces inside the pit and, some return via the seat into the cabin and, ultimately, to the community. (McCloy 1989, p. 10.)

According to McCloy, the very reasons that were advanced by the purposive communicator through the play for the adoption of this innovation rendered the innovation hazardous to the health of rural people. The old unvented latrines that some villagers had constructed prior to the promotion of the VIP toilet 'smelt less than these'. Backing his argument with technical data, he writes that negative ventilation takes place as often as 55% of the time on some latrines, yet donor agencies continue to promote and fund the construction of VIP toilets. He further highlights the dangers of unskilled and unregulated people 'dabbling' in self-help sanitation improvement. Sanitation, he writes, should be left strictly to the professionals.

This contradicts the messages transmitted by RSP through the Marotholi play, since the emphasis was on demonstrating how the villagers can design and build latrines themselves, without expert advice and workmanship. The response of the development experts, such as the Urban Sanitation Improvement Team, was that McCloy's article used limited and biased information,

> and did not look at economics . . . it posed no viable alternatives; it used spurious, melodramatic and fictitious reasoning; it did not look at hundreds and thousands of people with VIPs who are very happy with them; it did not look at user education and did not mention the massive improvements VIPs have made to the sanitation situation in Lesotho. If you bother to look at the alternative sanitation methods available to most people, then you would see that VIPs constitute a very significant improvement. (Blackett 1989, p. 2.)

While the debate continues, with McCloy further responding to Blackett in support of his position that VIP toilets as designed and constructed in Lesotho pose a health hazard to the community, mass media and interpersonal channels continue to be used, encouraging the adoption of the innovation. The rural communities, supposedly the 'beneficiaries' of the innovation, are not part of this debate. Their views are not sought, for the external agent with his superior knowledge has decided what is beneficial to them — in spite of the conflicting messages on the benefits of the innovation among the external agents themselves — and then proceeds to use his resources to promote it. Experimentation with the lives of the villagers, enabling each expert to test his theories, is characteristic of some innovations being diffused in the developing world.

Simultaneous dramaturgy: the *Agro-Action Play*

In the Lesotho experience of theatre-for-development, the *Rural Sanitation Play* was only the beginning of a movement toward theatre-for-conscientisation. The search for a theatre in which the shortcomings outlined above are eliminated led to further experimentation to find a method that would permit the audience to offer their own solutions to the problems presented in the play. The Agro-Action play, (see Appendix), created in support of the German Agro-Action Project with the members of communal gardens in the Mafeteng district, attempts to use the simultaneous dramaturgy technique of theatre-for-conscientisation.

Brief history of the *Agro-Action Play*
The play was created in 1988 at the request of the Food Security Assistance Programme (FSAP), a project sponsored and operated by Deutsche Welthungerhilfe/German Agro-Action, a non-governmental welfare

organisation based in the Federal Republic of Germany.

The German Agro-Action is the German National Committee of the Action for Development of the Food and Agricultural Organisation (FAO) of the United Nations. Its stated aim is to protect the interests of the rural population in the Third World, and to provide a lobby for the majority of the people in developing countries, who live in rural areas and are dependent on agriculture for their living. Its guidelines, therefore, emphasise those projects that shall benefit rural populations and underprivileged urban groups by removing the basic causes of underdevelopment through medium- and long-term measures. Preference is given to non-governmental organisations and local groups at grassroots level, who will be in charge of planning and implementing the projects. These projects should be in accordance with the 'real needs' of the people concerned, who will thus receive assistance towards self-reliance. The projects should continue even after the termination of financial assistance from German Agro-Action, and economic and technical progress should always result in improving social and, whenever possible, socio-political structures.

The assistance that German Agro-Action provides to grassroots organisations in developing countries comes in the form of funds and, if required, personnel. These funds — raised from private donations in Germany, from government grants, and from subsidies from the European Community (EC) — are meant to assist the poorest sections of the population in the promotion of agriculture and the improvement of nutrition, and as emergency aid in the aftermath of natural or man-made disasters, when the affected population has lost the economic basis for survival.

The German Agro-Action began its operations in Lesotho in 1982 by establishing the Food Security Assistance Programme, with the overall aim of improving agricultural production and the living conditions of poor rural communities in order to achieve a state of self-reliance in food production.

FSAP operates in 21 villages in the southern district of Mafeteng, and three in the Peka area of the northern district of Leribe. More than one thousand people, 90 per cent of them women, are participating in small-scale food-for-work projects. The staff consists of three German expatriates and 14 Basotho, nine of them extension workers.

The projects carried out by the villagers comprise:

- *Infrastructure improvements*: road construction and maintenance, dam construction, construction of storage facilities, construction of garden irrigation systems, and village water supply;
- *agricultural activities*: vegetable gardening, fruit tree cultivation, fish and duck production, dairy husbandry, fodder crop cultivation, extension of arable land, afforestation, and field erosion control;

- *improvement of basic structural conditions*: through extension services, training, loans, and conscientisation.

The FSAP is, therefore, an integrated rural development programme. It is supposed to create sources of income and employment primarily through labour-intensive and production-oriented activities at village level, thus providing a base for people to become independent of food rations and other types of outside assistance. The food-for-work element — where villagers who work in the project get periodic rations of food — is supposed to be a short-term measure until villagers participating in the programme have become self-reliant in food production. It is also an attempt to stimulate people to participate actively in the development of their own resources.

The FSAP covers not only the provision of food-for-work rations, but also material inputs such as tools, fencing material, irrigation equipment, initial sets of seeds, fertiliser and pesticides, as well as expertise.

The Marotholi Travelling Theatre was invited by the personnel of the FSAP after discovering that the people were unhappy about some aspects of the programme, but were unable to articulate their discontent. Soon, food rationing was going to be stopped, but the FSAP personnel doubted whether the villagers would be able to organise themselves and continue to work in order to maintain what they had already achieved, without food rations. The villagers seemed to be growing less motivated.

> Still, success does not always materialise because people often lack the motivation to participate continuously and maintain their achievements. Project planners realised too late that there was no opportunity for everyone to participate equally in dialogue, to express day to day problems with one's own words and to spend time considering and finding one's own solutions. (Ganter and Edkins 1988, p. 41.)

Furthermore, Ganter and Edkins, who were involved, respectively, in managing the activities of the FSAP and in documenting them, found that there was a strong element of mistrust among the people, brought about by the fact that from the inception of the programme there was no common agreement on the objectives — either among the 'beneficiaries', or between the community and the donors. These problems were compounded by the fact that,

> History has taught the Basotho that foreigners do not always act on behalf of the local people. There is also little reason for them to believe that aid projects only focus on the well-being of the poor. Too many mistakes have been made — the rich become richer, the poor become

poorer. Local government institutions are not excluded from this kind of mistrust. (Ganter and Edkins 1988, p. 40.)

The Marotholi Travelling Theatre was therefore required to assist in the creation of community dialogue on those issues that concerned the villagers in relation to communal gardens, and on the villagers' general participation in the activities of the FSAP. In the process, it was hoped, dialogue between the 'beneficiaries' of development actions and the donors would also be created.

After collecting information, through the official eye technique, from the staff of the FSAP, the members of the group went to the villages to gather information from the communal garden members while they worked in the gardens. This was the interviewing method, since formal interviews were held with designated people in the village — those who were members of the FSAP projects. The group decided that although the play they were going to create concerned members of the project, and was going to be devised and performed with them, it was necessary to involve all the villagers. Membership of FSAP programmes is open to all community members. But not all of them participate. The flooding method was used to collect information from as many community members as possible, irrespective of their membership or non-membership in FSAP programmes. The information gathered through these various methods indicated that the villagers had both positive and negative opinions about the project. These can be listed as follows:

A. Positive Views

1. The gardens develop the village.
2. The members can buy vegetables at cost.
3. They are paid with maize meal, beans, cooking oil and an amount of R5.50 each per fortnight.
4. They get clean water nearby from the taps, instead of walking long distances to the well or to the river.
5. They enjoy working together in a spirit of unity and camaraderie.
6. The market for the produce is good, so they are able to accumulate a lot of money.
7. They eat nutritious food.
8. They have gained experience in proper methods of gardening.
9. They intend to branch into poultry farming since they have accumulated enough funds from the vegetable profits.
10. After five years all the money will be controlled by them, and they will be managing their own affairs without assistance from the FSAP.

B. Negative Views

1. There are delays in bringing food rations to the village, and in paying them their fortnightly stipend.
2. There is a lot of work, but the stipend is very small.
3. There is lack of security, and people steal from the gardens, destroy the vegetables and throw them into the dam, and catch fish from the dam.
4. There is no market for their produce. [This contradicts No. 6 under Positive Views. The conflicting views are due to the fact that some villages within the Sephula-cluster have access to good market facilities, whereas others do not have the market for their produce.]
5. Storage facilities for the harvest are inadequate.
6. There is too much competition from other village communal gardens [each village in a cluster of 21 Sephula villages has its own communal garden].
7. The foreman does not work. All he does is eat. They do not want a man as a foreman since the vast majority of them are women.
8. They prefer to elect the foreman from among themselves, but Mojeremane [the FSAP staff] has instructed them to choose a man.
9. They fear that the work will not continue and the project 'will die' when they are on their own without assistance from FSAP, after five years.
10. They are forbidden to join other developmental organisations in the village.
11. The soil is poor.
12. Hail, drought and pests destroy their efforts.
13. They do not like *pitsos* regularly called by FSAP staff since they are a waste of time.
14. There are constant clashes between the committee and the other members.
15. Members of the committee are not happy that they have to work on Saturdays and Sundays without pay.
16. They are employees of Mojeremane. They don't know what happens to all the profits from the produce since all the money is given to Mojeremane.
17. The chief has given a field to Mojeremane while there are families without fields.

C. Reasons for Non-Membership

1. People work for long hours, and are paid low wages.
2. Young women have not joined because their husbands work in the mines and are able to send them money on a regular basis.
3. They are afraid to join because others mock and laugh at them that they are poor.

4. They have had a similar project run by the government, which failed.
5. They don't want to work for Germans. Men are particularly not happy about the involvement with Germans.
6. They are sickly and too old to work.

The picture that emerges from this data is that the villagers regarded themselves as employees of the FSAP. They did not view the project as their own, but were workers, hence the dissatisfaction with the low wages and long working hours. The FSAP on the other hand did not view themselves as proprietors of the project. As far as they were concerned, they were assisting the villagers to gain some measure of self-reliance in food production. The food they were rationing out, and the money they paid the workers, was not viewed by the FSAP as wages paid in return for the villagers' labour, but as a short-term measure to alleviate the immediate problems of poverty and to motivate the villagers to work even harder on their projects. The objective was to withdraw these incentives after a period, when the projects were self-sustaining and the villagers able to live from the profits of the produce. The incentives had an effect, however, opposite to the desired one, for they reinforced the perception that the villagers were labourers employed by German Agro-Action, who reaped all the profits accruing from their labour. This clearly shows that from the start of the programme in these villages there was no common agreement between villagers and donors.

Marotholi decided that a single play would not address all the problems. What was needed was a series of plays over a period, that would deal systematically with these issues. The first step in the data analysis stage was to prioritise the issues. The villagers were told that all the issues would be addressed, but were asked to choose those they thought most important, so that a play addressing them could be created. An attempt was made to explain the whole concept of theatre-for-development, since most of them did not understand what was required of them. On the very first visit of the theatre group for information-gathering, the communal garden women had welcomed them with an impromptu performance of song and dance, using their watering cans as drums. It was explained to them that the whole idea was to encourage such performances, and use them for discussing the problems, instead of just for entertainment and relaxation. Within these performances of song and dance we were going to create a story, and have people act using their own words to express their views about the problems.

Marotholi's inclination was to create a play around the problems caused by food aid when it is offered as a reward for participation in development programmes. In their tours of the villages they had discovered that in many instances villagers were most reluctant to involve themselves in development projects when there was no food-aid incentive. In some cases, villagers would refuse to prevent soil erosion in their own fields if they were not given cooking oil and maize meal. A whole 'food-aid culture' had been created over the years by government and donor agencies, through which a mentality of dependency had evolved. For these reasons, the Marotholi were inclined to addressing this problem with the villagers, in the hope that at the end of it all the dangers of food-for-work programmes would emerge, and the villagers would see the value of working in their own projects not to get food rations, but because they would be aware of the benefits that accrue from their own labour in their own projects. Marotholi wanted to break the ideology of dependence.

The villagers, however, did not view the food-aid problem as a priority. Their immediate problem was the theft and destruction of their work both by vandals and by those who stole out of need, but did not want to work in order to satisfy the need. Throughout the 21 villages in the Sephula area, the problem of theft was a major concern among the communal garden members. However, to examine the theft problem, it became necessary for them to analyse reasons for some villagers' reluctance to join the project — communal garden members felt that non-members were responsible for the vandalism. Three major reasons were identified for non-participation: dependency on remittances from the mines; public opinion ('people will think we are too poor'); opposition to working for Germans. The villagers decided that these issues must be incorporated into the play. There was also a strong feeling that the issue of the imposition of leadership (male foreman) on the (female) workers must be addressed.

The members of the theatre group then went back to base and created three basic storylines that simply presented the problem, leaving each sketch open-ended so that the villagers could provide solutions. Characters were created to advance the plot for each sketch, as in Table 6.1.

Table 6.1
The three basic storylines in *Agro-Action Play*

	Characters
Theft	Size
	Makhotso
	Chieftainess
	Communal Garden Members
Non-participation	
(a) Mine Remittances	Mpokho
	'Mapalesa
(b) Public Opinion	Her friend
Leadership	Chieftainess
	Communal Garden Members

The three storylines were then woven into a single play, and rehearsed by the theatre group without the villagers. It was taken for performances on five occasions, to the villages of Ha Khati, Ha Seetsi, Ha Sephula, Ha Motloi, and Tebang. Members of the communal gardens and other villagers from the neighbouring villages attended these performances. The solutions offered at different performances did not vary much, and were all reconciliatory in tone, although at Ha Khati the chieftainess (not the fictional one of the play) ended up crying when the villagers voiced their strong objection to her activities. She said she had not been aware that her people harboured such strong grievances against her.

The *Agro-Action Play* as conscientisation
Community decision from community participation: The role of Marotholi in the play is animatory or catalytic in that they merely facilitate the process of transformation which must be generated from within the community by the community members themselves. Theirs is not a persuasive role toward the adoption of desired practices. It is for this reason that in theatre-for-conscientisation the outside agents who work with the community members to create theatre are called animators or catalysts.

The technique of theatre-for-conscientisation that Marotholi attempted to use in the *Agro-Action Play* is simultaneous dramaturgy. They created scenes suggested by the villagers, each presenting the problem from the villagers' perspective. In the first scene the conflict is introduced between those who oppose communal gardens — Size, 'Mapalesa and her friend — and those who see the value of such projects in the village — 'Makhotso, the chieftainess, and the communal garden members. The first plot point in the dramatic curve happens in the second scene when a community decision is made that 'Makhotso should report her husband's activities to her fellow communal garden members. This was introduced in the play because the villagers were concerned that wives do not confide in fellow members, even when they are aware that the culprits are within their families. Unlike in an agitprop situation, where the play would have suggested a solution, the members of the audience debate the advantages and disadvantages of a number of possible solutions, and make a community decision on the best course of action to take.

A further community decision is made in the fourth scene, when the members of the audience agree that in their experience of communal gardens supported by the German Agro-Action, party politics have not played a role. Unlike in *Kopano ke Matla!*, the villagers' concerns about discrimination based on party affiliation are not dismissed by fictional characters as unimportant or non-existent. The villagers have their own experience of this situation, and they know exactly how previous development projects have operated in their villages. Immediately they are told something that is contrary to what they know to be true, they become sceptical of the whole message. In the *Agro-Action Play*, the villagers were able to express their experience of past discrimination, and to assert that such discrimination no longer exists.

The third community decision occurs in the same scene when the villagers, after discussing the neo-colonialist aspects of foreign aid, come to a conclusion that still they need the aid. The plot point shows the high level to which the Basotho in the rural areas have been politicised. The catalysts could have guided the villagers to develop this point even further, examining more closely the issues raised by the villagers. For example, after the villagers make a decision that they need foreign aid, a member of the audience suggests: 'But when they [foreign donors] come we must look closely at their activities, so that we don't find that one day we have sold ourselves and our land. A man does not see twice.' It is not clear how the villagers will 'look closely' at the activities of foreign donors so as to detect neo-colonial tendencies. For instance, what particular things will they look for? On finding them, what action will they take? What power do they have at community level to decide what projects will be permitted to operate in the villages? These questions would have been addressed if the catalysts had prompted the members of the audience to develop their discussion. The next chapter, on intervention, discusses the significance of prompting in the conscientisation process.

The fourth instance of community decision is on the rejection of imposed leadership. This issue is raised by the fictional communal garden members and their chieftainess. The members of the audience quickly take it up, and decide that a foreman must be elected by the members of the communal garden. The choice must not be based on gender, but on how capable the person is of fulfilling his or her duties to the project and its members. In this instance, the community hopes to achieve a greater control of its social, economic and political destiny. They want to control their institutions. The aspiration for democratic conduct of their affairs is in itself a process of development.

The climax, representing the main plot point that requires the audience to complete the play, is the court case. Size is accused of theft and vandalism. The spectators engage in a long discussion on what to do with the culprit. Various solutions proffered by audience members are thoroughly discussed, then rejected as unfeasible or adopted. In the course of the debate, constant reference is made to the actual events in the world of the community. The decision taken is that Size must be sentenced to work in the communal garden, and must be given a position of responsibility. This is in fact what community members say must be done to those people who steal and destroy in the garden. The solution in the play is also the solution in society.

The play did not strictly follow the simultaneous dramaturgy technique.

When the catalysts halt the action at a crisis point and ask the audience to offer solutions, the actors did not perform the actions on the spectator's orders. Instead there was a long debate among the members of the audience, with the catalysts and extension workers from the FSAP participating. For example, after the members of the audience have confirmed that they do have people like Size in the community, one woman from the audience suggests that the best solution is to take such people to the chief of the village. The action of the play should have continued. Size should have been taken to the chieftainess. Another woman says this does not help since the culprits 'look down upon the chief'. An old woman offers her suggestion:

> If the chief fails, then we must go to the government. Where I live in my village which is not far from here, the government had failed to provide us with any services. There was no road. There was no water. Until this German project came here. Our government for all these years has not done anything for us.

This was an opportunity to perform the old woman's suggestion. Size must be taken to the 'government'. (It is not clear what the old woman meant. She might have been referring to the police, or to any one of the government institutions responsible for rural development.) This, of course, will not remedy the situation, since another woman from the audience asks: 'Then if they have not done anything for us, how are they going to help if we take people who spoil our things to the government?' In this way the actors become like puppets, who perform strictly on the orders of the spectators. In the *Agro-Action Play* the actors become like puppets only in the final scene when Size becomes a changed man and works hard for the success of the garden, and Mpokho, his wife, and her friend become the most enthusiastic members. This is the end of the play the villagers wanted to see.

The play still functions as simultaneous dramaturgy, since the action and the debates are not deterministic, as everything is subject to criticism and rectification. Spectators are free to change anything at a moment's notice without censorship. Thus the play becomes a democratic vehicle for community dialogue and community decision.

Community decision-making did not exist in *Kopano ke Matla!*, and was minimal in the *Rural Sanitation Play*. In both plays, decisions were made by fictional characters on behalf of the audience. In the latter play, members of the audience could make decisions on peripheral issues, such as the use of dried faeces as manure. However, the central issue — the adoption of the VIP toilet — was engrafted in the play. This left the audience with only two options: to adopt or reject the innovation — the affirmation–negation option.

Community decision-making is a product of community participation in most or all of the stages of creating the play. The issues addressed in the *Agro-Action Play* were selected by the villagers themselves. The villagers were involved in the planning of the programme. They created the basic scenarios of the play; for instance, it was their suggestion that Mpokho should lose his job at the mine, should find that his wife has misspent the money, and should ultimately join the communal gardens. The catalyst's role was to order these suggestions in a coherent storyline. The catalysts became merely interpreters of the villagers' own views.

The villagers were not involved in the story improvisation and actual rehearsal of the scenarios they had created. This was done by the catalysts on their own. However, since the play created from this process was unfinished because it only posed the problem, the villagers were in fact involved in the process of dramatisation when they completed the play. Their involvement in this process was not through performance (except in song and dance). They did not become actors. Instead, they were co-authors, since they determined or modified the direction the play would take. It was a story of their composition that was being told.

Use of performance space: The advantages of the arena in facilitating a smooth interaction between the actors/catalysts and the audience/performers have already been discussed. As in the *Rural Sanitation Play*, the *Agro-Action Play* was staged in the round. Neither sets nor props of any kind were used. Even actions such as sweeping the room were mimed. This helped in the deconstruction of illusionism, which further promoted their participation in the play. It is in the nature of the villagers' own performance modes such as *lipina-tsa-mokopu* that no props nor sets are used. All the actions are mimed.

Naming, reflection and action praxis in the *Agro-Action Play*: Active audience participation for its own sake does not result in conscientisation. The dialogue must be directed towards the three stages of the conscientisation process: naming, reflection and action praxis. The three questions were addressed in the *Agro-Action Play*, since the villagers identified their problems, examined the sources of the problems, and made decisions on what course of action to take in order to remedy the situation. Table 6.2 illustrates how the process works in the *Agro-Action Play*. Active participation of the audience in this process was non-existent in both *Kopano ke Matla!* (which has already been identified as agitprop) and the *Rural Sanitation Play* (which falls under the new category of *participatory agitprop*).

Agro-Action Play as communication
The *Agro-Action Play* lacked the strong persuasive elements that were

Table 6.2
Three stages in the process of conscientization in the *Agro-Action Play*

Naming	Reflection	Action
Theft/ vandalism	a) Opposition to neo-colonialism	Culprits work in the gardens, and awareness of project value to community created
	b) Lack of understanding (of project value to community)	
Lack of participation	a) Dependence on mine remittances	a) Creation of awareness that mine employment does not last forever/ retrenched migrant joins communal garden
	b) Public opinion (fear of displaying own	b) Not satisfactorily dealt with
Imposed leadership	Misconception that male would manage project better	Introduction of democratic structures in the project

evident in both *Kopano ke Matla!* and the *Rural Sanitation Play*. None of the parties involved adopted an advocacy position, and Marotholi were not purposive communicators. The FSAP were purposive communicators inasmuch as they wanted the projects in the villages to succeed, and to explore ways in which this might be achieved. They were not being prescriptive in their purposiveness.

Unlike in the two previous plays, the message was created jointly by the villagers and the catalyst group. Since the villagers selected the campaign issues, they initiated the process of communication. They were involved in the planning of the programme, and had a say in what to include or exclude. Their role, then, was not only to respond to the messages created and transmitted by the theatre group, as was the case in *Kopano ke Matla!* and *Rural Sanitation Play*.

The optimal heterophily process: Although the catalysts did not insert themselves into the village, and live with the villagers for a period of time, they were able to achieve optimal heterophily by working closely with the communal garden members. Indeed the FSAP engaged their services as intermediaries because they were more homophilous to the community garden women than the FSAP personnel of foreign experts. The Marotholi are heterophilous from the communal garden members because of their high level of academic education, and the difference in class position. However, because of their rural origins and their commitment to development, they acquire greater empathic ability vis-à-vis the communal garden members. Their heterophily is therefore optimalised. The communal garden members, in turn, are able to achieve optimal heterophily with non-members. They belong to the same village, and are members of the same peasant class. This makes them homophilous. The communal garden members, however, are opinion leaders on the issues that relate to communal gardens and to other projects supported by the FSAP. As a result they have a degree of heterophily with the non-members. They can therefore be used by the members of Marotholi as intermediaries in communicating with the non-members. The situation is illustrated in Figure 6.2. The change agent has a more successful interaction with the communication medium organisation. They both share the desire for a social transformation of the target group. The change agent, however, has a very high level of heterophily with the target group, since the change agent is an outsider who does not share the same codes operating in the culture of the target group. Although the communication medium organisation shares some of these codes with the target group, it is more heterophilous to the target group than the target group's fellow-villagers, who have attained opinion leadership in the field of integrated community development projects. For this reason, the communication medium organisation is able to communicate more effectively with the target group through these intermediaries.

The four-step optimal heterophily process is essential in cases where the catalyst group is unable to join the community for a long period, and participate in all the aspects of community life. To get into the village, and work with the villagers, they need intermediaries. This was the case also in the *Rural Sanitation Play*. The change agent (Rural Sanitation Project), engaged the services of the theatre group, who in turn used village health workers to get into the villages, and to mobilise the villagers for performances.

It does happen that the theatre group itself or the catalysts themselves are both a medium organisation and change agents. This happens when they, on their own, without support or sponsorship from, say, a developmental agency, go out to the village with the aim of creating community dialogue on those issues that concern the villagers most. In that case the four-step process becomes a three-step process. They still have to find ways and means of getting into the village and mobilising the villagers to attend the performances, and possibly participate. An example is the Kumba workshop (Eyoh 1987, p. 11), where the catalysts achieved optimal heterophily by using a plantation owner who had developed 'a rather

Figure 6.2

The four-step optimal heterophily process

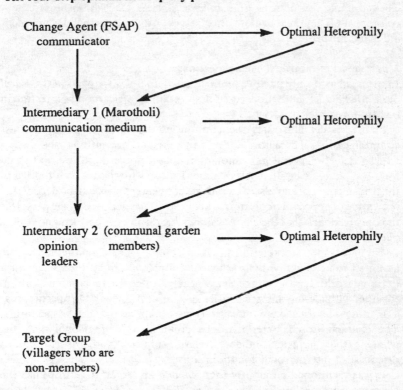

interesting rapport' with his workers. The workers were the target group. Because the plantation owner was an effective intermediary between the workers and the catalysts, the catalysts met with an enthusiastic following; the ground had been well prepared.

Diffusion of innovations: The *Agro-Action Play* lacked the diffusionist elements observed in both *Kopano ke Matla!* and the *Rural Sanitation Play*. The problems are examined from the perspective of the villagers, and there is no reliance on technical solutions characteristic of the paradigm. Instead historical, economic and political factors are examined in order to explain current rural problems. For instance, when the villagers discuss possible solutions to the problem of theft and vandalism, an old woman comments on the failure of the traditional leadership and of the government in meeting the developmental needs of the community. Elsewhere there is discussion on the discriminatory practices of the ruling party, as perceived by the villagers.

The villagers in the *Agro-Action Play* examine the structural causes of the problems not only at local level, but at national and international level. They discuss the politics of foreign aid and its relationship to neo-colonialism. They create among themselves an awareness that development aid is not altruistic.

A new model of theatrical communication

In as much as it only partly explained participatory agitprop in the *Rural Sanitation Play*, Elam's model does not explain theatrical communication in theatre-for-conscientisation.

Elam's model illustrates the continuous discourse of public address communication. The actors address the spectators continuously, during which period the spectators cannot interrupt the proceedings and contribute their own dialogic input. Their communication with the actors is limited to the transmission of signals (in sound and movement) that will be decoded as indicative of approval or disapproval of the events depicted in the play. It is the only feedback that the actors will receive during the performance of the play.

The actor–spectator relationship is an oblique one, in that the actors have assumed roles of individuals who communicate among themselves in a fictional world. It is the sum of this character-to-character communication, together with metonymic accessories such as costumes and properties, that constitutes theatrical communication between the actors and the spectators. The character-to-character dialogue creates an interpersonal dialectic, whereas the character–audience relationship lacks the discontinuous discourse of interpersonal communication.

It was mentioned previously that *Kopano ke Matla!* (agitprop) has the characteristics outlined above, and is therefore adequately explained by Elam's model. However, both participatory agitprop (as in *Rural Sanitation Play*) and the simultaneous dramaturgy technique of theatre-for-conscientisation (as in the *Agro-Action Play*) need a new model to be devised.

Figure 6.3 is a theatrical communication model that illustrates the three major elements of simultaneous dramaturgy:

a) *Theatrical context*: the performer–spectator transaction.
b) *Dramatic context*: character-to-character communication.
c) *Social context*: a range of four transactions as follows:

   i)   Spectator addresses character in the fictional world of the play [dramatic context];
   ii)   spectator addresses spectator outside the dramatic context;
   iii) actor [outside dramatic context] addresses spectator;
   iv)   spectator addresses actor [outside dramatic context].

This model takes into account the multiplication of communicational factors. The multiple *sources* of theatrical information are both the actor and the spectator. Other potential sources from Elam's model, such as set designer, lighting designer and costume designer, are eliminated. When these plays are performed no special lighting effects are used. This applies also to sets and costumes. The aim is to deconstruct the illusionism of conventional theatre. Composers of music and choreographers, on the other hand, may be regarded as other sources. They, however, are drawn from among the actors and the audience. Another source is the director, in those productions that have one (in some cases there is communal direction). In all the Marotholi plays discussed in this chapter there was a director.

The actors encode the information, and place it in a dramatic context, using symbols accessible to the audience, so that connection may easily be made between text and context. In the dramatic context there is a character-to-character transaction, which in turn is transmitted to the audience.

The *transmitters* are the voices of the actors, their bodies, and any musical instruments that may be used. For instance in the *Agro-Action Play* drums and accordions are used. The transmitters send *signals* in the form of sound, movement, smells and other impulses through the physical *channels* that are available for human communication, namely light and sound waves. Olfactory and tactile channels, may also be used, for instance, a play on nutrition where a cooking demonstration is actually made as part of the play. Smells become part of the signals. The *receivers* in this model are the ears, the eyes, the nose and the sense of touch of the spectator. These receive *messages* (speech, gesture, music) that are then decoded and interpreted as text at the *destination*. The spectator receives a complex of theatrical messages, in the theatrical context, and interprets them into a single text.

The spectator in this model creates his/her own messages, which are transmitted through the channels mentioned above and received by the actors in the social context, and the characters in the dramatic context. These messages created by the spectators may be in response to the actors'/characters' own messages, or may be altogether new.

An example of this social context/dramatic context interaction happens in the *Agro-Action Play*. The members of the audience, addressing the characters in the dramatic context, agree that Size must work in the communal gardens. An old woman objects:

> But I still do not agree. You see that man over there (points at him in the audience) was a leader of our workteam in our village. My fellow-villagers are my witnesses that he learnt about the work of the communal gardens, and about the ways of our operations, and then turned against us. The problems of the villages are not the same. He turned against us.

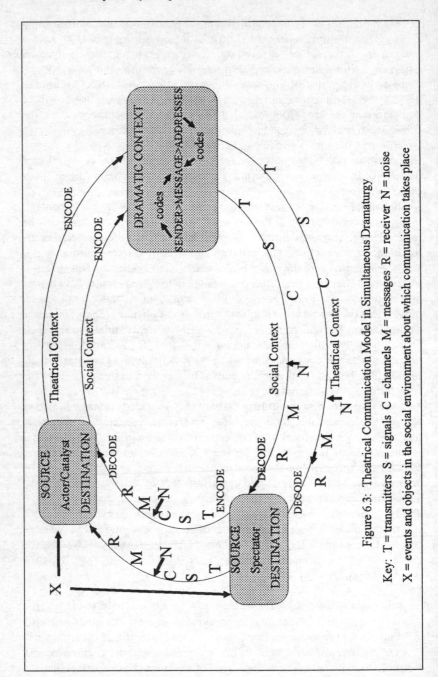

Figure 6.3: Theatrical Communication Model in Simultaneous Dramaturgy

Key: T = transmitters S = signals C = channels M = messages R = receiver N = noise
X = events and objects in the social environment about which communication takes place

He is now the one who eats the fish. He is now the one who destroys our
vegetables in the garden . . .

All at once the spectator addresses other spectators about events in the
fictional world of the characters, and relates them to the real-life events of
the society. Throughout the play this interaction between the contexts
happens. It is the interaction that is lacking in *Kopano ke Matla!*.

The concept of noise has been introduced in this model to encompass all
interference that may hamper the proper reception of the messages. It may
happen anywhere in the communication process. When the actors encode
the information, there may be noise if the theatrical and cultural codes they
use are not shared by the audience. In the transmission, noise may occur as a
result of lack of actors' ability. For example, if *lifela* sung by the main actor
in *Rural Sanitation Play* are not performed according to the conventions of
the genre as experienced by the villagers, the performance will be
meaningless to the audience. It will constitute noise. The noise in the
channels will include those factors that affect visibility and audibility. In the
Agro-Action Play there was a downpour during the second scene. It made so
much noise that the performance had to be transferred to a storeroom.
Other forms of noise may be the irrelevance of the content, or the audience's
lack of interest.

Forum Theatre: *The Trade Union Play*

It has already been mentioned that the *Agro-Action Play* attempted to use
the simultaneous dramaturgy technique of theatre-for-conscientisation. In
this technique the spectator can address the character in the fictional world
of the play, but does not lose his/her identity as spectator. In forum theatre,
another technique in theatre-for-conscientisation, the spectators gradually
become actors. They do not merely comment or debate from the sidelines,
but actually participate in the dramatic context of the play by becoming
actors, and then characters in the fictional world. In terms of the model
shown in Figure 6.4, they also encode information — using theatrical codes
common within their culture — into performance. They become participants in the character-to-character communication of the dramatic
context.

A brief history of the *Trade Union Play*
The heuristic nature of theatre-for-conscientisation was demonstrated with
the creation of the *Trade Union Play* (see Appendix). It was created at the
request of the villagers. In the *Agro-Action Play* one of the characters is
expelled from his job at the mine because he participated in a strike. Female

members of the audience evinced their displeasure at their husbands who participate in trade union activities. One woman said: 'I want to talk about the strikes at the mines. Now Mpokho has lost his job because of a strike. . . . Our husbands go to the mines to work for our families, and then join strikes.' These concerns could not be accommodated into the *Agro-Action Play*. Catalysts and spectators therefore decided that a new play must be created specifically to address these issues.

The first of the only two performances of the play was at Tebang village on a December weekend when a great number of migrant workers were home for a short holiday. Four catalysts (two males and two females) arrived at the village on a Saturday morning, and planned the first two scenes with their hosts, the communal garden women whose husbands were migrant workers. The scenes were rehearsed. Particular attention was paid to *lifela* in Scene 1. The catalysts had spent two weeks learning *lifela* from some *likheleke* in the Roma valley. They had approached these *likheleke* with the content, and had requested them to assist in weaving this into *lifela*. As a result the first scene had the humour and the pathos characteristic of those *lifela* created and performed by the highly talented *likheleke*.

In the afternoon a meeting was called. A loud-hailer attached to a minibus was used to invite people to the *pitso* ground. They were told that there was going to be a play with songs and dances. Men, they were further told, were particularly invited because the play was going to address the problems they experience at the mines. The announcement was confined to one village because the catalysts did not think they could manage a very big crowd.

About fifty people gathered at the *pitso* ground. There was 22 men, 21 women, and seven children. This was one of the very few performances in the experience of Marotholi where the majority of the audience were men. In most cases up to 90 per cent of the audience is female.

Almost all the women, and half the men, had seen the *Agro-Action Play*. It was explained to them that the new play would be different from the *Agro-Action Play*, since they were required to participate, not only in the discussion but in the actual performance. This was enthusiastically accepted by the villagers, although one of them said, 'I cannot act, for I did not learn [memorise lines and rehearse] what to say'. But the catalysts assured her that she could act. One of them told her:

You are talking with me now, but you did not learn those lines beforehand. When you go out of your house in the morning and meet your friend, you do not first memorise what you are going to say to her. She also has not memorised how she is going to answer you. All you have is the topic that you want to talk about, and you each express your views on it. It is exactly the same thing here. We have our topic. It is on the problems of strikes and the part played by trade unions in causing them.

All we have to do now is to create situations around this topic, and act them out. It is the same thing that we did in the *Agro-Action Play* where I saw you participating actively. [From author's own notes taken during the event.]

Before the actual play began, there was a performance of songs and dances by the catalysts and the villagers. Women sang *lipina-tsa-mokopu* which they said reminded them of their youth. *Lipina-tsa-mokopu* are usually sung by the girls rather than by married women. There were also performances of *mokhibo* and *mohobelo*. These performances of song and dance served three important functions:

- They created a festive atmosphere, where everyone participated in a care-free manner.
- They took the place of relaxation and breathing exercises that are necessary before a rehearsal or a performance.
- They helped in building self-confidence among the participants.

The total effect of the song and dance performances was to develop the group's confidence to improvise. These warm-up exercises are essential in breaking any barriers that might impede smooth interaction among the members of the audience, and between the catalysts on one hand, and the spectator-performers on the other.

The performance of the play continued for the whole afternoon, since from time to time the catalysts had to go back to previous scenes and change them to suit new suggestions from the audience. At the end of the day, both the catalysts and the members of the audience felt that a number of problems had not been resolved by the play. But everyone was pleased that issues had been freely raised and 'tabled' for discussion.

A similar play was subsequently performed at another village in the Mohale's Hoek district, and plans were laid to go back to Tebang for a follow-up play on the migrant labour issue, examining problems from the perspective of the women. The feeling was that women did not participate much in the play because in most scenes the setting was at the mines, an environment in which they do not feature. It was resolved that the next play should have its setting in the village, and the migrants should feature as players in the world of the villagers, rather than in the mine compounds.

The catalysts returned to Tebang village to create another play on the problems of wheat production in the district. A similar methodology was used.

Conscientisation in the *Trade Union Play*
The technique of theatre-for-conscientisation used in the *Trade Union Play*

is forum theatre. The stages in the creation of forum theatre are as follows:

a)   Participants (community members) tell a story with a social problem;
b)   catalysts and community members together improvise, rehearse and present it to the group as a skit;
c)   the audience is asked if they agree with the solution;
d)   any spectator is invited to replace any actor and lead the action in the direction that seems most appropriate;
e)   the best solution is arrived at by trial, error, discussion, then audience consensus — the members of the audience articulate their approval or disapproval of the solution.

In simultaneous dramaturgy, the catalysts halt the action at a crisis point and ask the audience to offer solutions. The actors become like puppets and perform strictly on the spectator's orders. In forum theatre, a solution is offered, and the audience has to discuss the merits and demerits of the solution, and members then perform what they think should be the correct solution. All solutions that are offered, tried and tested, are from the members of the audience, and not from the catalysts. The members of the audience do not merely discuss and direct the actors from the sidelines, but are gradually drawn into the fictional world of the play and become actors. A quintessential forum theatre is a theatre without spectators, since all the spectators ultimately become actors.

Community participation: The level of community participation in the *Trade Union Play* is much higher than it was in the *Agro-Action Play*. From the very start of the process of dramatisation, the audience is involved. They select the campaign issues, and make a decision on both the subject and the content of the play. Unlike in the *Agro-Action Play*, where the catalysts went back to base to improvise and rehearse the introductory scene on their own without the villagers, in the *Trade Union Play* those introductory scenes are created and rehearsed with the villagers. The whole of the morning session is spent creating these scenes with the villagers.

During the performance of the play in the afternoon session, the villagers are gradually integrated into the play. In the first scene, two catalysts prepare for the introduction of conflict by depicting through *lifela* the situation of poverty prevailing in their home village. They are labourers in the mines. They have left their wives and children at home, and express a deep longing for a normal family life. Some members of the audience begin their participation by ululating and performing the *tlala* dance. Another member of the audience spontaneously joins the catalysts on the stage and sings his own *sefela* about his travels through the mountains of Lesotho. This clearly illustrates the potency of incorporating the people's own performance modes in theatre-for-development. Even before the catalysts call upon the audience to assume roles in the play, some members of the audience have already led the way by instinctively joining the performance of their own accord.

The second scene introduces the conflict. The two catalysts are joined by the third, who is a member of the village community. The members of the theatre group decided to use him as a catalyst because of his long experience in the trade union movement in Lesotho. But like the members of the theatre group, he had no experience of the mining industry in South Africa, since he had never worked there. The conflict is between those who think trade unions serve the interests of the worker (represented by Motale and the shop steward), and those who think trade unions create more suffering for the worker (represented by Lebona). The latter view is, in fact, held by the majority of women in the audience.

It is during this scene that the first actor from the audience is introduced. After posing to the audience the question whether they agree with Motale and his shop steward advisor or with Lebona, a migrant worker comments:

> I was a member of NUM [National Union of Mineworkers]. I resigned because NUM is more concerned with the politics of South Africa, rather than with the problems of the workers. All we ever do is to sing political songs about Mandela. [ANC leader Nelson Mandela, in jail for 25 years when this play was performed, is a patron of NUM.]

At the time when these comments are made, the labourer is among the other members of the audience. The catalysts call him to the stage to participate in a new scene depicting the position he had just articulated. In simultaneous dramaturgy this issue would have been resolved through discussion and debate among the members of the audience, until there is general agreement on the solution. In forum theatre, however, views emanating from the audience are tried on the stage, with the members of the audience themselves participating in the performance.

In the third scene, the trade union rally develops the conflict. Here again we see more of the audience members participating. Gradually, more and more members of the audience are introduced as participants in the play, as various scenes depicting alternative solutions are tried on the stage. This happens right up to the end of the play, when the members of the audience resolve that migrant workers should join and participate in the activities of the trade unions because trade unions benefit the workers.

The audience in the *Trade Union Play* is, therefore involved not only in selecting campaign issues, but in planning the whole programme, and in the performances.

Naming, reflection and action praxis in *Trade Union Play*: Community decision-making happens throughout the *Trade Union Play*. Problems are identified, examined, and solutions recommended by the villagers themselves. Table 6.3 illustrates how the process of critical analysis works in the play. Critical analysis leads to critical awareness or conscientisation. By the end of the play more members of the audience have acquired a deeper insight into the role and function of a trade union than they had before. They are even aware of the need for a follow-up action in the form of another play that will address the same issues from the women's perspective.

Table 6.3
The three stages in the process of conscientization in the *Trade Union Play*

Naming	Reflection	Action
Loss of employment/loss of income	Unionization of migrant workers	Migrants must continue to join and participate in trade union activities
	Struggle for more pay, better working conditions, and abolition of racial discrimination	
	Strikes	Strike fund establishes income generation projects for workers who have lost jobs
	Dismissal from work	
Union only concerned with SA politics and not worker's problems	Structures that have created racial discrimination in the mines are political	Union should continue to address political issues, since an effective union cannot avoid politics
Undemocratic tendencies of the union (eg calling strikes without consulting the members)	Issue unresolved. Disagreement as to whether there have been instances of undemocratic behaviour	Union must be run by the workers according to their wishes
Lack of formal education of shop stewards	Shop stewards elected from among the workers themselves who have little formal education	Union as a worker's movement must continue to be run by workers elected by fellow-workers irrespective of educational status

Structural causes examined: In the *Trade Union Play*, rural problems are explained through an examination of historical, economic and political factors that have brought about the situation. The play does not attempt to offer technical solutions. Indeed, the nature of the subject itself makes it impossible to discuss it honestly without examining the structural causes at local, national and international levels. The question of the employment of Basotho workers in the mines, of their participation in trade union activities, and of their losing jobs as a result of strike action, does not affect only the individual workers. It affects the country which depends on the remittances from the mines for its survival. It also affects political relations between Lesotho and South Africa.

The economy of Lesotho depends on labour exported to South Africa. Prospects for economic growth depend on industrial relations in the mines. That is why the government is highly sensitive on the question of Basotho participation in the trade union movement. The statement made by a member of the audience that 'even Lekhanya [the government] said on the radio that you must not strike', reflects this growing unease in the government about the effects of industrial action in South Africa on the economy of Lesotho.

It is not only the government that discourages workers from participating in trade union activities. One character in the play says: 'The bosses have told us that trade unions are bad, and we must not join them. TEBA [The Employment Bureau of Africa, a mine-labour recruiting organisation owned and operated by the Chamber of Mines] told us the same.' This statement is supported by Cobbe, in his examination of economic aspects of Lesotho's relations with South Africa.

> Prospects [of increased mine employment of Basotho] after mid-1988 are very uncertain because they depend on industrial relations in the mines, Basotho participation in the black South African trade-union movement, and employer reactions. In the latter part of 1987, it appeared that TEBA and Anglo [the Anglo-American Corporation] were trying to warn Basothos not to participate actively in NUM, and that if they took part in strikes to do so quietly and unprovocatively. Clearly, there are large numbers of Basotho willing to respond to such messages — some 4,000 aspirants are reported to have gathered at Maseru TEBA offices seeking to replace dismissed miners during the strike. However equally there are many Basotho committed to NUM, and actual conditions in the South African mine compounds during industrial action make 'quiet' let alone non-participation of dubious practicality, because disputes in the goldfields have a history of leading to physical violence. (Cobbe 1989, pp. 86–7.)

The contradictions reflected in the play between those who support participation in trade union activities and those who do not are real-life contradictions that scholars like Cobbe have analysed in their academic papers. The play then takes the discussion from the realms of academia to a community analysis by the people concerned. They cease to be objects of analysis, but active participants in a self-analysis process.

Further evidence of Heuristicism in theatre-for-conscientisation: The *Trade Union Play* is a product of theatre-for-conscientisation's heuristicism. The play in turn had possibilities of engendering other plays. For instance when a woman in the audience says that the government has warned Lesotho miners to desist from strikes, a migrant worker angrily replies,

> He [the chairman of the Military Council] says that because he eats our money! When we put our money in *sakoeng* [deferred pay sent directly to Lesotho by the employers. It is a percentage of a miner's wages, and he can withdraw it only when he is back in Lesotho] where do you think the interest goes? It is eaten by Lekhanya. He knows that if we strike then he won't get our money.

This illustrates that the Basotho mineworkers are unhappy about the deferred pay system. They are aware of the exact amounts that are deducted from their wages and transferred to Lesotho. They are also aware that after months of back-breaking labour in the mines, when they withdraw their money in Lesotho it has not earned any interest. They are aware that money in the bank should earn interest, and that therefore their wages are earning interest for someone else. They have no problem in identifying that someone else as the government. Although they refer to General Lekhanya by name, they don't really mean him personally, but the ruling class in Maseru. Lekhanya is both a personification of the monolith that is government, and a representative of the ruling class. It is how Basotho express themselves. To them 'Lekhanya ke 'muso' or Lekhanya, is the government.

The new play would examine the workers' feelings about the deferred pay system. What really happens to the interest? Do they think the system benefits them? What new system would they recommend? What action must they take to remedy the current situation? What channels are they going to use to express their feelings to the government about this deferred pay problem? All these questions would be addressed by the new play. In this way community dialogue continues as play gives birth to play.

The *Trade Union Play* did in fact engender another play on a totally different subject. In the final scene, a question was raised relating to the problems of wheat production. Some members of the audience suggested that a new play should be created to examine the causes of poor wheat production in their village, and how this trend could be reversed. It was noted that for many years Mafeteng had been the foremost wheat producing district in Lesotho. However, of late very little wheat was being produced in the district, and generally the standard of agriculture had deteriorated.

The four catalysts who were involved in the *Trade Union Play* went back to the village and together with the villagers created a play, following the same technique and methodology used in the *Trade Union Play*.

What started off as an innocuous play — with extension workers from some development agencies participating in the performance and advising the villagers on various methods of wheat farming — ended up exposing the corruption of the chief. Apparently for some years he had been encouraging the peasants to sell their fields as residential sites. He received some commission from such transactions. Although the sale of land is illegal in Lesotho, huge tracts of previously rich farmland had been divided into small residential plots and people had already built their houses there.

It dawned on the extension workers that the poor harvest was due not to poor farming methods, but to land shortage. The community members resolved that sale of agricultural land should cease, and people should be allocated residential sites on the mountain slopes and rocky areas, in order to reserve arable land for wheat farming.

Once more the play presented ample evidence of the need to examine the structural causes of the problems, rather than to concentrate on a technical solution. If, for instance, the extension workers had pursued technical solutions, they would have solely taught the villagers better farming methods. But wheat production would have continued to deteriorate, owing to the diminishing areas of arable land, as a result of the chief's corruption. The play is further evidence that the theatre-for-conscientisation method is the most effective in the examination of structural causes of problems, since it does not give the outside agent the opportunity of proffering technical solutions without first examining the issues from the 'beneficiaries'' point of view.

Communicative aspects of the *Trade Union Play*

As in the *Agro-Action Play*, the catalysts do not play an advocacy role. However, unlike in the *Agro-Action Play*, in the *Trade Union Play* there is no purposive communicator. Marotholi Travelling Theatre were not engaged by any agency with vested interests in the results of the communication process. Of their own accord, under no auspices, they go to the village and create the play with the villagers.

Participatory communication in the *Trade Union Play*: The messages are created jointly by the villagers and the catalyst group. When the village women express their opposition to unionisation during the *Agro-Action*

Play, they are initiating the process of communication that culminates in the creation of the *Trade Union Play*. The resulting play does not beam messages in the form of directives encouraging people to support development projects. Instead, the message can emanate from any point, and can be added to, questioned, responded to, from any other point. Figure 6.4 illustrates this participatory communication process.

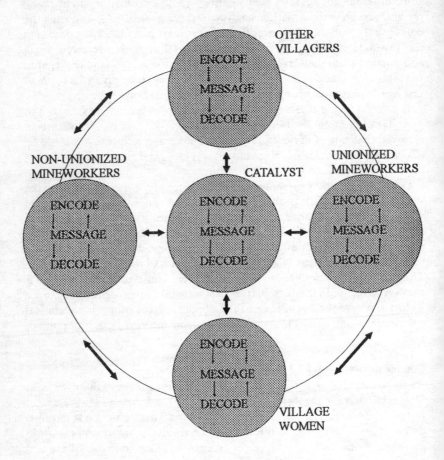

Figure 6.4: The Participatory Communication Process in the Trade Union Play

Basically there are five groups at the performance of the *Trade Union Play*. The first group is that of the village women who were displeased with the activities of the trade union movement in the South African mines. The second group is that of the mineworkers who currently hold membership in the trade union movement, and are likely to defend its activities. The third is a group of mineworkers not in favour of the trade union, or indifferent to it. The fourth is composed of sundry villagers who attended the performance, for example, the farmer who spoke just before the end of the play and expressed his appreciation of the fact that community dialogue had been created on a crucial issue. The final group is that of the catalysts, who are outside agents. In the model in Figure 6.4 they occupy a central role because of their ability to conduct the proceedings, to intervene, and to order the agenda in a more coherent manner. Their role is comparable to that of a chairman in a meeting.

The optimal heterophily process: Optimal heterophily was achieved in a manner similar to that in the *Agro-Action Play*. The Marotholi Travelling Theatre got into the villages through the women who were members of the German Agro-Action Projects. The whole programme was organised by these women and they mobilised the audience to the performance site. However, it was made clear to the prospective audience, through a loudhailer on a minibus, that the event had nothing to do with German Agro-Action. The communal garden women took a merely intermediary role because of their experience in the mode of communication. They had had previous exposure to theatre-for-development through the *Agro-Action Play*, and were well disposed towards it.

The four-step optimal heterophily process in Figure 6.2 becomes a three-step process in the *Trade Union Play*. The change agent, who is a purposive communicator, is eliminated. In this case, the theatre group plays the role of both the change agent and the medium organisation. The communal garden members remain intermediaries between the catalysts and the target group, which is composed of unionised and non-unionised mineworkers, as well as other villagers.

It may be argued that because the village women initiate the communication process, they are therefore purposive communicators, who use the outside agents as intermediaries. However, the initiation of the communication process does not of itself make the initiator purposive. Purposiveness in communication entails advocacy. Although the women begin with the impression that trade unions are bad because they cause strikes, they do not have enough information about the unions and the conditions in the mines. The lack of adequate information obviates their adoption of an advocacy position. For them the communicative event serves the function of giving them information on the work conditions in the mines, and the role of the trade union movement in the life of Basotho migrant mineworkers. It is from this information that they will either confirm or confute previously held views that trade unions are bad. Only then can an advocacy stance be adopted: either 'our husbands must participate in the activities of trade unions' or 'our husbands must not participate'.

Innovation-diffusion paradigm: Like the *Agro-Action Play*, the *Trade Union Play* lacks the characteristics of the diffusion of innovations. In the *Trade Union Play* there is no external or superior agent of change who decides (usually on technical grounds) what is beneficial to the target audience. Change, in the *Trade Union Play*, happens from below, rather than through a top-down imposition of ideas and values.

The new theatrical communication model

The *Trade Union Play* has very strong elements of discontinuous discourse. The individual catalysts and individual villagers speak alternately, becoming both senders and receivers. Anyone can interrupt, and the source cannot manipulate the effects on the receiver.

The new theatrical communication model in Figure 6.3 explains the process of the simultaneous dramaturgy technique. The spectators interact with the dramatic context through direct address to the actor/catalyst. The catalysts are addressed in their capacity as both actors and characters in a dramatic context. The audience has a vicarious participation in the world of the play, since it is limited only to their ability to determine the fate of the characters in the fictional world, while they remain outside that world.

The forum theatre model in Figure 6.5 adds a new dimension to the theatrical communication model. In this model the spectator not only interacts with the dramatic context through the actor/catalyst, but is able to encode his message into performance — using dialogic and non-verbal signs shared by the other members of the audience. The spectator therefore participates in the dramatic context in a direct manner, since he assumes a role as a character engaged in the discontinuous discourse of the dramatic context.

An example of the situation described above happens in the third scene, when Migrant 1 becomes a union leader and instructs the workers to strike. At another stage, in the fourth scene, Migrant 5 and Migrant 6 assume the roles of Motale and Lebona, who were previously played by catalysts, and engage in discontinuous discourse as follows:

Migrant 5/Motale: NUM is not only interested in singing songs of South Africa. Songs are sung to rally people.
Migrant 6/Lebona: But it is politics. It has nothing to do with the worker.

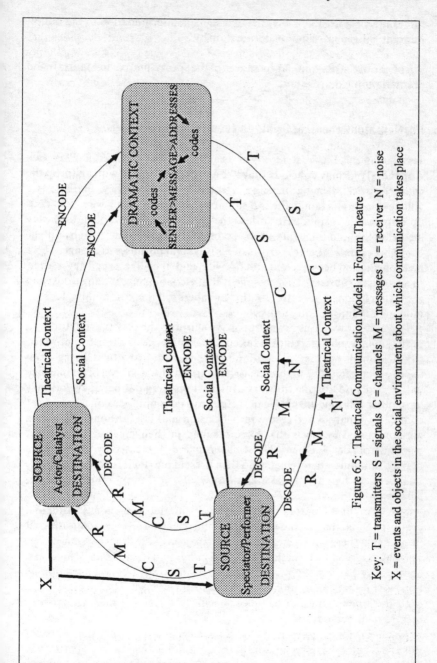

Figure 6.5: Theatrical Communication Model in Forum Theatre

Key: T = transmitters S = signals C = channels M = messages R = receiver N = noise

X = events and objects in the social environment about which communication takes place

Migrant 5/Motale: Do you agree that there is discrimination in the mine?
Migrant 6/Lebona: What discrimination?

Throughout the play similar instances of the spectators' participation in the dramatic context are found.

Participatory theatre/Comgen theatre: the *Alcoholism Play*

Terminological Inconsistency: On examining the *Alcoholism Play* (see Appendix) one may conclude that it is agitprop. It shares with agitprop the characteristics of being message-oriented and exhortatory. Pikilane is a village drunk. His family life is a shambles. He beats up his wife, who ends up crippled in hospital. He suffers the consequences of loneliness, heavy medical bills, and the wrath of the community. He is counselled by village health workers. He sees the errors of his ways and promises to change. There is reconciliation between him and his wife, and 'they live happily ever after' in a world of sobriety. The message is that alcohol abuse is dangerous, and the exhortation is directed to the members of the community to stop indulging in intoxicating drinks.

The play, however, is not agitprop. In agitprop the play is produced by a professional group, and is then taken to the audience as a finished product. ('Professional' here is not confined to those who earn their living from theatre, but refers also to those who have attained a high level of proficiency in the field, and are practitioners of the art on a regular basis, even if they have other full-time engagements.) Agitprop does not focus on a process of community analysis and community decision-making. Although the actors are committed to ideals that have resulted in their creating theatre, art comes before development. The *Alcoholism Play* is created by the members of the community themselves, who then present it to their fellow community members. In Lambert's classification (see Table 2.1, p. 50) it falls under *participatory* theatre.

The term 'participatory theatre' is problematic. As a classification in a group of three that includes agitprop and theatre-for-conscientisation, it implies that there is no community participation in the other two. However, as we have already seen in the *Agro-Action Play* and in the *Trade Union Play*, community participation is the essence of theatre-for-conscientisation — both as simultaneous dramaturgy and as forum theatre. There is therefore a need for a new term that will most accurately describe the participatory theatre methodology.

The most appropriate term would have been 'community theatre' since this is a theatre that emanates from the community itself, and is performed by community members for a community audience. The term 'community theatre' however, also becomes problematic. It has now become a generic term describing a range of different methodolgies; ranging from a theatre created by the community with the assistance and active participation of outside agents, or a theatre created by the community from their own efforts and resources, to a theatre created by outside agents using their own resources, but addressing issues of a particular community, and performed for that particular community. It therefore would not be possible to make a distinction between a participatory theatre methodology, and theatre-for-conscientisation, since under the current use of the term they can both be referred to as 'community theatre'.

The term used by Marotholi Travelling Theatre in their discussion of the methodology in question was 'community-generated theatre', which was ultimately reduced to 'Comgen theatre'. We find it more convenient to use this term for the particular methodology that Lambert (1982) and Boal (1979) refer to as participatory theatre. We further recommend the use of the term 'participatory theatre' for all theatre methodologies that involve the active participation of the audience in most or all of the stages of creating theatre-for-development — especially the process of dramatisation. Participatory theatre will, therefore, include Comgen theatre, theatre-for-conscientisation, and even participatory agitprop.

Brief history of the *Alcoholism Play*

Marotholi Travelling Theatre was invited by village health workers at Tebellong in the mountain district of Qacha's Nek to teach villagers theatre skills so that they might create their own plays. Three catalysts from Marotholi went to live with the villagers at Tebellong for two weeks.

Tebellong is in a remote part of the district, and inaccessible by road. The means of transport to and from the village are light aircraft or horseback. One could use a four-wheel drive motor vehicle, but one would have to park it about 15 kilometres from the village, cross the Senqu river by boat, and walk the rest of the way.

There is a community hospital run by the Lesotho Evangelical Church, which serves Tebellong and neighbouring villages such as Qabane. Nurses based at the hospital go out on horseback to visit clinics in the surrounding villages. The clinics themselves are private houses owned by village health workers, who usually allocate a room in their homes for use as a dispensary.

The catalysts cooked and ate their meals at the house of 'M'e 'Malitlhare, a village health worker, but slept at different neighbours' homesteads. They participated fully in the life of the community. For example, the male catalyst helped to fetch horses from the veld, and to see to it that the herdboys took care of the cattle. He also participated at the *khotla* where the chief and the men of the village were trying to settle a dispute between the clinic and some members of the community. Apparently villagers felt that they were no longer getting proper services at the clinic because the village health worker's husband, who owned the house, was not pleased when villagers came for assistance. He said that the village health worker should be attending to her family affairs, rather than assist people in primary health care for no remuneration. He was no longer willing to let his house be used as a dispensary.

The female catalysts also participated in the various activities in the village. They helped in cooking meals for the homestead, and in drawing water from the well. They went with the village health worker to act as midwives to a woman who was giving birth. They also attended the secret night dance called *litolobonya*, where men are not allowed.

Marotholi's objective was to equip the villagers with theatre skills, so that they would be able to create and perform plays on their own. They worked with a group of sixteen villagers — eleven women and five men. Five of the women were village health workers. More people had volunteered to be part of the workshops, but the catalysts found it necessary to limit the number to a manageable size.

According to one of the catalysts (interviewed by the author in Maseru on 3 October 1989) on the first day of the workshop, interaction between the catalysts and the villagers was difficult.

> Villagers were not keen to participate. They felt that theatrical activities were for children. They said that they could watch as spectators, but would not be willing to be actors. The majority of them had an idea of what a play is. They had seen 'sketches' performed by children in church and during school concerts. Others were regular listeners of *pale* [radio drama] on Radio Sesotho. But they felt that it was not something that they could do.

The villagers saw theatre as something far removed from the world of the community. It became necessary for the catalysts to rid them of this misconception of theatre by placing theatre in the context of the villagers' own performance modes. They performed songs and dances such as *mokhibo, lipina-tso-mokopu*, and *liphotha*. These were modes of performance that the villagers enjoyed most, and they participated with great enthusiasm. They even taught the catalysts a song and dance form called *sehalahala*. The catalysts were not familiar with this form; they thought that it was peculiar to that area of the country since they had never come across it elsewhere.

Interaction was further enhanced with Sesotho games and riddles. These were followed by story-telling. At first traditional folk-tales (*tšomo*) were told. Later the participants were required to invent their own stories. Then a simple analysis of the stories was made — the emphasis being on the structure. The stories had a beginning, a middle, and an end. There was always conflict between opposing forces. Each character in the story wanted to achieve a particular goal. Some of the stories were performed by the participants. Here they were taught how to improvise dialogue, and how to structure their scenes. They also learnt how to use their traditional songs and dances in their plays.

The workshop then dealt with the theatre-for-development process: information gathering, information analysis, story improvisation, rehearsal, public performance, discussion, and follow-up action. They were also taught how to incorporate the discussion stage of the process into the performance stage, by throwing questions to the audience in order to open up the play for audience participation.

The catalysts then asked the villagers to choose themes they wanted to address in their play. After interviewing a number of other villagers they drew up the following list.

- problems with modern daughters-in-law
- unemployment
- alcoholism
- immunisation of infants
- family instability, and divorce
- rural poverty

The villagers felt that these issues were of major concern in the village. They decided, however, to choose the theme of alcoholism, since they felt that most of the other problems were a result of excessive drinking.

The villagers created their play and performed it to audiences of fellow-villagers in the neighbouring villages of Ha Machesetsa, Pulane, Qabane and Ha Makoae. Later the personnel of Tebellong Hospital wrote the following report in their 'Summary of Evaluation Session for Theatre Workshops':

> ... Is theatre useful as an extension? It was generally felt that participatory theatre was an excellent variation on *pitsos*, it's more interesting, encourages participation of villagers in meetings, and is particularly good for villages where people are not active in development. Most importantly, it encourages the audience to come up with answers to their problems.
> ... Has there been enough training to allow us to continue to use theatre? There was some feeling that there hadn't been enough time for the extensionists to work with the Marotholi members, but overall feeling is that training has been sufficient to allow us to practice on our own and continue to use theatre methods. While performances will not have the polish of professionals, they will still accomplish the goal of entertaining and educating people we work with. (Libe *et al*, 1989).

The report further states that the villagers intended to continue to use theatre-for-development. They established a permanent theatre group called Liinoli (plural form of *seinoli*, a type of bird that lives on river fish).

The *Alcoholism Play* as conscientisation

This play is a clear indication of what the peasants are capable of doing on their own with a little assistance from outside agents. They planned their own programme, selected their own campaign issues, created their own play and performed it. The role of the outside agents was limited to equipping them with theatre skills, and exploring with them various methods that they could use in the theatre-for-development process. This means that in the Comgen theatre, as illustrated by this play, the local community has the utmost degree of participation in comparison to all the other methodologies examined in this study. They are in full control of the naming, reflection and action process of conscientisation.

Naming the problem: The villagers identified a number of problems in the community, which included rural poverty, unemployment, family instability and the high rate of divorce, and the problems of relationships between daughters-in-law and their in-laws. They then proceeded to identify excessive drinking of alcohol as the source of all these problems, and decided to create a play that would preach against alcohol. They did not examine the historical, economic and political factors that may contribute to, or even be the source of, the existence of these problems. In their 'scapegoating' approach, they blamed excessive drinking as the source, and did not consider the possibility that excessive drinking and alcoholism might be the result of the problems. Here the peasants blame themselves for the problems of poverty. If only they could stop drinking, they say, they would defeat poverty. They are not aware of the political and economic structures both at local and national level that have kept them in the state of poverty (for an analysis of these, see Chapter 3 on Lesotho and the problems of underdevelopment). This tendecy of the victims to blame themselves is consistent with what Kidd discovered at the Zimbabwe workshop on theatre-for-development:

> . . . all the sketches were lively and full of fun. However many of the sketches had a tendency to moralize. For example, a play on teenage pregnancy concluded with a girl losing a paternity case and being disowned by her father. To rub the point in deeper, the father then divorced his wife for failing to discipline the girl. (Kidd 1985, p. 186.)

The tendency to moralise, and to find the nearest scapegoat, in the naming of their problems is due to the fact that the peasants had not been equipped with the tools of critical analysis. They had been provided only with the technical tools of the theatre.

Reflection: After identifying their problem as excessive drinking, the villagers proceed to ask themselves through the play why this problem exists. We find that the only reason given for Pikilane's behaviour is that he has more money than the rest of the villagers, and therefore he has become a free-spending drunk. Again we find the dearth of analysis of the problems of alcoholism in the village that is evident in the naming stage.

It might be useful here to compare the *Alcoholism Play* with some aspects of *Ngaahika Ndenda* (published in English as *I will Marry When I Want*) by Ngugi wa Thiong'o and Ngugi wa Mirii (1982). This play was created by the two authors and performed by the peasants at the Kamiriithu Cultural Centre in the Limuru district of Kenya. The major problem addressed by the play is landlessness. The play asserts that people were robbed of their land, first by the colonialists, then by their collaborators, the emerging black capitalist class of landowners (some of whom were absentee landowners). Most of the Kamiriithu inhabitants have remained poor and landless.

On recognising the need to create critical awareness among these peasants, the two authors 'were charged with the task of writing a play for the people of Kamiriithu'. (*The Classic* 1983, p. 30). The 'charge' came from the committee of the Kamiriithu Cultural Centre, of which one of the authors was a member. The play was scripted and taken to the peasants for rehearsal. The peasants contributed their creative input in song and dance, and in criticising the language and content of the play.

Ngaahika Ndenda attempts to analyse the problems of Limuru by bringing about class consciousness through the exposure of class contradictions in the society. Among the issues it examines are the problems of unemployment, the mercenary role of the church in perpetuating rural poverty, disillusionment with the Kenyan style of independence, the exploitation of workers by national ruling classes, and the prejudice at all levels of society against women. It is an anti-sexist play.

The problem of alcoholism is examined not in isolation from the structural problems that beset the society. Characters in the play do not merely become drunkards because they are bad people. The society will not be redeemed by the transformation of the alcoholics to a state of sobriety. The play examines the macro-origin of the problem by illustrating that the state of landlessness and unemployment led to escapism in drink. The peasants, in their condition of poverty brought about by the political system in Kenya, find solace in alcohol and in escapist religions. Kamande, one of the characters, becomes a drunkard as a result of losing his job. Even Kiguunda, a farm labourer who starts off as a 'good' family man, becomes an alienated being, losing himself in drinking *chang'aa* (a potent homebrew) after losing his small piece of land to the wealthy Kanoru family.

Unlike in the *Alcoholism Play* created by the peasants of Tebellong, the peasants of Limuru were able to acquire a critical awareness of their problems, since their play afforded them a deeper analysis of their situation. In the *Alcoholism Play* this analysis does not exist. Pikilane is a drunkard. He beats up his wife. But there is no satisfactory reflection of his situation, and of the situation of the society beset by a problem of alcoholism.

Action: In the *Alcoholism Play* the action that the villagers decide upon is that alcoholics must be counselled to stop drinking, and shebeen owners must sell liquor only in the evenings. The villagers appreciate the fact that shebeen owners also have a living to make, but this must not be made during working hours. When a shebeen owner objects, the villagers decide that a law must be made to enforce their decision that liquor should be sold only in the evenings. The villagers thus resort to a technical solution. The reasoning behind this is that if a law is made, then people won't drink during the day. If people don't drink during the day they will go to work, and the problems of poverty will be solved. The solution does not take into consideration the fact that employment opportunities do not exist in the village. The solution therefore is similar to the proverbial act of putting the cart before the horse.

Guidance from catalyst group: The *Alcoholism Play* was created with minimal guidance on the treatment of the content from the catalyst group. The scapegoating in its treatment of the issues is similar to that found in other plays elsewhere in the continent that were created without guidance from catalysts. The women of Mwima, in Malawi, created a play without any guidance from a catalyst group.

> It presented an interesting contrast between effective modern medicine and ineffective traditional medicine. The catalyst group wondered whether the scapegoating of the *sing'anga* (herbalist) in the play was not a projection of what the local Mwima health committee felt the catalyst group wanted to see, rather than a genuine expression of popular sentiment.
>
> On the other hand, the Mwima villagers have shown an increasing confidence in handling drama as a medium. The plays have shown a syncretic vigour and a progressive mastery of theatrical resources. (Kerr 1988, pp. 179–80.)

Kerr's statement, as well as the *Alcoholism Play* experience, are a clear illustration that it is possible to have a lot of community participation in the theatre-for-development process, and yet achieve very little conscientisation. Like the Mwima women, the villagers at Tebellong showed great skill in handling drama as a medium. Without guidance from the catalysts they created and performed their play. This means that the level of their participation was the highest imaginable. Yet they attained little or no conscientisation. If participation *per se* does not lead to conscientisation, there must be some other variable that is essential for the process to happen.

The *Alcoholism Play* as communication

On the question of communication, the *Alcoholism Play* has characteristics of participatory agitprop already examined in the *Rural Sanitation Play*. However, there is one major difference, in that the *Rural Sanitation Play* was devised and performed by outside agents (hence the participatory agitprop label), whereas the *Alcoholism Play*, as comgen theatre, is the product of the local community. The communication process is initiated by the community, who seek the assistance of outside agents only in so far as they should teach the community members to use the communication medium. On mastering the techniques of the medium, they use the medium for their own purposes without further assistance from outside agents. They create their own messages and transmit them to other members of the community. They insert in their play elements of discontinuous discourse, as in the *Rural Sanitation Play*, and these enable other villagers, who are not participating in the performance, to participate in the discussion of the issues.

The performers and their audiences have achieved a state of optimal heterophily. The villagers are to some extent homophilous among themselves. However, the group that wants to see changes happen in the village has some level of heterophily by the mere fact that they are aware that change is necessary. This gives them optimal heterophily with their fellow-villagers. The catalyst group, on the other hand, attained optimal heterophily with the community by using the village health workers as intermediaries, and by living with the villagers for two weeks, and participating in all aspects of community life.

7. The Concept of Intervention

Participation and conscientisation

The relationship between participation and conscientisation that has emerged in the analysis of the plays is as follows:

1. Conscientisation happens as a result of the target community's participation in *naming* their problems, in *reflecting* on them by exploring the reasons for their existence, and in community decision-making on the course of *action* to take in order to solve the problems.
2. For conscientisation to happen the naming and the reflection stages of the above process must not be limited to an explanation of rural problems in terms of technical causes, and therefore technical solutions during the action stage. Structural causes (historical, economic and political factors) of the problems must be examined, not only at local level, but also at national and international levels.
3. Structural causes must be examined from the perspective of the target community, and for this to happen the medium must not use a marketing approach to communication (persuasive communication). This means that the target community must not only have an access to the communication medium, but must participate in medium programming.
4. Community participation, of crucial importance in conscientisation, happens during the process of dramatisation — the process of creating and performing the play. In the agitprop *Kopano ke Matla!*, the community is not involved in the process of dramatisation. Therefore little or no conscientisation happens through this play.
5. It is possible to have community participation, and yet little or no conscientisation. The *Alcoholism Play* is an example of this. The local villagers had maximum participation in the dramatisation process, yet the resulting play did not become a vehicle for critical analysis, and therefore did not bring about critical awareness.

It is important to note that there is a good reason for positing the above observations in terms of community participation, rather than audience participation. In most cases the two will mean the same. The members of the target community become the audience, and their participation is therefore audience participation. However, in other cases the members of the community might create their play, and present it to an audience of their fellow community members. There is an audience that is distinguishable from the performers. This sector of the community that now comprises the audience may or may not participate in the performance. There is still community participation in the dramatisation process since the play is created and performed by members of that local community. An example of this situation is found in the creation and performance of the *Alcoholism Play*.

Participation and intervention
The observation that community participation may not necessarily lead to conscientisation means that there is an essential variable that must operate within the process of participation in order to get conscientisation. The variable is *intervention*.

Intervention happens during the dramatisation process when catalysts interrupt the proceedings of dramatisation to contribute their views, or to guide the participants. Intervention is directorial, and serves the following functions in the dramatisation process:

• To keep order and coherence in the play;
• to facilitate a deeper analysis;
• to contribute technical expertise on the medium itself, and on the content.

In comgen theatre, as evidenced by the *Alcoholism Play*, there is little or no intervention, since the catalysts did not play any role in the dramatisation process. They simply equipped the community with theatre skills. Because there was minimal intervention, there was little or no conscientisation, in spite of the fact that there was maximal participation.

In agitprop theatre, on the other hand, there is minimal community participation, as evidenced by *Kopano ke Matla!*. Throughout the process of dramatisation the community members are not involved. The theatre group, on their own, create a play and take it to the community for performance as a finished product. During the performance, the members of the community are not involved in contributing their views on how events should occur, or in performing. Agitprop therefore becomes a classic case of maximal intervention, because throughout the play it is the members of the theatre group who are playing a role. The dramatisation process is continuous, right up to the end of the play, so that the members of the target community cannot 'get any word in edgewise', and therefore cannot participate. During this period the members of the theatre group are the only ones engaged in the discourse. Continuous discourse can therefore be interpreted as maximal intervention.

Examples of intervention from the plays

Whereas in agitprop the whole play comprises maximal intervention, and in comgen theatre there is minimal intervention, the other three plays examined in the previous chapter show varying degrees of intervention. The greater part of the *Rural Sanitation Play* consists of intervention. The community members are not involved in the creation of the play. In the performance of the play some parts are open to audience participation. The catalysts use the technique of opening up dialogue with the audience in the course of the play, rather than during discussion time. There is some degree of community participation in the performance component of the dramatisation process. In this play there is more intervention by the change agent/catalyst and less participation by the members of the target community.

The *Agro-Action Play* presents a situation where the participation of the community is increased, and the intervention by the catalyst group decreases. The members of the community are involved in creating the play, and indirectly in performing it. The community members decide on the issues that must be addressed, and on the storyline. The members of the catalyst group rehearse the first few scenes, but leave the play unfinished. The members of the community, during performance, give directions on how the play should be completed. But throughout this process of dramatisation the catalyst group intervenes to contribute its views on various aspects of dramatisation, and on the content. For instance, in the discussion of discrimination based on political party affiliation a woman from the audience said: 'No, this project does not involve political parties. It is for everyone irrespective of political parties. It is for the whole nation.' The matter would have ended there, and the play would have proceeded to address other matters, if one of the catalysts had not asked: 'But can you say there are some people in the village here who believe that politics is involved in this project?' Audience members admitted that there were people who believed so. The catalyst further asked, 'Why do they believe so?' It turned out that the village had an unpleasant experience of discrimination against those who did not support the ruling party. When development projects were introduced in the village, only those who were card carrying members of the party would be allowed to participate. As a result, villagers had become sceptical of all development projects, even when they were funded and managed by non-governmental organisations.

Because this matter had been brought to the open, through the prodding of the catalyst, the villagers were able to discuss it, and to make a community decision that favouritism of any kind should not be tolerated. This is an example of an intervention that facilitates a deeper analysis.

Intervention to facilitate a deeper analysis also happens throughout the *Trade Union Play*. For instance, in the third scene a trade union rally is held, with members of the community taking the roles of workers and union officials. A union leader instructs the workers to go on strike. He says in his speech to the workers:

> Comrades, I have to tell you that there is going to be a strike. We are now tired of working in these mines for low pay. So, I am telling you now that all of you must begin the strike immediately.

The meeting is over, and the workers prepare to strike. That would have been the end of the matter if a catalyst had not asked if that was really how things happened when strikes were called. Some men from the audience said it was exactly how strikes were called. The catalyst said, 'Well, I am glad I didn't join the trade union if things are like that . . . if a man from the union just comes and tells you to strike!' A migrant worker answered:

> No, it is not true. I am a member of NUM, and I know it is not true. When a strike is called it is after all the members have met, and it is the members themselves who decide to strike or not. Ramaphosa [secretary-general of the National Union of Mineworkers] does not just tell us to strike. We hold meetings, and we tell him that we want to strike.

After this a long discussion ensues as to whether strikes are called by the workers or by the union officials. Various mineworkers relate their own experiences of strikes in the different mines where they work. The women also contribute their views to the effect that it is not important whether strikes are called by the workers or by union officials, 'strikes are bad because children starve'. At the end of it all a resolution is made that workers should be vigilant that the trade union is democratically run. They say:

> The union [officials] should not be the boss of the workers, for in that case the union will be acting like the employers who always bully the workers. A union must be run by the workers according to their wishes.

This deeper analysis would not have happened if the catalyst had not intervened. Most of the people who had never worked in the mines, and were without any experience of how the workers' movement functions, would have left with the impression that the union officials dictatorially call strikes without consulting the workers.

This scene also illustrates how intervention works to keep order and coherence in the play. After the discussion on whether strikes are called by the workers or by union officials, a catalyst who plays the role of a shop steward steps forward and says:

> I think we shall not agree on this matter now. Let us leave it until the end of the play. Then we shall come back to it. We shall not just leave it like that because it is important. Where do we go from here?

Intervention here serves a directorial function. The catalysts are aware that for it to be entertaining, a play must maintain its narrative structure. Their role in this case is that of ordering any digressions, and fitting them properly in places where they belong. This means that the play is being created and directed during performance. Plays of simultaneous dramaturgy and forum theatre are in a perpetual state of rehearsal.

This directorial function is also observed in the beginning of the play. After the catalysts had sung their *lifela*, a migrant comes to the stage and sings his. His *sefela* is very long. A catalyst requests him in the form of another *sefela* to shorten his. If this had not happened there would not have been any time left to perform the play.

In the *Agro-Action Play* an example of this directorial intervention is found after a man from the audience has asked this question: 'Is is not true though that when these overseas countries give us aid it does not come naked? It comes with something else. It is their way of coming to rule us.' There is a shouting match between those who agree with him, and those who disagree. The catalysts try to restore order by beating the drums, and one of them shouts, 'Let us listen to one another! If we all speak at once we shall not understand one another!'

An example of intervention that functions to provide the participants with technical expertise happens when a catalyst who is also an extension worker from German Agro-Action says:

> This shows that your committee was not strong enough. I always say that a weak committee will have such problems. Your Size was not supposed to be in the money. When these people say Size must be given responsibility they mean that he should see to it that people go to work at eight, and knock-off at four. Not that he should look after the money. He should look after garden implements and see to it that they are kept in proper condition.

This intervention happens after the community had revealed a lack of expertise on committees and on the function of each member who holds a portfolio in the committee.

Theatre-for-development practitioners have long been conscious of the role that intervention plays in conscientisation. This study only serves to concretise current practice by identifying and ordering the characteristics of intervention. An example of intervention that facilitates a more profound analysis of the problem is found in Kidd's description of the dramatisation process at a Zimbabwe workshop for theatre-for-development. After the peasants had created their play on teenage pregnancy with little intervention from the catalyst group, the catalysts felt that the play tended to moralise. The girl loses the paternity suit, and is disowned by her father. The father also divorces the mother for failing to discipline the girl.

> In the day's post-mortem we agreed that we should try to *move* the villagers beyond this kind of moralising to a more complex interpretation of the issues involved. We speculated that the problem of teenage pregnancy was more than just a matter of 'the erosion of traditional values', an 'over-indulgent mother', or 'poor discipline at boarding school'. It also involved pressures on unemployed, poorly educated young women whose options after primary school were very limited, creating the potential for sexual exploitation. We also noted that the pressures on men to go to towns for work put a greater burden on the women who remained behind in the villages. (Kidd 1985, p. 186.) [Emphasis mine]

The causes of teenage pregnancy stated above are from the catalyst group's speculation. They did not surface as a result of the villagers' own analysis of the problem. The catalysts felt that they had to intervene and introduce these speculations into the villagers' play in order to facilitate a deeper analysis.

Another instance at the same workshop happened during the creation of a play on water supply problems in the village. The villagers could not get water from the school borehole. The school committee insisted that people pay a water fee. Those too poor to afford the water fee suffered because they couldn't use the school borehole. The solution presented by the villager's play was that the school committee chairman should be voted out of office.

> We intervened: 'Is this realistic? And anyway, will it solve your problem?' They agreed it was unlikely; they felt they had little influence. We suggested they organise a public meeting with the school committee to review the policy. (Kidd 1985, p. 193.)

The intervention then facilitated a deeper analysis of the problem.

The intervention–participation–conscientisation relationship

The intervention–participation relationship

It was noted that more intervention by the catalyst/change agent means less community participation. For instance in agitprop there is maximal intervention, and minimal participation. In comgen theatre on the other hand there is minimal intervention and maximal participation. The relationship can therefore be diagramatically explained as in Figure 7.1. In this model, it must be noted, no values are assigned to the variables, as both have not been measured. The function of the model is not to quantify the process, but to determine the position of each methodology of theatre in relation to intervention by change agent/catalyst and participation by community members.

Figure 7.1

The intervention-participation relationship

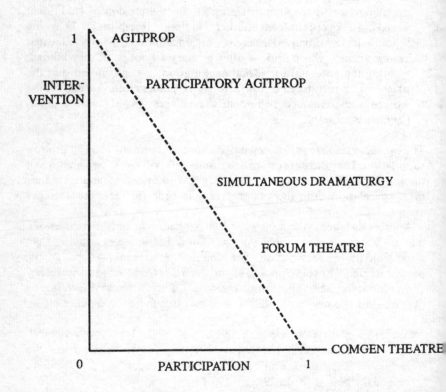

The participation–conscientisation relationship

The relationship between participation and conscientisation can be illustrated by the curve in Figure 7.2. The figure illustrates the rising level of conscientisation with the rising level of participation, until optimal participation is reached. From this optimal participation point, more participation engenders less conscientisation until a stage of maximal participation–minimal intervention is reached.

Figure 7.2
The Participation-Conscientisation Curve

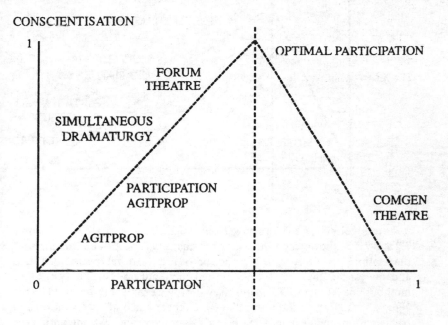

The intervention–conscientisation relationship

The curve in Figure 7.3 illustrates the relationship between intervention and conscientisation. We noted that in agitprop there was maximal intervention, and minimal conscientisation. In comgen theatre, there was minimal intervention, and minimal conscientisation. The degree of intervention decreased as we went through participatory agitprop, simultaneous dramaturgy and forum theatre, while at the same time conscientisation increased. However when reaching the least interventionist situation, conscientisation falls to a minimum. Minimal intervention engenders minimal conscientisation. Maximal intervention on the other hand, also engenders minimal conscientisation. Optimal intervention is the ideal balance between intervention and participation that engenders the highest level of conscientisation.

Figure 7.3

The Intervention-Conscientisation Curve

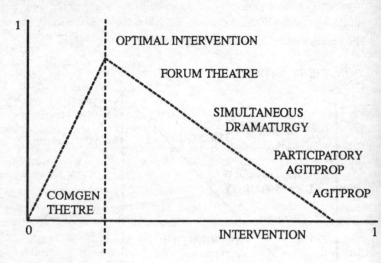

CONSCIENTISATION

As in Figure 7.1, no values have been assigned to the variables in Figures 7.2 and 7.3, as the objective here is not to quantify concepts, but to represent the relationships. Only those methods of theatre-for-development identified and analysed in this study are positioned on the curves. There may be other methods not yet identified, in use elsewhere. An example is that used by the Ngugis at the Kamiriithu Centre, in which there was both intervention and participation, and also an indepth analysis of the problems confronting the peasants of Limuru.

The Kamiriithu method cannot, however, be classified under any of the methodologies discussed in this study. The play was scripted by the two authors in the conventional manner that playwrights compose plays, and was taken to the peasants for rehearsal. In the course of producing the play,

> many of the people whose talent had been lying fallow suddenly became sharp and constructive critics of the language and content of the play. They changed and innovated at will. A whole marriage sequence incorporating some song and mime was 'written' by some of the women participants. (*The Classic* 1983, p. 30.)

The local villagers did not conceive nor create the play. Their role was limited to modifying what had been created by the two authors. Two of the elements necessary for conscientisation were present: the local community's participation in performance; and the analysis that examined the causes of problems at local, national and international levels. The play, however, had a very high level of intervention in the form of the pre-created script. As a result it is not clear how much the peasants were involved in the naming–reflection–action process, and how much the play served as a vehicle for conscientisation. The location of the Kamiriithu methodology on the curve will be determined by the level of conscientisation attained.

Optimal intervention

Theatre-for-development practitioners, in their dramatisation work with local communities, should create a balanced situation that will result in optimal intervention. Optimal here refers to the most favourable or desirable condition. Optimal intervention would therefore mean the best compromise between the opposing tendencies of participation and intervention. As in the case with optimal heterophily, there cannot be set a standard of what optimal intervention is. All that can be said is that it is attained at that point when intervention is just sufficient to serve the three functions — naming, reflection, action — and does not go to the extent of imposing the catalyst's own views and values on the process of dramatisation. The point will vary from community to community, and from catalyst to catalyst, depending on the proficiency of the catalyst in utilising the medium, and on the level of critical awareness of both catalyst and community.

This finding places a great responsibility on the catalyst. It confirms an assertion previously made in this study that catalysts must have a higher level of social consciousness than the villagers. Without this higher level of social consciousness — and of critical awareness — they cannot play their interventionist role effectively, and the villagers will remain unconscientised through the theatre.

Optimal intervention and community control

When the participants of the Zimbabwe workshop held an evaluation session of their work with the peasants, they found that some of the community's own plays were overrun by the ideas of the catalyst group (Kidd 1985, p. 196). This means that the level of intervention was too high to permit the villagers' own perspective to surface. The catalysts controlled the process of community dialogue. Optimal intervention, however, is not the same as control. The village community retains control of the process; they choose the priorities and decide which issues should be raised. The catalyst intervenes in a process that is determined and controlled by the community. *The Rural Sanitation Play* is, on the other hand, a clear example of change-agent control. Although the villagers participated in the play, they did not decide on the issues to be raised, nor did they choose the priorities. The outside team, as in some instances at the Zimbabwe workshop, 'shaped the process, leading it and suggesting through our questions the direction it should go . . .' (Kidd 1985).

Optimal intervention should serve the function of drawing out the villagers' own analyses, rather than imposing the catalyst's own thinking on the villagers.

Community control on its own, however, is no guarantee that progressive change will happen, as shown by the *Alcoholism Play*, in the same way that participation *per se* does not guarantee progressive change. For progressive change to happen there must be informed intervention.

Community control is essential, however, in ensuring the continuation of community dialogue through theatre even when the catalysts have gone back to base. Participatory theatre takes time to mature; that is why 'Workshop participants [catalysts] must be sure that they leave behind local structures which could continue to work, although this would require constant backstopping and support.' (Eyoh 1987, p. 14.)

This support will involve intervention, and it will continue until the members of the community have acquired such a high degree of critical awareness that they do not need catalysts. The most effective theatre-for-development is achieved when the community itself assumes the function of catalysts. Only at that stage will comgen theatre be a theatre for conscientisation.

Intervention and domestication
A theatre for domestication reinforces the structures that oppress the disadvantaged members of the community. It perpetuates the exploitative relations between the disadvantaged communities and the ruling classes. Domestication in theatre comes in three guises:

- An agent consciously seeking to influence people to accept or even promote the very structures that oppress them. Here an impression is created that the exploitative structures serve the interest of the oppressed
- an innocuous situation or event in a play meant to liberate, but domesticates in the process
- censorship and self-censorship.

Through intervention it is possible for catalysts to create a theatre for domestication, particularly if the catalyst's own level of critical analysis and therefore critical awareness is not high. In the same way that Kidd says his group 'moved' the villagers beyond moralising to a more complex interpretation of the issues involved, catalysts with less critical awareness may 'move' the villagers into a false interpretation of the issues involved.

A false interpretation is one of the major factors that lead to domestication. An example of this is found in the 'blaming the victim' syndrome of *Kopano ke Matla!*. When rural poverty is blamed on the laziness of the villagers, the true causes of rural poverty are concealed from the rural communities. The structural causes are not examined. The villagers who are 'lazy and traditional', but who, strangely enough, have always worked hard in their fields or as labourers digging the roads and building both Lesotho and South Africa, are blamed for poverty. They are prevented from examining the class contradictions in society. The concealment of facts is an act of domestication because the peasants who are unconscientised will not be able to identify the source of their problems, and will therefore not fight to remedy the situation.

The same characteristics of theatre for domestication are found in the *Alcoholism Play*, where the villagers were not able to identify the problems of alcoholism in their village from a structural perspective, but made a false interpretation of the problem. However, it must be noted that this kind of possible manipulation is minimised by the level of the audience's own experience of the issues at stake. For example, in the *Trade Union Play*, if the catalysts represented interests such as TEBA, the Anglo American Corporation and the Lesotho government, all of whom benefit from the labour of the migrant workers and would not like to see strikes happen, the effort for domestication would have failed. The mineworkers have a firsthand experience of the world of the mines, and the exact nature of oppression there. No amount of manipulative intervention by catalysts would make them see those structures in a different light.

An example of domestication through censorship or self-censorship can be found in *Kopani ke Matla!*. It was observed earlier that there was a conscious effort on the part of the director to avoid a discussion of any 'political' issues. He said he did not want the play to become a 'political forum'. This means that issues pertinent to the subject of the play were not discussed. Peasants were told to accept unquestioningly the situation as presented by the theatre group.

From the above arguments, it is clear that the critical awareness of catalysts is an important factor in theatre-for-development. Depending on the catalyst's level of consciousness and intentions, it is possible for theatre-for-development, particularly of the agitprop kind, to become an instrument of oppression. Just as we must distinguish between communication media as instruments of domination, and communication media as instruments of liberation, so we must between theatre as an instrument of the domination of the peasants through the ideology of the ruling classes, and theatre as an instrument of liberation. This last point is discussed further in the next chapter.

8. Conclusions

This chapter focuses on the salient points that have emerged in this study. It summarises those issues most crucial in either confirming or refuting current thought and practice in theatre-for-development, or in the evolution of new paradigms.

The efficacy of theatre in development communication

The study has illustrated that theatre can be effective as a medium for development communication. The work of Marotholi Travelling Theatre analysed in this study has confirmed some of the assertions made by theatre-for-development and development communication practitioners and scholars on the relative efficacy of the medium in conscientising a rural population, and in disseminating development messages. The work particularly confirms the findings of the Telu Workshop in Sierra Leone, of which the workshop director writes:

> Today, Theatre for Development has been identified by many in the Third World as an effective two-way communication process predicated on dialogue and genuine participation on the part of the researchers and the researched. If properly used, it can perhaps be a most efficacious instrument for conscientising and enabling the masses and for propagating development messages using the people's language, idioms and art forms. (Malamah-Thomas 1989.)

It is significant that Malamah-Thomas adds the qualification 'if properly used' to his statement on the efficacy of theatre. Like all other media, theatre's effectiveness in development communication depends very much on the proficiency of the practitioner. In theatre-for-development the proficiency should not only be in the creation of highly polished productions of great aesthetic merit; the practitioner must also have clarity of what development and development communication entail. Both *Kopano ke Matla!* and the *Alcoholism Play* illustrate this point. Both plays were artistically produced: the former approaching its theatre from a Western perspective, and the latter from the perspective of the traditional performance modes. But both plays failed as vehicles of development communication, and of conscientisation.

The plays that evinced efficacy were those that concentrated not only on the artistic product, but also on the process of analysis from the rural community's perspective. The practitioner must find the balance between aesthetics and function. This study has shown that the two are not in opposition. Indeed, it was clearly illustrated that those works which were of high aesthetic quality in the utilisation of popular performance modes such as *lifela* were the most effective in drawing people to participate in a critical analysis process. In those plays, then, theatre-for-development was able to serve the following functions:

1. **Mobilisation in support of national development**: People were motivated into effective participation in programmes geared towards people's self-reliance. *The Agro-Action Play* illustrates how villagers were mobilised into effective participation in communal gardens and fish husbandry. They critically examined the nature of such programmes, and set their own guidelines for effective participation in the programmes.
2. **Conscientisation**: In all the plays where there was community participation and catalyst intervention, the villagers were able to question some of the contradictions in society. The villagers examined the contradictions at local level (the chief's corruption, the lack of democratic dispensation in the *Agro-Action Play*), at national level (the dissatisfaction with the deferred pay system in the *Trade Union Play*) and at international level (the neo-colonial nature of aid programmes in the *Agro-Action Play* and the relations between Lesotho and South Africa in the *Trade Union Play*).
3. **A two-way communication process with inbuilt feedback**: Through the plays, dialogue was developed among the members of the community themselves, and between the community and extension workers from governmental and non-governmental agencies. Each side had an opportunity to express its views, and to learn the other side's perceptions and priorities. Government was able to have feedback on its policies, and the peasants had a say in their own development.
4. **Community discussion and community decision-making**: The plays gave the villagers the opportunity to discuss their problems, to decide solutions, and to implement the solutions.
5. **Intervillage and intravillage solidarity**: The performances fostered intravillage solidarity since community members were able to discuss

their common problems, and to work out solutions together as a community, rather than as individuals. Intervillage solidarity was fostered with villagers from one village attending and participating in performances in other villages. This happened a great deal in the _Agro-Action Play_, where villagers from the Sephula cluster visited neighbouring villages to attend performances there, and to share their problems with villagers from neighbouring villages.

6. **Revitalisation of the people's own forms of cultural expression**: The plays provided a stimulus for the villagers' cultural activity.

These functions are not new discoveries of the efficacy of theatre-for-development, but, as has already been stated, a confirmation of the work that has been widely done in Africa. In addition to the experience of the Telu Workshop, Kidd (1985) also reports on the Zimbabwe Workshop, which made similar findings.

This study's position is that of all these functions, the most important is that theatre-for-development gives the periphery access to the production and distribution of messages. It was shown that critical analysis, and therefore conscientisation. happens only when the periphery is able to produce and distribute its own messages.

Problems of underdevelopment

The study has shown that current mass media practice in Lesotho bars the periphery access to production and distribution of messages. As a result, the problems of underdevelopment are addressed from the perspective of the ruling classes.

In the meantime skewed development continues, with the centre getting wealthier while the periphery sinks further into poverty. Lesotho has not fed itself for many years. All the basic food grains are imported.

> Particularly relevant are the consumption patterns of 'the better off', which are similar to those of persons with roughly comparable incomes in South Africa, and hence heavily dependent on imports (e.g. petrol, kerosene, milk and dairy products, meat, various processed foods not made in Lesotho). (Cobbe 1989, p. 17.)

As the problems of food security remain unresolved, it is the periphery that suffers the most, since the centre can afford to live on imported goods. The periphery depends mostly on agriculture. Although agriculture is the main economic activity in the periphery, it accounts for a small portion of total national income. Hence we find the paradoxical situation where the country has a predominantly agricultural economy, but is unable to feed itself, and has to import most of its grain and other staples from the countries of the centre.

The government has not succeeded, despite its rhetoric, in addressing the inequity. Some scholars feel that this is not a government priority at the moment.

> As regards domestic economic policy, it appears that the government is perhaps even less concerned about income distribution issues in practice (as opposed to rhetoric) than was the Jonathan regime: the total emoluments of Ministers have reportedly reached levels rivalling those in some of the less-restrained Homelands. (Cobbe 1989, p. 80.)

The study further discussed the failure of foreign aid to remedy the situation outlined above. Indeed foreign aid has reinforced dependency, and has not promoted self-reliance. It benefits the centre more than the periphery.

> Foreign aid, in the form of loans, grants, expertise, food and other commodities, is being dumped into our country Lesotho, supposedly in response to our poverty. What is the result? A minority of the Basotho become millionaires, while the rest are becoming poorer and poorer. Foreign aid is being sought in the name of the poor, and the rich sign loans for the poor to repay. Must the poor sit and watch while this happens, or can they do something for themselves? (*Work for Justice* 1989, p. 1.)

The view that aid programmes benefit the ruling classes more than the peasants in the periphery is further confirmed by McAnary (1980) whose work was discussed in the study. He writes that bureaucrats and government officials in developing countries often use information about aid to divert foreign aid to areas where they have interests.

It is in the light of these conditions that the periphery's own perspective is necessary in addressing the problems. The reasons for addressing periphery issues from the periphery's own perspective are thoroughly addressed in this study, and are supported by Pavlich, who writes,

> The assumption [for advocating that problems must be enunciated endogenously by the community] here is that people who experience and live in a certain set of circumstances are most competent to espouse their salient features. This cannot be sensitively accomplished from a qualitatively different environment, or through general and rigid theories. It is necessary to enter the community and, using the language

of the community, the researcher should commence the task of defining problems from the perspective of local inhabitants. (Pavlich 1988, p. 604.)

The work of Marotholi Travelling Theatre has proved that theatre is an effective medium for this endogenous enunciation of periphery problems. The villagers' ability to analyse their situation, when they are armed with the proper tools of analysis, was clearly illustrated in, for instance, the *Agro-Action Play*, when they addressed such issues as foreign aid and the problems of neo-colonialism.

On combining political and technical analysis

The study illustrated that it is not only theatre-for-development practitioners and scholars who are concerned with community participation for self-reliance and equity, but development communication scholars as well. Both these groups believe that communication can serve as a vehicle for redressing inequity and dependency by addressing the macro-origins of the problems of rural poverty — and macro-origins are by nature structural. McAnary (1980, pp. 6–7), for instance, writes of the necessity to combine both political and technical analysis, and Shore (1980, p. 21) asserts that communication must strive to change the structures of domination and dependence. He says that the role of communication researcher and practitioner is not only that of defining what communication can accomplish under present restrictive conditions.

Through theatre the villagers were able to analyse the structures of domination and dependence, to make their own resolution in response, and to decide the best methods of implementing the resolutions. Theatre proved to be most suited to this task because it enabled the villagers to produce and distribute messages from their own perspective.

Indispensability of mass media

The study has made the following points:

- Live theatre is not mass communication.
- Some theatre is interpersonal communication, or has strong elements of interpersonal communication (for example, forum theatre, simultaneous dramaturgy, and to some extent participatory agitprop).
- Not all theatre is interpersonal communication (for instance, agitprop lacks the crucial characteristics of interpersonal communication. Agitprop can be best described as public address communication).

One major problem with theatre is that it is not multiplicative. Mass media, on the other hand, can multiply a message and make it available in many places. Radio, for instance, is much in use in Lesotho. Its advantage is that it can overcome distance and time. Radio signals reach the widely dispersed homesteads in the remotest areas of the country. At 62.2 per cent, radio set ownership is high for a developing country. This means that the majority of the people in Lesotho can be reached through the radio. Theatre, on the other hand, can only be performed in one place at a time. This means that, in spite of its advantages over mass media, theatre can never replace it.

The advantages of interpersonal channels in fostering conscientisation have been amply demonstrated by the work of Marotholi Travelling Theatre. So have the advantages of involving the audience in media programming. For mass media to be effective they must therefore introduce the interpersonal element, and must involve the audiences in the creation and distribution of messages. Boafo has written that existing media systems in sub-Saharan Africa are poorly and inadequately structured to serve the needs of development.

> [D]emocratised media systems can facilitate a more effective application of the media to stimulate vertical and horizontal communication, encourage and strengthen critical awareness, discussion and sharing of experiences and opinions as well as to generate grassroots participation in determining and establishing development policies, objectives and priorities. (Boafo 1988, p. 48.)

Because of its democratised nature, some of the theatre created by Marotholi was able to serve these functions, but it was not able to reach as many villagers as would be reached by a mass medium such as radio.

Current practice on Radio Lesotho is undemocratic. The broadcasters' approach is at worst a market-oriented one, closely following the dominance model that regards the communicator as propagandist and the audience as target market. At best, the approach follows the diffusionist model with all its technical solutions. A lesson that can be learnt here by a communicator using the radio is that for the medium to be a truly democratic development communication tool, it must involve the audiences in the production and distribution of the message. This can be achieved by decentralising production structures to the periphery, and by introducing radio forums where people can discuss the issues broadcast over the radio and can in turn broadcast their own messages. This would be a more effective combination of face-to-face and mass media communication. This, however, is a subject for another study.

Assets and liabilities of different methods of theatre-for-development

Agitprop: Its major disadvantage is that it engenders little or no conscientisation since the audiences do not participate in producing and distributing the messages. The theatre is produced by an outside agent, but is oriented towards the people. It is either diffusionist or persuasive communication (market approach). But until constraints of time and manpower have been solved, agitprop will continue to have a role in theatre-for-development. It was noted that the other methodologies take time since catalysts have to live with the community and create plays with them. In agitprop the spectacle is presented as a finished product, and then there are informal post-performance discussions. The theatre group is therefore able to tour from village to village within a very short time. However, all they will be doing is disseminating messages from development agencies, without creating any critical awareness of the objective situation from the villagers' own perspective.

Agitprop is also well-suited for packaging for radio and television. Indeed Marotholi have produced many television films on such subjects as AIDS, TB, and breastfeeding, all using the agitprop method.

Participatory Agitprop: Compared to agitprop, participatory agitprop engenders a higher level of conscientisation. This is because of the interpersonal element, albeit in a predetermined product. Kamlongera notes in his study the advantages of opening up dialogue within performance time.

> The advantage of this is that issues are debated within 'play' atmosphere, while at the same time alternative courses are being looked at. The audience do not only sit to be entertained, but to participate in a debate for which theatre is only a catalyst. This dispenses with the 'cold' after performance discussions common to the more traditional uses of theatre. (Kamlongera 1989, p. 245.)

Like agitprop, participatory agitprop is easy to tour from village to village. Since it is more effective than agitprop, it is probably the best method in those instances where there are constraints of time and manpower, and the catalysts are unable to stay with the villagers and create theatre with them. Participatory agitprop can meet the immediate communicational needs of extension workers, while a long-term theatre-for-conscientisation takes place at its own pace in the villages.

Theatre-for-Conscientisation (both simultaneous dramaturgy and forum theatre): Of all the methodologies identified and discussed, simultaneous dramaturgy and forum theatre are the most effective in conscientisation. The study has developed a new theatrical communication model explicating the interaction through messages between catalysts and audiences in theatre-for-conscientisation situations. In this method, the plays are produced by and for the people without spectators, since the spectators ultimately become actors. Improvisation happens throughout the play, and the direction the play takes is never pre-planned. Etherton's assertion (see chapter 2) that people need to learn the conventions of what he calls 'the well-made play' before they can improvise and create theatre-for-development, is shown to be a fallacy.

By presenting two strongly conflicting views, the catalysts provoke the people to participate. Ideally, community participation and community control should increase as catalysts pull out. The ultimate goal is that villagers take over until there is no need for catalysts. This will be a point of convergence of forum theatre and comgen theatre.

Theatre-for-conscientisation is, however, a time-consuming process, which works over a long period. It therefore cannot deal with immediate country-wide communicational needs since resources (of personnel, for instance, who must stay in a single village for some time) are limited.

The work of Marotholi has illustrated that theatre-for-conscientisation is most effective in a small group. The small audience of about 50 people was ideal in the *Trade Union Play*, whereas the large audience of a thousand people that gathered for the performance of the *Rural Sanitation Play* at Ketane Ha Nohana could not have participated meaningfully in theatre-for-conscientisation.

An adaptation of this method should be used in electronic media. For instance, in a situation where there are radio forums, radio plays can be left unfinished, and radio forum participants can then discuss how best to complete the story. The information is fed back to the production unit, and the next serial will reflect the ending that has been determined by the listeners. The same technique may be used for drama on small-format media and on television.

Comgen Theatre: The work of the villagers of Tebellong illustrated that local communities in the vilages may have the means of producing theatre, but without the guidance of catalysts in analysing the problems, the theatre does not become a vehicle for conscientisation. Villagers isolated problems and treated them as inherent and internally generated, for which they themselves were to blame. This indicates that although comgen theatre is the least expensive method — it does not involve a touring group of performers, but is created and performed by the locals — it does not serve as a vehicle for conscientisation. For comgen theatre to serve as a vehicle for critical analysis, and therefore critical awareness, catalysts must visit the village from time to time to enhance the level of analysis. This can be done through workshop sessions using the simultaneous dramaturgy and the forum theatre techniques. In this way comgen theatre and theatre-for-conscientisation will ultimately converge, as the villagers themselves ultimately become catalysts. The process is a time-consuming one, and the catalysts will have to make many visits. It was observed in the Tebellong experience that even after two weeks, the villagers felt that they had not received enough training.

What Marotholi were doing, in order to have the theatre activity in all the villages of Lesotho, was to hold workshops for village health workers. All villages have village health workers, and workshops can be held only for a small group at a time. The village health workers then go back to their villages and create theatre with their fellow villagers. This becomes an 'each one, teach one' process, where those who have been trained in workshops train other village health workers from neighbouring villages. In this process catalysts should travel from village to village and work with the established groups there to enhance their level of analysis. In this way both grassroots control and grassroots participation will be maintained, while critical analysis will increase until comgen theatre becomes theatre-for-conscientisation.

Efficacy of popular and traditional media
The study has, through the analysis of the work of Marotholi in this area, illustrated that popular and traditional media can be effective in development communication. However, some modes of traditional performance do not lend themselves well to such uses, since they would be out of their social context in a theatre-for-development situation.

The practitioner of theatre-for-development and of development communication must take great care to ensure that, if and when traditional and popular modes of performance are used, they are used proficiently. It must be remembered that among the villagers there are people who have attained a high artistic standard in the practice of these performance modes. People know a mediocre product when they see one, and they will only be attracted to watch and participate in an event that evinces a high level of artistic merit. It is therefore important to pay particular attention to the aesthetics of the performance modes for them to have any effect.

For this reason the Marotholi were engaged in a programme of learning from *likheleke* of *lifela*. Those members of the group who have potential have undergone some training from *likheleke*, at the same time exploring with them how *likheleke* themselves can use *lifela* not only to reflect their world and protest against injustice and exploitation, but also as a vehicle of conscientisation and resistance.

Intervention

The study has shown that theatre is not a self-generative communication medium that automatically becomes effective. For theatre to be effective it needs informed intervention. Theatre-for-development practitioners may fall into the dangers of romanticising the democratic aspects of theatre-for-development, and the ability of peasants to identify and solve their problems. The *Alcoholism Play* experience showed that intervention by catalysts is essential in a theatre-for-development process. Peasants may identify their problems, but a solution will elude them if they have not gone through a process of critical analysis of the problems. It must be remembered that all forms of exploitation and domination have been heaped on the peasants — first by the colonialists, and then by the African ruling classes who took over from colonialists and perpetuated the structures of domination. As a result a number of peasants have internalised oppression and domination, and live in what Freire (1972) calls a 'culture of silence'. Intervention helps to extract them from that culture of silence, and unleashes in them a critical analysis that will lead to a critical awareness.

The study has evolved a new paradigm of intervention. The paradigm explains the relationship between intervention and participation. The two variables are dependent on each other in that if one increases, the other decreases. The paradigm further explains the relationship between participation and conscientisation. It places the various methodologies of theatre-for-development that have been identified on a curve. The curve portrays the rising level of conscientisation with the rising level of participation, until optimal participation is reached, then the level of conscientisation decreases as participation increases. From this point of optimal participation more participation engenders less conscientisation until a stage of maximal participation–minimal conscientisation is reached. Another curve portrays the relationship between intervention and conscientisation. The picture that emerges here is that minimal intervention engenders minimal conscientisation. Maximal intervention on the other hand also engenders minimal conscientisation. Optimal intervention is the ideal balance between intervention and participation that engenders the highest level of conscientisation.

The study concludes that for catalysts to play an effective interventionist role they must have a higher level of critical awareness than the villagers.

Domestication and other constraints

The study identified three traits of domestication: one is domestication that arises from an innocuous situation intended to liberate, the second is domestication that happens as a result of a conscious effort from an agent who seeks to domesticate, and the third happens through censorship and self-censorship. In all cases domestication's vehicle is intervention or lack of it.

Writing on folk media, Lent made these observations:

> As Third World governments use folk media and interpersonal
> communication channels to transmit the developmental message to rural
> peoples, it becomes apparent that they have in their hands a truly
> grassroots propaganda machine capable of being harnessed to also
> promote non-developmental interests. Therefore, because the dividing
> line between developmental, governmental and political ends can be
> hair-thin, it is possible (and is happening) for folk media to be misused to
> promote the development of national leaders, rather than the
> development of national policies and programmes. That, indeed, would
> be unfortunate in a world where governments already control so many
> mass media used to promote their own ends. (Lent 1982, p. 15.)

Lent is writing of a situation where the government consciously uses the
medium for the purposes of the domination and exploitation of the
oppressed rural people. Governments are capable of enforcing domestication
also by preventing theatre-for-development from being a truly democratic
vehicle. In Malawi, for instance, practitioners have to go through the ruling
political party structures in order to carry out their work in the villages.
There will therefore be constraints of both censorship by the party hierarchy
and self-censorship by the theatre practitioners.

It is all very well to talk of examining structural causes of problems. In
some countries this may not be possible since it would invite the wrath of the
rulers to descend upon the heads of the catalysts. Not many theatre
practitioners and development communicators are prepared for martyrdom.
Few of them have such a high commitment to social and political
transformation that they would follow the path of exile taken by Ngugi wa
Thiong'o and Ngugi wa Mirii of the Kamiriithu Educational and Cultural
Centre. Others are just as highly committed as these two gentlemen, but
prefer to explore various strategies that they can use in their theatre so that
they may continue to work with the peasants while at the same time avoiding
a confrontation with the ruling classes.

In the Kumba workshop (Eyoh 1987) a letter from the Presidency of the
Republic of Cameroon authorising the workshop warned the participants
against the development of themes of a political nature. The participants
had to design strategies to negotiate this. Eyoh does not say what these
strategies were. It is possible that they involved self-censorship, since that
was what was demanded by the Presidency. Kidd, on the other hand, reports
that in Zimbabwe the situation is different:

> Part of our success in this work was due to the particular political
> situation and historical experience of Zimbabwe and the receptiveness to

this kind of work. The war's radicalization of the rural areas and the experience of people's theatre during the liberation struggle made fertile ground for the workshop. The Zimbabwe's government commitment to dialogue, consultation, conscientization, and mobilization provided a clear mandate and focus for the workshop. (Kidd 1985, p. 198.)

In Lesotho the work of Marotholi has not been restricted through either censorship or self-censorship. The theatre group has even undertaken assignments from government ministries with a clear understanding on the part of all involved that in their mobilisation of the peasants for participation in development programmes, political and social structures will be analysed. However, there can never be any guarantee that this state of affairs will continue. Perhaps Marotholi has been fortunate in that, although the government often commissioned them to do campaigns in the villages, no one in the government really took a close interest in their work.

Since some governments are not very pleased with a conscientised peasantry, theatre-for-development practitioners who want to avoid the wrath of the authorities should use participatory agitprop. In participatory agitprop intervention will qualitatively and quantitatively control structural analysis of the problems to the level that the catalysts may deem safe. Other practitioners may prefer to devise subversive strategies in participatory agitprop. Theatre-for-conscientisation, the experience of Marotholi found, will undoubtedly open up the proverbial can of worms.

Another constraint on theatre-for-development, which may also have overtones of domestication, pertains to financial support. Theatre groups such as Marotholi Travelling Theatre depend on international donors, and on government sources when they undertake work in support of government development campaigns. Such financial support may compromise the liberating quality of the work. One of the questions posed at the Kumba workshop was on this very issue.

> Can workshops of the kind organised in Murewa and Kumba effectively take place without all sorts of support mechanisms from the state and international sponsors, and does the existence of such support mechanisms not compromise the liberating quality of the work, thus rendering the process domesticating? (Eyoh 1987.)

Marotholi had, until they went their different ways, not compromised their work to meet the domesticating demands of a sponsor. However, they did realise that such possibilities existed. For this reason they were engaged in a programme that would make them financially self-reliant. Like the Travelling Theatre in Malawi (Kerr 1983) which created *Nchira wa Buluzi*, and the Sistren Theatre of Jamaica (Lambert 1982), they performed plays in urban areas for which admission was charged. The proceeds subsidised the free rural performances. However, these funds accounted only for a small portion of their budget, and they still depended heavily on sponsorship from donors.

Evaluation

Communication programmes need to be evaluated to find out what they have accomplished and how they can be improved. The work of Marotholi Travelling Theatre was very weak on evaluation. The only recorded evaluation is of the *Rural Sanitation Play* at Majaheng in the Berea district, which showed positive results on the impact of the campaign, and of *Kopano ke Matla!* at Ha Ratau in the Maseru district, which showed some impact, but to a lesser degree. However, since this is not meant to be an empirical study of theatre-for-development, but a theoretical one, it would be a digression to deal with these evaluations. The Marotholi explored ways of using *formative evaluation*. In this method all evaluation is integrated into the normal project activities. This allows the planner to change the course of the programme if early evaluations show that something is not working as planned. Often a theatrical performance is used to evaluate previous performances.

Whatever method of evaluation is adopted, it is crucial that projects of this nature should contain a constant evaluative component.

Appendix

The Plays

Kopano ke Matla!
Rural Sanitation Play
Agro-Action Play
Trade Union Play
Alcoholism Play

Kopano ke Matla!

Characters:

    A Miner
    A Lazy Man
    Friend of Miner
    Co-operative Treasurer/Teacher
    Miner's Wife
    Shebeen Queen
    2 Members of the Co-op
    IEMS Advisor

Scene Breakdown (with dialogue extracts)*:

Scene 1: *Four women come from fetching water and discuss the increasing*

* The Scene Breakdown is from Appendix A of Horn and Davenport (1985), and extracts of dialogue have been translated by the author from a picture-story book of the play. Unfortunately the video of the play which had been produced by the Instructional Material Resource Centre, Maseru, and held by their library got destroyed there. This author attended the performance at the Royal Village of Matsieng in September, 1984.

cost of living. The prices have escalated tremendously and it is difficult to make ends meet.

WOMAN 1:
Women! Things are so expensive . . .

WOMAN 2:
Do not even mention that, woman. You know only the other day I went to the shop with a ten maloti note [*Lesotho currency*]. But when I came back I had nothing.

WOMAN 3:
Your case is just like mine. It is because of this big monster called sales tax.

WOMAN 4:
When I saw the cold of this morning, I said to myself let me go and buy shoes for my little daughters. Do you know how much these shoes cost? Thirty maloti!

WOMAN 3:
How do you think we are going to survive?

The women then discuss the fact that a neighbouring village has established a co-operative society. One woman objects to co-ops because of the corruption they generate; another on party political grounds.

WOMAN 4:
I think there is no other way. I think we have to do like the people of Lintjeng village. I saw one buying at the store with a lot of paper money. She said she got the money from the co-operatives. Let us also establish our own co-operative, so that we may defeat problems.

WOMAN 3:
Co-operatives? No! They are bad. Those who are at the head eat our moneys. They cheat the people out of their fields. Also there is a lot of politics there. When you belong to the ruling party you are the king. Another thing is the church. Always you will find that the Catholics are right in front, and the Protestants far behind.

WOMAN 4:
No, 'Masek'hona, you do not understand. The woman I saw from Lintjeng village said there are no political affairs nor church wranglings in the co-operatives. What is there is the unity of the village. That woman is a widow whose husband died many years ago. I am advising you, let us establish a co-operative society.

Scene 2:   *Villagers are drinking in a shebeen. Miner arrives showing off his wealth.*

SHEBEEN QUEEN:
You people must really buy today. As you can see, I have brewed the strongest beer as I have seen that the wealthy miners are here.

MINER (*coming in*):
Hei bo! This is Manocha of 'Mamanocha entering. This is the bad dog who comes from the mines of Kloof, from the field of boys and girls. I am the boy with money, the dog who eats maloti. I say peace to you all, children of Basotho [*people of Lesotho*]. I am greeting you.

The patrons of the shebeen are very happy to see him, for he has a reputation of freely spending his money.

MINER (*to the sheebeen queen*):
Give everybody here some beer! I am Manocha. The money that I get is like the stars, my child. It fills buckets. Let us drink, Basotho!

The miner's wife has also joined the drinking party. A villager, who is also the local school teacher, shows the patrons a newspaper article about the new technology being introduced in the mines, leading to redundancies. The miner rejects this as nonsense.

MINER'S WIFE:
But my husband, I do not believe that this money will last us a lifetime. When it gets finished what are we going to do?

TEACHER:
That is true 'Mamanocha. In fact I have read in the newspaper here of the problems facing Basotho in the mines.

MINER'S WIFE:
Read for us, teacher.

TEACHER (*reading from a newspaper*):
'Because of the machines that the mine owners have bought, it is reported that great numbers of Basotho miners will have to come home. The machines will take the place of the workers. Also because of poor political relations between Lesotho and South Africa, a number of Basotho workers are unable to cross to South Africa. When the mines need more labour, they will get it from the black people who live in the South African homelands.' That is why I have been insisting that we establish our own co-operative society in order to improve our own economy through agriculture and livestock. It is the only way to survive.

MINER'S WIFE:
I agree with you, teacher. That is exactly what I have been saying.

MINER (*angry*):
Hei, you little teacher you! That little paper of yours is dreaming! And you are also mad. Your co-operatives are just a trick to rob us of our money and of our fields. And to steal our wives too!

LAZY MAN:
That is true, Manocha! Co-operatives will also deprive us of our freedom. It is a way to make us toil for nothing, so that we'll not even have time to bask in the sun. Now that I hear that this little teacher comes with nonsense, I am going away to enjoy the sun by the rockside.

SHEBEEN QUEEN (*angry*):
Get out of my house, all of you drunkards! Do not come and fight in my house. Get out at once!

Scene 3: *At the miner's house. He disagrees with his wife over co-operatives. He forbids her to get involved.*

WIFE:
What is the matter with you, Manocha? I see you moving up and down like a hen that is being burnt by an egg.

MINER:
I am pacing the floor because I am sick and tired of all this nonsense about co-operatives that you people have been prattling about. I forbid you to join such nonsense, do you hear me?

WIFE:
But co-operatives are useful. They will bring us money even when you are not working in the mines.

MINER:
I can see that you are also mad. Before I go back to the mines I am going to tell your mother that you run around in drinking parties of co-operatives. She must see to it that you stop this kind of behaviour.

WIFE (*very angry*):
Manocha! Do not talk rubbish! What right do you have to talk to me like this? I am going to join the co-operatives. In fact from now you will cook for yourself, you little devil.

Scene 4: *A village meeting has been called. A poultry and vegetable co-op is set up, but without experienced advice.*

TEACHER:
Mothers, we are all happy that you have taken the trouble to come to this meeting today.

WOMAN:
This is a very important day in our lives.

Lazy man also joins the meeting.

LAZY MAN:
Peace to you, our people. I delayed to wake up today. I said to myself let me accompany the morning just for a short distance. Well, I am now here as well.

TEACHER:
Today we are establishing a co-op for our village. We'll first talk about the subscription that each person must pay. We'll also discuss the activity that we'll do in order to create our own wealth. We'll all have to do something, to work, and not just to sit. Let us agree first about the money. Let it be thirty maloti for each person.

SHEBEEN QUEEN:
I do not think there is any problem, teacher. I think we all understand. In fact here is my thirty maloti.

TEACHER:
Now we have started, my people. This is a good example from the mother who sells liquor. We thank you.

OLD WOMAN (*crying*):
Jo! I am a poor widow woman. I like co-operatives, but what am I going to do? I do not have even a penny for subscription. If only my husband was still alive.

SHEBEEN QUEEN:
Let me lend you money, grandmother. Do not cry. The co-operative will pay it back. (*She pays for the widow.*)

MINER'S WIFE:
We must open a savings account at the bank. We'll know that our money is kept safely.

TEACHER:
Banks? Banks are terrible, and are a lot of bother. Everyday when you go there you must wear a tie. And also when we need our money at night what are we going to do?

WOMAN:
Yes, banks are no good! The people at the bank eat our money. Also you must go there with a passport which costs five maloti. And what do you do when your passport is lost?

LAZY MAN:
Co-operatives are a pain. Should I work? No! For what should I pay money? When will I drink and also relax? Remain deceiving one another, and continue to work. I will eat with you, when you have harvested.

The co-operative is established and the teacher becomes the treasurer.

TEACHER:
Our people, we have now finished. We are going to have hens that lay eggs, and plant vegetables. Peace! Rain! Prosperity!

Scene 5: *Co-op members come to tend chickens, but discover that eggs and some chickens have been stolen. They find that only one bag of feed is left. All members gather. The Treasurer is accused. Advice is sought.*

WOMAN (*when she gets to the fowl-run*):
My God! What has happened to the eggs? Some hens are missing too! Also there is only one bag of feed. The treasurer said he bought ten bags.

Co-op members gather, and one is sent to fetch the treasurer.

SHEBEEN QUEEN:
'Mamanocha, come with him immediately. He must explain himself.

The treasurer, now big-bellied, comes.

TREASURER:
Peace to you, mothers. What has happened?

SHEBEEN QUEEN:
You are the one who must explain to us what has happened.

TREASURER:
I will explain. I think the eggs have been stolen. Last night I heard dogs and cats barking. Also I bought four bags of feed.

WOMAN:
Do you say cats bark?

TREASURER:
The feed is finished all over in Maseru, except at the Manpower Development Secretariat. Even there I paid a lot of tax which is called

When People Play People

pay as you earn sales tax. [*Here the treasurer is using a lot of 'big' words that he knows the villagers will not understand.*]

MINER'S WIFE:
They are all blue lies.

TREASURER:
I also paid a subscription for Provident Fund.

SHEBEEN QUEEN:
Provident Fund? You are the father of lies! Thief! You are going to vomit all our money. I am going to beat you up. You steal our money and then say provident fund, provident fund! You witch! We are going to fetch the police.

TREASURER:
Police? Oh, please, I pray you! Let me tell you the truth. I used the money to pay school fees for my children. I slaughtered some of the hens to make provision for my relatives. Please forgive me, I beg you.

SHEBEEN QUEEN:
Okay, we are going to forgive you just this once, provided you pay back all the money you have stolen from the co-operative. But from now we must get proper advice as to how to run our co-operative. Let us ask the department that deals with adult education at the university [*the Institute of Extra Mural Studies*] to help us. It is said that they have courses on co-operatives.

Scene 6: *A meeting. A representative from the Institute of Extra Mural Studies explains to members how to re-establish the co-op effectively, and how to protect themselves.*

TREASURER:
This gentleman here, Mr Lekau, works with co-operatives.

IEMS ADVISOR:
You must keep your money in a savings account at the bank, and must have monthly meetings where the treasurer will give a full report about money. You must register your society, so that it will be protected by law. You must also see to it that you elect a new committee each year, so that one person will not lead others all the time.

TREASURER:
Your speech was very important, Mr Lekau.

MINER'S WIFE:
Yes indeed. If only we had got this information before starting our co-operative, instead of learning through problems.

Scene 7: *It is after two years, and co-op members are drinking in the shebeen. They have just shared out profits. All clearly look more prosperous, and are expensively dressed. Even the shebeen looks better furnished.*

WOMAN (*to Shebeen Queen*):
Your home looks very beautiful.

SHEBEEN QUEEN:
All these things come from our co-operative. They are the fruit of our labour.

Someone mentions that Lazy Man has not been seen for a couple of days. A woman enters with news that Lazy Man has been found dead in his house.

WOMAN:
Lazy Man has been found dead! A pile of co-operative cabbage was found under his blanket. Since he refused to join the co-operative he had been very weak from malnourishment.

ANOTHER WOMAN:
People have heard him say that warnings against eating cabbage that has been sprayed with insecticide before it has been properly washed were only meant to frighten off thieves and children. He must have stolen some cabbage, and ate it without washing it. He gave himself poison.

The Miner arrives. He is very depressed and cannot buy drinks, since he has been out of work for the past six months.

TREASURER:
In truth those who refused to join the co-operative when we started it look as though success has escaped them. Just look at how poor Manocha is. Do you think he can buy us beer as he used to?

The Miner goes off, and is followed by Friend with whom he discusses his problems.

MINER:
Really, my cousin, work is finished for me. The mines are now using machines. So we were told to go back to our homes. Now I am only left with fifty maloti.

FRIEND:

> My cousin, it would be useful if we ask the members of the co-operative if they will accept you, even though you talked to them very rudely last time.

They both re-enter the shebeen.

FRIEND:

> Manocha and I have a suggestion . . . a request that we want to make. Our people, how would it be if we allow Manocha to join the co-operative, please? The work is finished for him. He will live a difficult life.

TREASURER:

> No! This is the same Manocha who insulted us, when he thought he was clever. I say if he joins I am resigning! I am resigning!

MINER'S WIFE:

> Who are you to talk like that? Have you forgotten that we forgave you when you made a mistake?

WOMAN:

> I think Manocha should be accepted into the co-operative. Indeed a man does not see twice. I think he should join. But Manocha, why are you quiet? Talk for yourself.

MINER:

> Indeed, our people, I am in big trouble. It is true that I want to join the co-operative because machines have taken our place in the mines. Please allow me to join.

After some debate he is finally admitted. They will call a meeting where the Miner will be officially admitted into the co-operative.

TREASURER:

> Once more we are a nation of peace. How beautiful it is when warmth reigns.

The play ends with song and dance, performed by all the members of the cast. Each scene is punctuated by a song of the genre monyanyako. *(These are celebratory songs that are performed at any happy occasion, and are most popular among school children at all levels. They feature strongly in school concerts, and adult choral music concerts.)*

Rural Sanitation Play

Characters:

Sek'hoek'hoe	-	a villager
Manchoati	-	his wife
Nchoati	-	their daughter
Mankhoe	-	a diviner
Malipere	-	a village health worker
Liloche	-	Sak'hoek'hoc's neighbour
Liloche's wife		
Shebeen Queen		
Liloche's Friend		
Technical Assistant		

Scene Breakdown (with dialogue extracts)*

Scene 1: *Sek'hoek'hoe arrives home from a distant village where he had gone to get a diviner to help his daughter who is seriously ill after having had an attack of diarrhoea. He walks among the members of the audience who have formed an arena, towards the acting space in the centre, singing a* sefela. *During this time Manchoati and the ailing Nchoati are centre-stage where the mother is trying to comfort her daughter.*

SEK'HOEK'HOE:

He! ka ithoka, ka ithoka,	Hey, I am singing my praises
Ka ba ka ithoka.	And sang them once again
Thibela! Thibela!	

* Transcribed and translated by the author from a video of the performance recorded at Ketane Ha Nohana in the mountains of Mohale's Hoek district on 1 August 1986. The author was also present at this performance.

Thibela oa hoa a sale.
'Na oa ka ke mamonotoana
Ea tlhako li sesane.
'Maka litaba.

Stop, stop yours [*wife*] so that she should remain.
Mine is the one with beautiful thin legs.
The one who causes quarrels.

Taola ee-ee!
Taola boela haeno u holile,

U phaka li mafume
Ke ho laisha

U noka litala
U nkha boqheku.

Oh, Taola!
Taola go back to your home you are now old,
Your arms have grown rusty
Because of loading heavy loads [*in the mines*]
Your legs are green
You reek of old age.

Tsirr . . . tsipa!

[*ideophone for something that moves very fast and then penetrates or pierces*]

Majoana oe Majoana,
U ne u liselitse hokae maobane?
Ke ne ke liselitse 'Makatse lekhalong.
E itse ha ke fihla 'Makatse lekhalong
Ka rinyarinya ka otla fatse

Hoa tsoa letolo le likoecha mahlong.

Majoana oh, Majoana
Where did you herd cattle yesterday?
I herded them at the 'Makatse gorge.
When I arrived at the gorge of 'Makatse
I repeatedly pounded and struck the ground
From which emerged thunder [*and lightning*] that displayed anger in its eyes [*an allusion to his prowess in the practice of traditional medicine and magic associated with witchcraft*]

Ke mashapa-shapane
Ke shapile linyane la pela selomong.
Bo — 'm'alona ba tla ba tse-tse-tsema
Ka ba ka timelloa ke ho bua Sekhooa

I am the one who strikes hard
I beat up the young of a rock-rabbit at the precipice.
Its mothers swiftly and stealthily attacked me
I even forgot how to speak English.

(*In normal speech tone which gives the words the effect of an aside*)

Homme se bile se ntsoanetse, banna,
Empa he nka na ka tsamaea ke se leka.

And how the language suits me, men!
But, well, I can still try.

Ke ne ke matha ka lerumo Mantsonyana.
I used to run with a spear in Mantsonyana

Ke le mothapo a motso mpeng.
I had a black vein on my stomach.

Khomo li khaotse teu tsa pele;
The first oxen have cut-off from the span;

'Na ha ke na taba le tsona
But I don't care for them

Khomo tseo,
Those cattle,

Hoba ke tsoere koto ea matlanka-chitja.
Because I am holding a round *knobkierie* that hits hard.

Nka tlanka motho mantsiboea.
I can hit a person in the evening.

Hoa iketloa! Hoa iketloa!
There is happiness, there is comfort.

Hoa iketloa ke bana ba lireng.
There is good life among the children of the enemy.

Rona mafutsana ra tla ra sotleha
But we the poor are suffering.

Bana ba ka ba jeoa ke'eng,
What is eating my children,

Jo-o-nna Mankhoe-ee!
. . . Mankhoe!

Bana ba ka ba jeoa ke'eng.
What is eating my children,

U cheka oe-e-e!
Even though you have been digging the herbs?

Maobane mona
Only yesterday,

Ke re maoba e itse ke robetse
I say only the night before yesterday when I was asleep,

Ke hahapisa mahanana,
Snoring very hard,

Ke tsohe se ke tsosoa ke seboko,
I was woken up by a loud scream,

Banna! Seboko se bohloko hakaalo!
Oh, men! What a plaintive wailing!

Ere ha ke re kea tsoha,
When I did wake up

Ke nke mechesi ke laeti,
I took the matches and lit the lamp,

Ke fumane mosali a tletse mofufutso.
I found my wife full of sweat.

Ngoana a kula!
The child was ill!

A kula ngoana oe-e-e!
Oh, the child was ill!

E ka ba bana ba ka ba jeoa ke'eng Mankhoe-e-e!
What can be eating my children, oh Mankhoe?

Leha ho le joalo kea u tsepa.
But I do trust you still.

Tloho u tl'o tla bona bana,
Come and see my children,

Mankhoe-e-ee!
Oh, Mankhoe!

At this point Sek'hoek'hoe arrives home (centre stage), and finds the child in a worse condition. He tells his wife that the diviner, Mankhoe, is on his way. Sounds of the drums. The diviner and his acolytes enter singing and dancing.

The members of the audience join in the song, and the ritual of divination
(tlhophe) *is enacted. In the course of the ceremony Liloche enters and sits
down. Immediately he settles down the ritual stops for there is a stench in the
room. The foul smell emanates from the shoes of Liloche who unknowingly
stepped on some human faeces while crossing the local defecating ground on his
way to Sek'hoek'hoe's house. He is subsequently driven out of the house amid
his protestations. The ritual continues. Mankhoe points out that the child has
been bewitched, and gives the parents some herbs for enema. Mankhoe and his
acolytes dance out. Sek'hoek'hoe leaves strict orders that the child should be
given enema according to the instructions of the diviner. All leave the stage,
taking with them props.*

Scene 2: *Liloche and a friend visit a shebeen for a drink. There are other
customers as well, including the local village health worker, Malipere. During
the conversation Liloche relates his encounter with the diviner.*

LILOCHE:
I say I had only gone to the *tlhophe*. But the people made so much noise to
me about shit.

SHEBEEN QUEEN:
You are not even ashamed to tell us that you had stepped on shit.

THABANG:
It is quite possible that it was your own shit. I always see mine so I don't
step on it.

MALIPERE:
I have been saying for a long time that we must build toilets.

LILOCHE:
So now we should take the defecating ground from the dongas into the
house?

MALIPERE:
Toilets are for good health.

LILOCHE (*asking a member of the audience*):
Mother, do you think I am not healthy when I don't have a toilet?

AUDIENCE MEMBER:
You are quite healthy, father.

ANOTHER AUDIENCE MEMBER:
You are not healthy. You don't live well at all. See how you swim in shit.

LILOCHE:
Okay, in future I'll be careful that I don't step on it.

The village health worker tries to explain the danger posed to health by human faeces and the role of flies in the transmission of diseases. An argument erupts between Liloche and the village health worker, with the other customers joining in and taking sides. A fly falls into Liloche's beer. He retrieves it from the container with his fingers, throws it away, and continues to drink his beer.

MALIPERE:
You must not drink that beer where a fly swam.

LILOCHE:
It is my beer, not the fly's.

MALIPERE (*to the audience*):
I ask you, mothers, and fathers, is this right? You saw what this man did. Is it right?

Some members of the audience say it is unhealthy while others feel that there is no harm in what Liloche has done.

MAN FROM THE AUDIENCE:
Of course it is right. He can even suck the beer from it before he throws it away. Or swallow it. After all a fly has no bones.

ANOTHER MAN FROM AUDIENCE:
I say, what do you expect Liloche to do? Throw away his beer? We live in times of famine. We cannot waste food.

NURSE FROM THE AUDIENCE:
The fly has hairs all over its body with which it carries germs. It sits on all sorts of filthy things. Before it eats it vomits what it had eaten before. It can sit and eat faeces, and then vomit on your food.

LILOCHE:
Look at a big woman like you being concerned with a small innocent thing like a fly.

The argument deteriorates into a shouting match between Malipere and Liloche. Liloche, his friend and the other customers leave, taking with them some props on the stage. The shebeen queen clears the remaining props while complaining that the village health worker is driving her customers away.

Scene 3: *Sek'hoek'hoe's house. Enter Sek'hoek'hoe and Liloche discussing the sick child's situation. Malipere arrives to enquire about the sick child. She tries to convince them to seek medical help for the child. Manchoati arrives from the defecating ground, and without washing her hands starts serving those* *present with food and drinks. Malipere refuses to touch the food since she says Manchoati did not wash her hands first.*

MANCHOATI:
Hey woman, I did wash myself in the morning. How many times a day do you want me to wash?

LILOCHE:
You are not even ashamed to tell a woman in her own house that she is dirty she should wash!

The question is taken to the audience:
is it reasonable to expect Manchoati to wash her hands?

MAN FROM AUDIENCE:
Yes, she must wash her hands.

WOMAN FROM AUDIENCE:
But she is weak. A person who is so weak will not be able to wash her hands.

ANOTHER WOMAN FROM AUDIENCE:
It is wrong because the germs from the defecating ground will get into the food.

The village health worker wants to see the child, but she is told that the child is sleeping since she has been given an enema. Liloche on the other hand says that Malipere must not be allowed to see the child for she is a witch who creates confusion wherever she goes. She leaves. They all exit, with Sek'hoek'hoe saying he is taking his race horse to the village well to drink.

Scene 4: *Liloche, on returning home, discusses his recent experiences with his wife. The wife cautions him to take the advice of the village health worker seriously since she had been attending a series of health training courses. She is a volunteer, and is not paid for her services. But, in turn, the community must assist her in any way it can, such as helping her in her fields or drawing water for her, since she spends her time visiting the sick and advising people on primary health care. Liloche is then convinced that village health workers are indeed good for the village. He finds out from the audience if they know about village health workers.*

LILOCHE (*to audience*):
Are there village health workers in your village?

AUDIENCE:
Yes!

LILOCHE:
Do you help them, since you hear that they help us free of charge?

WOMAN FROM THE AUDIENCE:
Yes, the one we have in the village, we help her.

LILOCHE:
With what do you help her?

SAME WOMAN FROM AUDIENCE:
Anything she needs.

ANOTHER WOMAN FROM AUDIENCE (*angrily*):
No, we don't help her because she is a whore who spends all her time whoring at the dispensary. We do not help her. We attend to our own work.

LILOCHE'S WIFE:
So some help, other don't. I for one would suggest that she should be helped.

Liloche's wife then explains that she has acquired new information about toilets, particularly the VIP (Ventilated Improved Pit) latrines. The VIP toilet has a pipe to take the smell out of the toilet, with wire gauze to stop the flies from flying in, and to trap those that might have come in through the door when it is opened. Liloche is convinced that VIP toilets are good, and suggests that they must immediately see a VIP toilet builder in the village who must come and demonstrate the workings of the VIP latrine to them. He will be leaving for the mines soon, and will be sending money to the wife who must see to it that the toilet is built. They both exit.

Scene 5: *A technical assistant (a fictional one from the play) arrives at the home of Liloche and explains how a VIP latrine works, as well as its advantages over other types of latrines. He then calls a real-life technical assistant from the audience to explain how the toilet is built. Sek'hoek'hoe and Manchoati have also arrived.*

TECHNICAL ASSISTANT:
To dig a proper hole you must first measure with a tape . . . The hole must be nine feet deep . . . This is how you build the foundation . . . You can purchase concrete slabs from us at the clinic . . . You should use a black pipe instead of white. Black absorbs the heat, and when there is heat in the pit the smell goes out . . . You can also build a double-pit latrine . . .

SEK'HOEK'HOE:
So one pit is used during the week and the other one is for Sundays?

TECHNICAL ASSISTANT:
No, you use the other pit when the first one is full. It may be full after four years. After some time you can take out the now dry faeces and use it as manure in the garden.

The members of the audience express consternation that human faeces can be used as manure. There are questions from the audience to the technical assistants (both the fictional one and the real-life one) on what material to use; if one already has a toilet with a white pipe can it be painted black, etc. However some are still not happy about the manure issue.

OLD MAN FROM AUDIENCE:
Are you telling this nation assembled here that we should use our own shit as manure to plant vegetables that we'll eat and sell to other people?

TECHNICAL ASSISTANT:
That is what we encourage.

OLD MAN:
To sell my own shit, so that people should eat it?

TECHNICAL ASSISTANT:
But it is no longer faeces after all these years. It is now manure.

OLD MAN:
I tell you, man, I have worked in Johannesburg for many years. I stopped eating cabbage when I saw that in their fields they use shit. A big field, from here to that hill over there . . . you will find mountains of shit in their fields. That is why to this day I do not eat cabbage. Sis! (*He spits in disgust.*)

ANOTHER MAN FROM THE AUDIENCE:
Tell me father, you, during this season of farming, don't you ever use manure of cows and horses from your kraal in the fields?

OLD MAN:
It is not the same. It does not come from human beings.

There is general agreement among the members of the audience, expressed through varied exclamations, that they will never use human faeces in their fields. The cast sings a monyanyako *song, and some members of the audience join to sing and dance. The lyrics are on VIP toilets and water taps.*

Matloana a VIP	VIP latrines
A thibele bohlasoa.	Stop carelessness,
Lipeo tsa mafu,	Germs that spread diseases.
Menko le litsintsi	Smells and flies.
A thibela bohlasoa.	They stop carelessness.
Lipompo li molemo	Taps are useful
Li kengoe metseng eohle.	They must be constructed in all villages.
Lipeo tsa mafu,	Germs that spread diseases,
Litsintsi, menko.	Flies, and smells.
Li thibela bohlasoa.	They stop carelessness.

Scene 6: *Liloche is trying to convince Sek'hoek'hoe on the benefits of VIP latrines. Nchoati is getting worse, and Liloche thinks they must get the village health workers. But Sek'hoek'hoe insists that they must get Mankhoe instead. Manchoati agrees with Liloche. Sek'hoek'hoe gets angry and accuses the two of them of having a love affair. He subsequently drives Liloche out of his house.*

Scene 7: *Nchoati's situation is deteriorating, and Manchoati and the village women express deep concern. Sek'hoek'hoe arrives. He did not get Mankhoe, for he has gone to another town. In desperation he offers to go and fetch Malipere, the village health worker. On arrival she quickly assesses the child and recommends that the child be rehydrated immediately. She calls a real-life village health worker from the audience, who demonstrates how to prepare a homemade sugar and salt solution for oral rehydration therapy, and administers this to the child. After some time the child begins to show some signs of improvement. The village health worker advises the parents on the proper food that the child should eat. Members of the audience ask questions about oral rehydration therapy, and these are answered by the village health worker and nurses in the audience. Sek'hoek'hoe says he has learnt a lesson because 'I have now seen that stubbornness devours its owner.'*

Scene 8: *Sek'hoek'hoe and Liloche are having further discussions on the VIP latrines, when Manchoati enters. She offers them water to wash their hands and then serves them with food. They all continue to have the discussions. Sek'hoek'hoe, the audience learns from the discussion, is a changed man. He wakes up in the morning to work on the communal projects for improving the village. They cover and protect water wells, and have formed a workparty to dig latrine holes for each family, for if some do not have toilets the diseases will spread even to those who have them. Even those who are in the mines must be encouraged to send money to build toilets. An audience member suggests that a credit union should be established to give loans for toilet building. Those who are interested will register their names after the play. The play ends with a monyanyako song and dance, performed by the cast and audience.*

Agro-Action Play

Characters:

Size	- a villager
'Makhotso	- Size's wife
Mpokho	- a mineworker
'Mapalesa	- Mpokho's wife
'Mampho	- a communal garden member
Chieftainess	
'Mapalesa's friend	
The accordion player	
3 communal garden members	

Scene breakdown (with dialogue extracts)*

Scene 1: *Members of the communal garden are waiting for the theatre group to arrive. Most of them are women, some with babies on their backs. The heavily overcast weather does not dampen the festive atmosphere. The group arrives in an open truck singing to the accompaniment of the accordion and drums. They jump down from the truck and are joined by the villagers in song and dance. The song is of the* seoeleoelele *type, and the dance is a variation of a dance that is normally performed at weddings. In the meantime, while dancing, some members of the cast prepare the acting space, arranging the few chairs to form an arena. Others help to direct the audience to sit or stand around the acting space, while the cast remains at the centre. When the song stops, the action in the arena begins. Mpokho has made a feast. The chieftainess, Size, his wife, Mpokho's wife, her friend and some villagers are present.*

---

* Transcribed and translated by the author from a video of a performance recorded at Ha Sephula in the Mafeteng district on 13 February 1988. The author attended this performance.

CHIEFTAINESS:
We are happy for the invitation to this feast. We no longer get such invitations because these days feasts are far apart and unusual occurrences in the village. Times are bad because of the famine that is covering this village. You and your wife should be grateful that you still have the strength to make such feasts.

MPOKHO:
The aim of this feast is to thank those who are down [*underground, the ancestors*] for the promotion that I have received. I am now a baasboy [*foreman*] at the mines where I work.

The two men perform the mohobelo *dance, while the women, including those in the audience, sing and clap hands. At this stage some women from the communal garden — one of them is 'Makhotso — come to fetch their fellow-workers who are supposed to be working in the garden. The women reluctantly leave the feast to work in the garden. Those who remain discuss communal gardens, and their varied attitudes towards them emerge.*

CHIEFTAINESS:
Those women must go, for they have signed an agreement with Mojeremane [*the German, meaning the German Agro-Action Project*] that they will work for five days a week.

MPOKHO:
I do not understand what these communal gardens are all about. When I left for the mines there were no communal gardens in the village.

SIZE:
I feel great pain when I see the things that are happening in this village. Our wives have been turned into slaves, into bulldozers that have breasts. They wake up in the morning working for the Mojeremane. This is German exploitation of our women. I remember how beautiful our women used to be!

CHIEFTAINESS:
You, Size, are still young. The only thing you know best is to go from shebeen to shebeen drinking *hopose* [*a home brewed alcoholic concoction*]. Since the communal gardens came to the village we have insulted hunger.

'MAPALESA'S FRIEND:
It is because Mojeremane fills your stomach so that he should be able to steal your country.

SIZE:
I knew that the first person who will stand up to defend the Germans is

you, chieftainess, because the chiefs have always been our oppressors. True blood-suckers! When the white people first came to this country, they came through chiefs.

In the debate that ensues 'Mapalesa and her friend indicate that they despise the women who work in the communal gardens, and regard them as inferior. 'Mapalesa's 'superiority' is based on the fact that she receives a regular income from her husband who works in the mines. She in turn supports her friend with some of the money. The feast ends without any conclusion being reached about communal gardens.

Scene 2:   *Size is quarrelling with his wife at home.*

SIZE:
Why did you disgrace me at the feast yesterday? We were sitting happily enjoying our beer, and you came to destroy other people's feasts.

'MAKHOTSO:
Don't you know I am the secretary of the communal garden? I have to see to it that people meet their commitment . . . people work . . .

SIZE:
Yes, you have now joined the traitors.

Mpokho arrives, and Makhotso goes out to prepare food for them. Size tells Mpokho about the 'madness that has attacked our village women'. He confides in him that to frustrate the women's work he has destroyed the garden fence, and has let his horse into the garden to eat the vegetables. He has thrown some of the vegetables into the dam. He has also caught some fish from the communal dam. 'Makhotso enters. She has heard part of the conversation, and confronts Size about it. They quarrel once again. The miner leaves for he does not want 'to involve himself in other people's business'. Size threatens the wife that if she ever reveals to anyone that he is responsible for the damage in the garden, he is going to kill her. He exits. Makhotso remains alone, debating with herself on what course of action to take about her husband's activities. She takes the problem to the audience.

WOMAN FROM AUDIENCE:
In a court of law thieves are sentenced and are made to pay damages.

OLD WOMAN FROM AUDIENCE:
In my village we had a man like your husband Size. When he was caught we took him to the chief, and he was instructed to pay the damages. This did not help. The extension worker advised us to report him to the police,

and a criminal charge has been laid at the local court. So far we see that
theft has stopped.

'MAKHOTSO:
    I see, mother. But now here is the thief. He is my husband. How do I deal
    with this matter? I find that taking him to the police will be a difficult
    matter. Also you heard how he threatened me . . .

YOUNG WOMAN FROM AUDIENCE:
    I think that since the thief is your own husband, so that you pay back the
    damages, let him be sentenced to work in the garden. Let him join the
    workparty in the communal garden . . .

*Different views were proffered by the members of the audience on how this
matter should be handled. Finally it is decided that 'Makhotso should take the
matter to her fellow community garden members. Women who are confronted
by a similar problem should not keep it to themselves, but must take it to their
colleagues who will take a joint decision on what step to take next.*

Scene 3: *There is now a drizzle, but the play continues. 'Mapalesa and her
friend are boasting about the new dresses that they are going to buy in town.
Mpokho enters and tells them about the fight at Size's homestead. The fight is
over communal gardens.*

MPOKHO:
    But I don't understand what these communal gardens are, that can even
    cause such fights in the family.

*However 'Malerato and her friend cannot explain. They are not interested
either. 'Mampho enters, visiting 'Malerato. As she is a communal garden
member, Mpokho asks her to explain to him about the project. She begins to
explain, but the two women are bored, and they leave. At this stage the drizzle
has become a downpour. Size comes to the stage playing his mouth organ and
singing* lifela.

SIZE:
    Basotho, as you can see the Lord has blessed us with rain. What shall we
    do now? Perhaps we should stop the play until it stops raining.

*The villagers suggest that the play should continue in a shack which is used by
communal garden members to store their garden implements, fertilisers and
seeds. The play proceeds in the shack. 'Mampho explains how communal
gardens were formed.*

'MAMPHO:
When we saw that there was hunger in our homes, we came together as people of this village. We decided to approach the village development committee, for we wanted to start a communal garden from which we would get food, and sell some of the vegetables for money. The development committee went to Mojeremane in Maseru who provided us with money, seeds and implements. Now, as you can see there are roads in the village which we constructed ourselves. There are water taps, and we also have a big dam where we have a lot of fish. We plan to do more projects for ourselves.

Mpokho is impressed that communal gardens are a good idea.

Scene 4: *The rain is much louder on the corrugated iron roof of the shack. Mpokho tells 'Malerato what he has learnt of communal gardens and other projects that can improve their family and the village. He advises his wife to join them. But 'Malerato is not interested.*

'MALERATO:
I am not going to join these things of the Nationalists [*Basotho National Party which ruled Lesotho from 1966 to 1986*].

MPOKHO (*to audience*):
'Mapalesa says these things are of the Nationalists. Is it true?

WOMAN FROM AUDIENCE:
Somebody says that these projects belong to political parties . . . to the National Party or the Congress [*Basutoland Congress Party*].

ANOTHER WOMAN FROM AUDIENCE:
No, this project does not involve political parties. It is for everyone irrespective of political parties. It is for the whole nation.

MPOKHO:
But can you say that there are some people in the village here who believe that politics are involved in this project?

SOME AUDIENCE MEMBERS:
Yes, they believe so.

MPOKHO:
Why do they believe so?

OLD WOMAN FROM AUDIENCE:
It is true my child that these days we do not trust these things that are brought here by you modern people. Your politics have brought divisions in the village.

ANOTHER WOMAN FROM AUDIENCE:
Yes. Every time development projects came to the village, there was discrimination against those who did not support the government [*the ruling party*]. Only those who belonged to the National Party ate, and the rest of us remained the poor people who eat lice.

YOUNG WOMAN FROM AUDIENCE:
That's how things used to be. But this is not a government project. Things have changed now. I am a member of the communal garden at Ha Setenane. People support all parties there. Some support the new government of the soldiers, others are Nationalists and Congress members, while others don't belong to a party. But we all work together in the same garden. It is not like in the old days of discrimination.

The members of the audience agree with her that in their experience of the communal gardens that are supported by German Agro-Action, party politics have not played a role. Size enters. Mpokho tries to convince him to join communal gardens. But Size thinks that Mpokho has gone soft in the brain.

SIZE:
Young man, I see that the whites with whom you work in the mines have destroyed your brain. The white man came to this country and ruled us. All of a sudden there were resident commissioners and high commissioners who lived in splendour in the towns, while we suffered in the village. Then heroic men came and fought for our independence, and indeed we got it. Now that we have independence we must lead our happy lives in peaceful relaxation. The government is the one that must do things for us. It must work for us because it is our government.

MPOKHO:
But who is the government? (*To the audience.*) Is he not the government? Are we, the people, not all the government?

MAN FROM AUDIENCE:
No we are not the government. The government are those people who are eating our taxes in Maseru. And our deferred pay from the mines.

ANOTHER MAN FROM AUDIENCE (*heckling*):
Where do you come from? Tax was long abolished!

YET ANOTHER MAN FROM AUDIENCE:
Is it not true though that when these overseas countries give us aid it does not come naked? It comes with something else. It is their way of coming to rule us again.

MEMBERS OF THE AUDIENCE:
Yes! Yes!

OTHERS:
No! No!

The actors try to restore order, by beating the drums.

SIZE:
Let us listen to one another. If we all speak at once we shall not understand one another.

WOMAN FROM AUDIENCE:
We have been working in these gardens with the help of Mojeremane for a long time now. But we have not seen Mojeremane make decisions for us.

After some discussion the people decide that they do need help from 'these people who come from across the seas'.

MAN FROM AUDIENCE:
But when they come we must look closely at their activities so that we don't find that one day we have sold ourselves and our land. A man does not see twice.

Scene 5: *The chieftainess is with 'Makhotso, 'Mampho and three other communal garden members. They are waiting for Size who has been summoned to answer charges of theft. 'Mampho complains about the foreman who was appointed by the chieftainess on the basis that he is a man, while all the other participants are women.*

CHIEFTAINESS:
I appointed the foreman because I felt that as a man he will enforce more discipline. He will work hard and will see that the work proceeds well.

'MAMPHO:
He does not work. Anyway why should members of the committee be appointed by you instead of being elected by us?

The question is taken to the audience, who quickly agree that the foreman must be elected by the members of the communal garden, and not imposed on them by the chief (or chieftainess in the case of those villages whose traditional leaders are women). The foreman must be somebody who is dedicated to the project. The choice must not be based on sex, but on capability. Size arrives and the case begins. He is accused of grazing the horse in the vegetable garden, and of illegally fishing in the communal dam. At first he denies the charges but when one woman gives evidence to the effect that she actually saw him one night, and his wife reveals what she heard him tell Mpokho, he admits.

SIZE:
Yes I did it, because I am helping you. It is said that at his home a prophet is hated. I destroy these things because I see that Basotho are like people who are sedated. I am helping you . . . to save you. I am liberating you.

CHIEFTAINESS (*to the audience*):
He has admitted that he is responsible for the damage. Mothers and fathers, do you have this situation in your village . . . of people like Size?

WOMEN FROM AUDIENCE:
Indeed we have! They are many!

CHIEFTAINESS:
What do you do with them?

WOMAN FROM AUDIENCE:
We take them to the chief of the village.

CHIEFTAINESS:
Then do they stop when you take them to the chief?

ANOTHER WOMAN FROM AUDIENCE:
No, they do not; for they look down upon the chief.

CHIEFTAINESS:
What happens then since the chief is ineffective?

OLD WOMAN FROM AUDIENCE:
If the chief fails, then we must go to the government. Where I live in my village which is not far from here, the government had failed to provide us with any services. There was no road. There was no water. Until this German project came here. Our government for all these years has not done anything for us.

WOMAN FROM AUDIENCE:
Then if they have not done anything for us, how are they going to help if we take people who spoil our things to the government?

OLD WOMAN FROM AUDIENCE:
I am talking about what Size says we are being exploited. We had no water before. No taps. No roads. Even here in Samaria where the Romans [*Roman Catholic Church*] have their mission. But now you were able to drive your trucks into the village on the roads that we have

constructed ourselves. The government has said that development is necessary, but it is us who must do things for ourselves — not the government. Each one knows the problems of his/her [*same Sesotho word is used for these pronouns*] village. Since the government says we must do things for ourselves it must then see to people like Size, who destroy our efforts. The chief is not the owner of development. People are the owners of development.

ANOTHER WOMAN FROM AUDIENCE:
What I say is that since this is your village (*referring to fictional chieftainess*), and Size is your person [*subject*] in this village, and this development is in your village, and Size is ruled by you, you have all the right to force Size to go and work in the garden where he has been doing the destruction.

It seems a large number of the audience members agree with this suggestion since there are shouts of, 'Yes, let it be like that!'

YOUNG WOMAN FROM AUDIENCE:
What if he destroys more of the vegetables?

CHIEFTAINESS:
There may be some other views. Let us explore all the possibilities. Perhaps some people may disagree with the mother who has just spoken. Wait, there is somebody there who has something to say.

WOMAN FROM AUDIENCE:
I just want to say that I agree with the mother who has just spoken. But I want to add that Size must not only work, but must be given a responsibility — a position of leadership.

EXTENSION WORKER FROM AGRO-ACTION:
Somebody said that he will destroy more from the inside. Will he not destroy . . .

ANOTHER WOMAN FROM AUDIENCE:
When he is inside he will see the value of the work that these women are doing.

Once more the members of the audience agree that must be the solution of the play. Size must work. After some time when he has enjoyed the fruits of his labour, he will see the value of communal gardens, and will go out of his way to encourage others to join. The actors on the stage are about to exit, in order to come back for a new scene that will depict this solution, when one old woman expresses her objection.

7777

7777777

777777

OLD WOMAN FROM AUDIENCE:
But I still do not agree. You see that man over there (*points at him in the audience*) was a leader of our workteam in our village. My fellow-villagers are my witnesses that he learnt about the work of the communal gardens, and about the ways of our operations, and then turned against us. The problems of the villages are not the same. He turned against us. He is now the one who eats the fish. He is now the one who destroys our vegetables in the garden because now he has all the inside information about how we work, and where we keep our things. Ntate Mathaba [the Agro-Action extension worker] knows all about him. I am asking myself that when Size knows all our ways, won't he be like our Size in the village?

MAN FROM AUDIENCE:
Let us try to answer this question. It is a very important question. Who can help us with an answer to this problem?

CHIEFTAINESS:
What I want to know is, what steps did you take about your own Size in your village?

OLD WOMAN FROM AUDIENCE:
We have had many Sizes. The first Size was the one who was our leader that I have told you about. But before I talk about him, let me understand you correctly (*referring to the actors on the stage*). At first you said your chieftainess is the one who chose your foreman. You did not elect him yourselves.

ACTORS:
Yes.

OLD WOMAN FROM AUDIENCE:
This means that the chieftainess nominated somebody who she put on top of you, and this person did not do any work . . .

ACTOR:
Yes, instead he destroyed and stole the produce, and some of the implements.

OLD WOMAN FROM AUDIENCE:
It was a person who was in the position of leadership who did that. My question is, after you have chosen a new leader in the name of Size, who is already a known thief, what is going to happen? Will there be a remedy? I forget some of the things you said in the play, but I think it was mentioned that it is important that the participants in the communal gardens should choose their own committees . . . their own leaders. These must not be imposed on you by the chief, because you know one

another. My other question is, now that the village is big, and not all the community members are members of the communal gardens — they only come when there is a feast, to eat the food — should they also participate in the election of the committee?

WOMAN FROM AUDIENCE:
No. People who elect are those who work in the communal gardens. Those whose names appear in our books as members.

ANOTHER WOMAN FROM AUDIENCE:
Also when you asked if there will be any remedy if the committee is elected rather than nominated, I would say yes, since each member of the committee will have his/her own responsibilities, and will not interfere with the work of others. Each person is responsible for something. The treasurer is responsible for the money, the secretary keeps the records and so on. When spades are missing we know who to ask.

EXTENSION WORKER FROM AGRO-ACTION:
My point is that if we take Size and make him a leader, we know that he is a thief and a destroyer, we are going to put our eye on him. To make an example about the man the grandmother was talking about, we put him into the work and he stole. But now we have caught him because we know among us how we catch them. One was in the committee, but when she was no longer a committee member she became a Size. We caught him still. We told him, 'No Size, do not destroy our work just because you are no longer in the committee.' Let Size work. We shall catch him if he steals.

The members of the audience shout their agreement.

CHIEFTAINESS:
It seems that you all agree that this is the best way to deal with Size. And that our play should end with Size as a changed man who encourages others to participate in developmental activities.

GIRL FROM AUDIENCE:
The people on the other side do not agree.

ANOTHER WOMAN FROM AUDIENCE:
I refuse! When our own Size was given responsibility in our village, that is the time when he took from our garden bags of potatoes, using his donkeys. He took all our money and went to Durban.

CHIEFTAINESS:
Do you mean your Size was put in an overall leadership position to the

extent that he had access to all your property . . . or did you give him a responsibility to work under supervision?

SAME WOMAN:
Size is a very clever person. When he is given responsibility you will find that he works his way through. All of a sudden the money is kept by him . . . everything is in his hands.

MAN FROM AUDIENCE:
Where is the committee when all these things are happening?

SAME WOMAN:
He cheated the members of the committee in a way that we did not understand. We found that those who kept the money were in cahoots with him.

EXTENSION WORKER FROM AGRO-ACTION:
This shows that your committee was not strong enough. I always say that a weak committee will have such problems. Your Size was not supposed to be in the money. When these people say that Size must be given responsibility they mean that he should see to it that people go to work at eight, and knock-off at four. Not that he should look after the money. He should look after garden implements and see to it that they are kept in proper condition.

WOMAN FROM AUDIENCE:
If I understand the suggestion well, Size will not be a committee member, for the committee is there. It has been elected by the members of the garden. The suggestion is that Size must work, and be supervised by the committee.

ANOTHER WOMAN:
He is not taking anybody's place in the committee.

ALL:
We agree. Let Size work.

The scene ends with a monyanyako *song and dance by the cast and the members.*

Scene 6: *Months later 'Mapalesa and her friend are drinking beer at home. Mpokho has been sending money home to contribute towards some development projects, but his wife has been spending it on drinks and clothes for herself and her friend. Mpokho comes singing* lifela *about the strike at the mine. When he gets home he tells the wife that he has lost his job because of the strike that is happening at the mines. But his consolation is that since he has* *been sending money home, he will be able to live from the investment. He is shocked to find that his wife has spent all the money. The members of the audience advise him to join the communal gardens. But an angry woman interrupts.*

WOMAN FROM AUDIENCE:
I want to talk about the strikes at the mines. Now Mpokho has lost his job because of a strike ... Our husbands go to the mines to work for our families, and then join strikes.

ANOTHER WOMAN FROM AUDIENCE:
It is because of the trade union. It causes all the strikes.

WOMEN:
Trade unions are bad! Our husbands are fools to join them! Our children are hungry! You say Mpokho should work in the communal garden, but he would still be having his job at the mine if it were not for the trade unions! I don't see why Mpokho's wife can be blamed. Trade unions should be blamed. Yes, let us talk about trade unions!

DIRECTOR OF MAROTHOLI:
This is a very important matter you bring. Unfortunately we cannot talk about many things at the same time. Today we want to solve our problems in the communcal gardens. Maybe next time we should come back and make another play about trade unions.

It is agreed that a play on trade unions must be created. A man suggests that a day when migrants have come home on a long weekend should be chosen.

Scene 7:   *A village meeting. Mpokho tells the people of their achievements since they joined the communal gardens. Size and Mpokho's wife are among the most enthusiastic workers. They have learnt the errors of their ways. Song and dance with drums and accordion.*

Trade Union Play

Characters:

Motale   - a miner from a Lesotho village
Lebona   - another miner from the same village
'Mamotale   - Motale's wife
'Malebona   - Lebona's wife
Shop Steward [played by villager who became a catalyst]
Villagers who play various roles

Scene Breakdown (with dialogue extracts)*

Scene 1: *Motale and Lebona have just emerged from the mine shaft. They are competing in the singing of* lifela. *In their* lifela *they express their greatness, the beauty of their village, the drought that pervades their homeland, the cattle that are dying, the lack of employment opportunities in their country, and the longing they have for their wives and families. As they sing* lifela *women in the audience ululate, and from time to time a man jumps up from among the audience and crosses the stage performing the* tlala *dance. It is obvious that the men in the audience are moved by this scene, for the catalysts learnt their* lifela *from reputed* likheleke, *and spent weeks practising them. A man from the audience comes forward and sings his own* safela. *Although it has very little to do with the mines, but deals with his travels from village to village throughout the districts of Lesotho, the audience are quite pleased with it. His* safela *is very long. In the form of another* safela *the catalysts request him to cut his short since 'a cow does not defecate all the dung at once'. They want to proceed to the second scene.*

* Transcribed and translated by the author from his notes and the audio of the performance recorded at Tebang in the Mafeteng district on 17 December 1988. The author was one of the catalysts.

Scene 2:   *Motale is in his dormitory in the mine compound. He is singing while looking at a letter. Lebona enters.*

LEBONA:

Child of my mother, you are singing as though the world is at peace with itself.

MOTALE:

It is at peace, child of my mother, I have just received a letter from my wife. It says my daughter has passed with a first class. She will be going to high school next year.

LEBONA:

You are a foolish man, Motale. You educate daughters who will marry and leave your family. They will enrich their husband's families with all that education.

MOTALE:

These are modern days, Lebona. I don't want that my daughter should suffer when the inlaws mistreat her. She will go and work for herself. You know, she wants to be a nurse or a miss [*school teacher*].

LEBONA:

How are you going to afford the school fees?

MOTALE:

There you are talking. These times are hard, child of my mother. When our wages are raised by R5.00, things at the shops are raised by R10.00. We cannot cope any more.

At this stage a trade union shop steward enters. He tells them about the advantages of being union members. The union is fighting for more wages for the workers.

SHOP STEWARD:

It is necessary that all workers should unite so that we can speak with one word. In that case we shall achieve what we want.

MOTALE:

I think I agree with this man. I am going to join the trade union.

LEBONA:

I am not a fool. The bosses have told us that trade unions are bad, and we must not join them. TEBA told us the same.

At this point the catalysts stop. The question is taken to the audience: who is right? There are shouts: some agree with Motale while others agree with Lebona.

MOTALE:
Fathers and mothers, it would be better if we listen to one another. Let us hear one person.

MIGRANT 1:
I was a member of NUM [*National Union of Mineworkers*]. I resigned because NUM is more concerned with the politics of South Africa, rather than with the problems of the workers. All we ever do is to sing political songs about Mandela!

LEBONA:
It is exactly as I see it. Come, my elder brother, come join us here and we show the people how it happens.

The migrant reluctantly goes to the stage. He is egged on by the other members of the audience. The actors are now four on the stage. They discuss how the scene should proceed to reflect the migrant's concern. There are various suggestions among themselves and from the audience. It is suggested that the next scene should show a trade union rally, and the trade union leaders must tell the workers that a strike has been declared. The migrant must be the union leader since he knows what happens there.

Scene 3: *A trade union rally. Lebona, Motale, the migrant (who will now become a union leader), the shop steward, and a few other members of the audience who have decided to join the rally. They are singing and shouting slogans: Viva! One union, one federation! Some dance the* toyi-toyi *dance [a rhythmic jogtrot dance performed to call-and-response chants by the youth at political meetings and rallies in South Africa]. At the end of the song and dance the union leader speaks. But a woman from the audience stops him.*

WOMAN:
But Lebona has no truth in himself. We heard him tell Motale that he was not going to join the union. What is he now doing at this meeting of the people of the union?

LEBONA:
Yes. I think the mother is right. I forgot that I said I was not going to join the union.

He leaves the stage and joins the audience.

MIGRANT 1/UNION LEADER:
> Comrades. I have to tell you that there is going to be a strike. We are now tired of working in these mines for low pay. So I am telling you now that all of you must begin the strike immediately!

The meeting is over.

MOTALE:
> So now we are going on strike. We want more wages. Should we strike? No, let me not ask that, for we are going to strike. You heard at the meeting that we are going to strike. What will happen if we strike?

WOMAN FROM AUDIENCE:
> You will be expelled from work. You know very well that it always happens like that.

MOTALE:
> And then what will happen?

ANOTHER WOMAN FROM AUDIENCE:
> Your children will starve.

MOTALE:
> Maybe then we should show how things happen at home. In our next scene we should show how the women and the children are . . .

WOMAN FROM AUDIENCE:
> But there are no big children who will act here. Who is going to be the child in your story?

MOTALE:
> We'll see about that. We'll hear some suggestions.

LEBONA:
> But before we go to the scene that shows the women at home, I am not happy with this scene. Is this really how things happen when strikes are called.

MEN FROM AUDIENCE:
> Yes!

LEBONA:
> Well, I am glad I didn't join the trade union if things are like that . . . if a man from the union just comes and tells you to strike!

MIGRANT 2:
> No it is not true. I am a member of NUM and I know it is not true. When a strike is called, it is after all the members have met, and it is the members

themselves who decide whether to strike or not. Ramaphosa [*secretary-general of the National Union of Mineworkers*] does not just tell us to strike. We hold meetings and we tell him that we want to strike.

Some people from the audience agree with him.

MIGRANT 1:
I know what I am talking about. In 1985 the union officials went to negotiate with the Chamber of Mines, and when they came back they reported there was a deadlock, and if it was not resolved by the first of October there would be a strike.

MIGRANT 3:
They asked the members first. At Western Deep Level where I work they asked . . .

MIGRANT 1:
They did not ask the members whether there should be a strike or not. Indeed, without any voting by the members, a strike was called on the first of October.

There are two sides to this issue. The women feel that it is not important whether strikes are called by the workers or by Ramaphosa, strikes are bad because children starve.

SHOP STEWARD:
I think we shall not agree on this matter now. Let us leave it until the end of the play. Then we shall come back to it. We shall not just leave it like that because it is important. Where do we go from here?

MOTALE:
We said we are going to show how things are with our wives. I am now expelled from work because of the strike. But I haven't reached home yet.

Scene 4: *'Mamotale and 'Malebona (both catalysts) are talking about their problems at home. Generally these are problems dealt with in the* lifela *of the first scene. However they are lucky, they say, since they have husbands who work in the mines. Their situation is not as bad as it is with other people who do not get any money from the mines. At this point Motale and and Lebona arrive. They are arguing about the strike. They have both been dismissed from work.*

LEBONA:
It is all your fault you clever people. Right now, even with us who were not involved in the strike, we are going to suffer.

They explain to their wives that all the workers have been told to go home. Some of them will be called back to work. They were told to listen for their names on Radio Lesotho. Lebona is sure that he will be called back to work, for he had made it clear to the bosses that he was not part of the strike.

LEBONA:
> The strike is for the people of South Africa. We are guest workers in that country. We must not get involved.

MOTALE:
> But we work there. It is our labour that these people are exploiting. We must be paid fairly for it. What do our people say about this?

MIGRANT 4:
> I say the same thing again, that was said by that elder brother from Kloof, or is he from Western Deep Levels? I forget. But he said your NUM is only active in singing songs of South Africa. It is interested in overthrowing the government of the Boers. And who gets killed?

MIGRANT 5:
> This man is talking shit. I think he is one of the *mpimpis* [*sell-outs*] of the Boers.

MIGRANT 4:
> Do you hear this boy insult me?

MOTALE:
> Please let us not fight. We do not want a situation where the quarrel of a man is settled with a stick. Rather let us act this out. Both of you fathers come to the stage and act your differences out. You be Motale, and this elder brother here is Lebona.

But the man who has been insulted is no longer interested in participating. He leaves, fuming. All attempts to call him back fail. The other man is still prepared to act. He agrees with Motale, so that is the role he will play. Another man from the audience volunteers to be Lebona.

MIGRANT 5/MOTALE:
> NUM is not only interested in singing songs of South Africa. Songs are sung to rally people.

MIGRANT 6/LEBONA:
> But it is politics. It has nothing to do with the worker.

MIGRANT 5/MOTALE:
> Do you agree that there is discrimination in the mines?

MIGRANT 6/LEBONA:
What discrimination?

MIGRANT 5/MOTALE:
Are you going to tell me that the money you are paid is equal to that of the white man?

'MALEBONA:
What does it matter if it is equal or not equal? Can you get that money here in Lesotho?

MIGRANT 5/MOTALE:
Women don't understand these things. I do not talk to women.

'MAMOTALE:
I think you must answer her. Women have a right to know. It is our children who starve when you have been expelled from work.

MIGRANT 5/MOTALE:
And you, who are you now?

'MAMOTALE:
I am 'Mamotale, and you are Motale. In this story I am your wife.

Migrant 5 seems to enjoy the fact that he has this newly acquired 'wife'. He laughs for a long time.

MIGRANT 6/LEBONA:
The question is difficult for him. He cannot answer it.

MIGRANT 5/MOTALE:
I am the one who asked you a question. Is your pay the same as that of a white man?

Migrant 6 admits that it is not the same.

MIGRANT 5/MOTALE:
Do you know why it is not the same? It is because of the law that is made by the Boers in their parliament in Pretoria [*Cape Town, actually*]. Is that not politics? It is the politicians of the Boers who decide in their law that you are not equal to the white man. You know some of them come as 'new-ones'. They don't know anything about the mines. We teach them the work. They get more money than us. Soon you find that they are our bosses.

Migrant 6 admits that is the case, but 'that is how things are'. They cannot be changed through an engagement in South African politics. Migrant 5 on the other hand feels that discrimination is a result of politics. For the union to be effective in fighting it, it must deal with the system that has created discriminatory laws. 'An effective union cannot avoid politics'. The question is taken to the audience, who debate it at length.

MIGRANT 7:

What I see is that NUM is most active when it comes to demanding increased wages. For instance, they now demand a raise of 55 per cent. This means that the owners of the mine will only get 45 per cent. The mine owners will get less than the workers. It seems now the workers want to own the mines.

The debate continues in this vein, with the two actor–migrants exchanging views with the members of the audience. During this period, women seem to be left out of the discussion. The catalysts call upon women to come to the stage to state their point.

'MAMOTALE:

Men are not the only ones who are affected by these problems. These are our problems — all of us. What I want to know is:
here I have a child who has passed with first class. She must go to school. But here is Motale. He has come back from work because he has been expelled. How am I going to cope?

WOMAN FROM AUDIENCE:

Ntate Motale says that the whites become their bosses. Even there it is the fault of NUM. My husband told me that NUM has always been quiet about white people who come to the mines and are trained by blacks, only for those whites to become bosses over the blacks. NUM is quiet on this issue because it is only interested in fighting for money.

MIGRANT 7:

Yes, NUM is no good. I have passed matric, but I found that at the mines the shop stewards are people who don't even have a Standard Six certificate. They mislead the miners.

The catalysts observe that a number of unresolved issues have emerged. Some of the issues are emotive, and a shouting match has developed among the opposing sides. They decide that a number of sketches must be created, each depicting the problem, and a resolution reached by the audience.

Scene 5: *The scene deals with the strike at the mine. The migrants and the catalysts play different roles. Some are workers, union officials, and mine* *bosses. Union officials negotiate with employers for a wage increase. They are not able to reach an agreement. Migrant 7 who plays the role of the employer is adamant that the workers want to own the mines. The union officials show him that his 55–45 per cent arithmetic is faulty. The union wants the wages to be raised by 55 per cent. This means 55 per cent of their current wages. The union officials report back to the workers that an agreement has not been reached. At this point all the other members of the audience become the workers in a mass meeting.*

MOTALE/CATALYST:
What must we do now? We have failed to reach an agreement with the bosses.

Again there are two sides. One shouts that a strike must be called, while another side says the workers must not strike.

WOMAN:
We heard that in the mines salaries have been raised twice as much. Why do you want more? Even Lekhanya [*the chairman of the ruling Military Council*] said on the radio that you must not strike.

MIGRANT 8:
He says that because he eats our money! When they put out money in *sakoeng* [*deferred pay sent directly to Lesotho by the employers. It is a percentage of the miner's wages, and the miners can only get it when they are back in Lesotho*] where do you think the interest goes? It is eaten by Lekhanya. He knows that if we strike then he won't get our money.

One migrant says that it is not only the issue of money that the migrants are unhappy about. The working conditions are not good. When asked to provide an example of what he means, he talks about safety, and the number of workers who are injured or who die. Do these women who say workers must not strike want their husbands to die? The money that is paid is not enough for the work that the people are doing. The 'mine owners' get a lot of profit, while the workers remain poor. Do those who are against the strike want to perpetuate this situation?

LEBONA/CATALYST:
Perhaps the father says these things because he is a union official. You heard the elder brother say that the union officials in the mine are not educated, and therefore mislead the workers.

People dismiss this assertion with much contempt and ridicule.

WOMAN:
> Is the union not a worker's movement? Are the workers in the mines not our husbands who have not been to school? Who should run the movement if not the workers themselves?

MIGRANT:
> So now you agree that the union is good.

WOMAN:
> At first I did not understand what its work is. Yes, now I agree that it is good.

It seems she has won some women to her side, although there are still many who think that a strike must not be called. The catalysts decide that there must be two more scenes: one to show what happens when a strike is not called, and another when a strike is called.

Scene 6:   *The migrants and the catalysts once more assume different roles. A strike is not called. They go down to work. They work very hard. They are mistreated by the bosses, who even physically abused them. At first the catalysts had thought that this was going to be a very boring scene, since they did not know exactly what it would show. But it turns out to be hilarious. Work songs are introduced, some of which the catalysts had never heard of before. A lot of mime. At the end of the month the workers find that the money they get is so little that they cannot send any home. Some workers die in underground accidents.*

Scene 7:   *A strike is called. Lebona says he will not join the strike. But all workers are dismissed from the mine. They go back home. What are they now going to do?*

WOMAN:
> When people are expelled like this what does your Ramaphosa do?

MIGRANT 7:
> Nothing! They are only interested in fighting for money.

MIGRANT 8:
> It is not true. The union continues to negotiate with the employers to re-employ the workers.

LEBONA/CATALYST:
> Looking at these two situations then, which one do you think is better. When there is no strike, or when there is a strike?

Members of the audience feel that both situations are not good. But most say that it is better for the workers to fight for their rights rather than be humiliated. The question now is how do the unemployed miners cope? What should they do to make ends meet? One man suggests that there should be a fund established to help the strikers. He is told by others that there is such a fund.

MAN:
The fund must help Motale to establish a business. All the people who have been expelled can come together and form a co-operative.

WOMAN:
What about Lebona?

MAN:
No, the fund cannot help Lebona. He is not a member of the union!

ANOTHER WOMAN:
But he has been expelled because of the union.

The migrants are so angry with Lebona that they don't care. 'He must see for himself', they say.

Scene 8: *Motale/Catalyst is with some of his friends (migrants from the audience). They are planning how to go about establishing their new business. At first they decide to form a wheat farming project. The members of the audience point out that wheat is no longer the major crop that used to make Mafeteng rich. All of a sudden the members of the audience want to discuss the wheat issue. 'What happened?' someone asks. 'We used to supply the whole country with wheat.' The catalysts suggest that this matter cannot be discussed now since 'we want to solve the problems of Motale and Lebona. Let us put it aside for a moment'. Some members of the audience suggest that the matter is so important that a new play must be made about it. Motale and his friends settle for brickmaking — perhaps because someone suggests that in the Quthing district migrants have actually established their own brickmaking factory through the assistance of a strike fund from NUM. It is decided that Lebona should be called back to work in the mines. Because some members of the audience are eager to see him suffer, they suggest that when he is back there he should break his leg, come back home with little or no compensation, and find Motale prosperous. Others suggest that to show that the union is powerful and does negotiate for the expelled members to be re-employed, Motale should also be called back to the mines. But because he is doing well at his business he must refuse to go back. However it is now getting late, and there is no time to create scenes depicting these suggestions.*

'MALEBONA:

Because it is now late our play must end here. We have not resolved all the issues, but I think we have come to an agreement on others. Indeed I agree that for our play to be really complete it must show the two suggestions about Motale and Lebona. But what I want to say is that I am not happy that we did not hear from the mothers. When we did the *Agro-Action Play* it was the mothers who were most active with their views.

The women say that the play was mostly set in the mines, a situation which is foreign to them. They suggest that next time a play should be created which will be set in the village, and examine these same problems from the point of view of the women.

'MAMOTALE:

It is a good idea. What I want to know, in what we have discussed so far, do you now see why your husbands join trade unions?

A big section of the audience agrees that trade unions are good for the workers. A small section of the audience, led by the migrant who claimed to have passed matric, disagrees. He insists that the play 'did not tell the truth because strikes are decided upon by Ramaphosa, and not the workers themselves.' There is some disagreement on this issue among those who have worked in the mines. Some say that there was never a strike that was not authorised by the members. The catalysts do not have any information as to whether this is true or not. However it is agreed that 'the union should not be the boss of the workers, for in that case the union will just be acting like the employers who always bully the workers. A union must be run by the workers according to their wishes.'

People show their approval by clapping hands and ululating, after which an old peasant comes forward.

PEASANT:

I think this play taught us a lot. It was good. I have never been a miner myself, for I believe in the land. I am a farmer. You can ask them all about the wheat I produce in my fields. I just want to say to that young man (*pointing at the migrant who has matric*) that he does not know what he wants. He talks as if it is a bad thing to fight for more money. I do not know why he is working. To be poor? At first he complains that the white man gets more recognition at work. Even though he is inexperienced he is made the boss. Again he complains that your union is only interested in demanding more wages. Is recognition of one's work not shown through money?

At the end of this performance the spectators-cum-performers make a resolution that migrant workers should join and participate in the activities of a trade union because trade unions benefit the workers. There is a minority which is adamant that Basotho miners have no business in South African affairs. They are like beggars in someone else's country, and must not participate in the politics of that country. They must realise that they go to the mines to earn money for Lesotho and for their families. The play ends with a general performance of songs (monyanyako) *and dances, accompanied by accordion and drums.*

Alcoholism Play

Characters:

    Pikilane   - village school teacher
    His wife
    Village health worker
    Shebeen patrons

Scene breakdown*

Scene 1: *A shebeen. Shebeen patrons are singing and drinking. One of them is Pikilane, a well-known village drunk, who is also the local school teacher. Because he is more educated than the other villagers, they regard him as being well-off, and crowd around him. He freely buys the women drinks.*

Scene 2: *Pikilane arrives home. He is very drunk. His wife wants to know why he comes home drunk, so late in the night. His wife works for a village water supply project, but Pikilane wants her to resign. There is a quarrel between the two over the two issues: his drunkenness and the wife's involvement in a development project. Pikilane beats up his wife, who has to be taken to hospital.*

Scene 3: *Village women are hoeing in the field, while they sing the following worksong:*

---

* Compiled from notes taken by the author from an interview with one of the catalysts. Although the author did not see this performance, he listened to an audio tape recorded during the creation and performance of the play at Tebellong, Qacha's Nek in July 1989.

Call:	Ha ba noele	when they have drunk
	Sebapa-le-masenke	[a very potent home-brewed alcoholic concoction]
	Ke Lerato la limpompong	Their love is a cheap one
Response:	Ha se lona!	It is not true love
	Ha se lona!	

They take a short break from hoeing and discuss Pikilane's problem. His wife has been admitted in hospital with serious injuries. They conclude that the source of the whole problem is liquor. They then discuss the dangers of liquor on the human body, the adverse effects of alcohol on the social fabric of their village, and the conditions of poverty caused by liquor. They take the question to the audience: How should problems of excessive alcohol consumption be solved in the village? How should Pikilane solve his family problem? To the first question the members of the audience suggest that alcohol should be abolished from the village. No one opposes this view at this stage of the play. To the second question they say that Pikilane must stop drinking. His family problems will be solved. The women go back to their hoeing and singing.

Scene 4: Pikilane stays alone at home because his wife is in hospital. He is a very lonely man, and shows signs of great suffering. A village health worker visits him, and advises him to stop drinking. She explains to him the dangers of alcohol in his body. Pikilane says he regrets his past activities, and from this very moment he will stop drinking. The question is taken to the audience as to whether Pikilane's wife should go back to her husband. The audience decide that the wife should go back, provided Pikilane goes to the doctor for a programme of alcoholism rehabilitation. He says he will indeed see the doctor. He regrets that his wife is now crippled, and he is faced with heavy medical bills. The next question that is taken to the audience is what should happen to places that sell liquor in the village. 'Why do shebeen queens sell these destructive beverages to our husbands?' The members of the audience say that shebeen owners have to live too. Selling liquor is their way of earning a living. The solution is that shebeen owners should only sell liquor in the evenings. A real-life shebeen owner objects. She says she earns her living by selling liquor, and she cannot restrict the hours. 'The fault is with the people who overdrink,' she says. The villagers resolve that if shebeen owners refuse to comply, then there must a a law to enforce the restriction. They will see the 'authorities' to find out if a law can't be made to restrict the drinking hours. The play ends with song and dance.

Bibliography

(Please note that for books, dates refer to the edition consulted rather than to the date of first publication.)

Abah, Oga S. (1989) *From Celebration to Survival: Report of the International Workshop on Theatre for Integrated Development (TIDE) 7–22 December 1989 in Onyuwei Otobi and Adankari Benue State, Nigeria*, NPTA Report Series No. 02.

Ake, Claude (1981) *A Political Economy of Africa*, Harlow Longman.

Banham, M. and Clive Wake (1976) *African Theatre Today*, London, Pitman.

Barthes, Roland (1979) 'Theatre and Signification', in *Theatre Quarterly*, Vol. 9, No. 3.

Bassnett-McGuire, Susan (1980) 'An Introduction to Theatre Semiotics', in *Theatre Quarterly*, Vol. 10, No. 3.

Becker, Samuel L. (1983) *Discovering Mass Communication*, Glenview, Illinois, Scott, Foreman & Co.

Berger, John (1983) *Ways of Seeing*, London, BBC and Penguin.

Berrigan, Frances J. (1979) *Community Communications: The Role of Community Media in Development*, UNESCO Reports and Papers on Mass Communication, No. 90.

Bjorkman, Ingrid (1989) *'Mother, Sing for Me': People's Theatre in Kenya*, London, Zed Books.

Blackett, Isabel (1989) 'Privy Secrets?', in *Sethala*, Vol. 3, No. 25.

Blumler, Jay G. (1978) 'Purposes of Mass Communication Research: A Trans-Atlantic Perspective', in *Journalism Quarterly*, Summer.

—— and Elihu Katz (eds) (1974) *The Uses of Mass Communication: Current Perspectives in Gratification Research*, Beverly Hills, Sage Publications.

Boafo, S. T. Kwame (1985) 'Utilizing Development Communication Strategies in African Societies: A Critical Perspective (Development Communication in Africa)', in *Gazette* (International Journal of Mass Communication), Vol. 33, No. 2.

—— (1988) 'Democratizing Media Systems in African Societies: The Case of Ghana', in *Gazette* (International Journal of Mass Communication), Vol. 41, No. 1.

Boal, Augusto (1979) *Theatre of the Oppressed*, London, Pluto Press.

Burke, Kenneth (1945) *A Grammar of Motives*, New York, Prentice Hall.

Byram, Martin L. and Frances Moitse (1985) 'Theatre as an Educational Tool for Extension Work: A Training Strategy', unpublished paper presented at the International Conference on Theatre for Development, Maseru, Lesotho, 24 February–2 March.

Cameron, Kenneth M. and Patti P. Gillespie (1980) *The Enjoyment of Theatre*, New York, Macmillan.

Central Planning and Development Office (1986) *The Situation of Children and Women in Lesotho*, Maseru, CPDO, Government of Lesotho.

Chifunyise, Stephen J. (1985) 'Theatre for Development in Zimbabwe', unpublished paper presented at the International Conference on Theatre for Development, Maseru, Lesotho, 24 February–2 March.

Classic, The (1983) 'Open-Air Theatre of the Landless and Poor', in *The Classic*, Vol. 2, No. 1.

Cobbe, James H. (1989) 'Economic Aspects of Lesotho's Relations with South Africa', in *The Journal of Modern African Studies*, Vol. 26, No. 1.

Comte, Auguste (1915) *The Positive Philosophy* (trans. Harriet Martineau), London, George Bell and Sons.

Coplan, David (1983) 'Editorial: Popular Culture and Performance in Africa', in *Critical Arts*, Vol. 3, No. 1.

—— (1985) *In Township Tonight*, Johannesburg, Ravan Press.

—— (1989) 'Basotho Working-Class Literature and the Meaning of Sesotho', seminar paper presented at the Institute of Southern African studies, National University of Lesotho, 3 May.

Cosetino, Donald (1982) *Defiant Maids and Stubborn Farmers: Tradition and Invention in Mende Story Performance*, New York, Cambridge University Press.

Crow, Brian and Michael Etherton (1982) 'Popular Drama and Popular Analysis in Africa', in Ross Kidd and Nat Colletta (eds), *Tradition for Development: Indigenous Structures and Folk Media in Non-Formal Education*, Berlin, German Foundation for International Education and International Council for Adult Education.

Croyden, Margaret (1974) *Lunatics, Lovers and Poets: The Contemporary Experimental Theatre*, New York.

Curran, James, Michael Guverich and Janet Woollacott (1982) 'The Study of the Media: Theoretical Approaches', in Michael Guverich *et al* (eds), *Culture, Society and Media*, London, Methuen.

Dalrymple, Lynn I. (1987) 'Exploration in Drama, Theatre and Education: A Critique of Theatre Studies in South Africa', Ph.D. thesis, University of Natal.

Davidow, Mike (1977) *People's Theatre: From the Box Office to the Stage*, Moscow, Progress Publishers.

Deutsch, Karl W. (1974) 'Theories of Imperialism and Neocolonialism', in Steven J. Rosen and James R. Kurth (eds), *Testing Theories of Economic Imperialism*, Lexington, Mass., Lexington Books.

Deutsch, Morton and Robert Krauss (1965) *Theories in Social Psychology*, New York, Basic Books.

238   *When People Play People*

Deutschmann, P. J. (1957) 'The Sign-Situation Classification of Human Communication', in *Journal of Communication*, Vol. 7, No. 2.

Dinh, Tran Van (1979) 'Nonalignment and Cultural Imperialism', in Kaarle Nordenstreng and Herbert I. Schiller (eds), *National Sovereignty and International Communication*, Norwood NJ, Ablex Publishing Corporation.

Dondis, Donis A. (1981) *A Primer of Visual Literacy*, Cambridge, Mass., MIT Press.

Duerden, Denis (1977) *African Art and Literature: The Invisible Present*, London, Heinemann.

Echeruo, Michael (1979) 'Dramatic Limits of Igbo Ritual', in *Critical Perspectives on Nigerian Literature*, London, Heinemann.

Elam, Keir (1980) *The Semiotics of Theatre and Drama*, London, Methuen.

Epskamp, Kees P. (1989) *Theatre in Search of Social Change: The Relative Significance of Different Theatrical Approaches*, The Hague, CESO.

Erven, Eugene van (1989) *Stages of People Power: The Philippines Educational Theatre Association*, The Hague, CESO.

Etherton, Michael (1982) *The Development of African Drama*, New York, Africana Publishing Company.

Eyoh, Hansel Ndumbe (1987) 'Theatre, Adult Education and Development, A Workshop at Kumba (Cameroon)', in *Ifda Dossier* 60, July/August.

—— (1991) *Beyond the Theatre: Interviews*, Bonn, German Foundation for International Development (DSE).

Felstehausen, Herman (1973) *Conceptual Limits of Development Communication Theory*, Madison, University of Wisconsin Land Tenure Centre.

Ferrino, H., N. L. Radtke *et al* (1980) *South African Outlook*, special issue on community theatre, July.

Finkelstein, Sidney (1976) *How Music Expresses Ideas*, New York, International Publishers.

Fisher, B. Aubrey (1978) *Perspectives on Human Communication*, New York, Macmillan Publishing Co. Inc.

Fiske, John (1982) *Introduction to Communication Studies*, London, Methuen.

Ford-Smith, Honor (1981) 'Women's Theatre, Conscientization, and Popular Struggle in Jamaica', in Ross Kidd and Nat Colletta (eds), *Tradition for Development: Indigenous Structures and Folk Media in Non-Formal Education*, Berlin, German Foundation for International Education and International Council for Adult Education.

Freire, Paulo (1972a) *Cultural Action for Freedom*, Harmondsworth, Penguin.

—— (1972b) *Pedagogy of the Oppressed*, Harmondsworth, Penguin.

—— (1973) *Education for Critical Consciousness*, New York, Seabury Press.

—— (1974) *Education: the Practice of Freedom*, London, Writers and Readers Publishing Co-operative.

—— (1978) *Pedagogy in Process: The Letters to Guinea-Bisseau*, New York, Seabury Press.

Galtung, Johan (1971) 'A Structural Theory of Imperialism', in *Journal of Peace Research*, Vol. 8, No. 2.

Ganter, Elvira and Don Edkins (1988) *Marotholi: Theatre for Another Development*, Maseru, Village Technology Information Services.

Gasper, C. (1980) *Creative Dramatics: Trainer's Manual*, Philippines, Mindoa-Sulu Pastoral Conference Secretariat.

Gerbner, George and Marsha Siefert (eds) (1984) *World Communications: A Handbook*, New York, Longman.

Gibbons, Arnold (1985) *Information, Ideology and Communication*, Lanham, University Press of America.

Gidengil, Elisabeth (1978) 'Centres and Peripheries: An Empirical Test of Galtung's Theory of Imperialism', in *Journal of Peace Research*, Vol. 15, No. 1.

Gleeson, Denis (undated) 'Theory and Practice in the Sociology of Paulo Freire', reproduced from *Hard Cheese: A Journal of Education*, third issue, held at the University of Cape Town library.

Griswold, Wendy (1982) 'Education as Transformation: Commentary and Replies', in *Harvard Educational Review*, Vol. 52, No. 1.

Grotowski, Jerzy (1969) *Towards a Poor Theatre*, London, Methuen.

Guback, Thomas (1974) 'Film as International Business', in *Journal of Communication*, Vol. 24, No. 1.

—— (1980) 'Imperialism, Neo-Colonialism and the Exportation of Culture: American Films Abroad', unpublished paper presented at the Seventh Annual Symposium on Literature, Film and Society in Africa, University of Illinois Urbana-Champaign.

Gugelberger, Georg M. (1985) 'Marxist Literary Debates and their Continuity in African Literary Criticism', in Georg M. Gugelberger (ed.) *Marxism and African Literature*, London, James Currey Publications.

Gupta, Sankar Sen (1982) 'Folklore: Mass Media: Communication: Can Folklore Convey Modern Messages?', in *Folklore*, Vol. 24, No. 1.

Gurevich, Michael, Tony Bennett *et al* (eds) (1982) *Culture, Society and the Media*, London, Methuen.

Hadland, Adrian (1988) 'Learning to Read Africa's Wisdom', in *Weekly Mail*, Johannesburg, 25–30 March.

Haket, L. (1991) *Theatre for Development: Annotated Catalogue of Documents Available at CESO Library and Documentation Section*, The Hague, CESO.

Hamelink, Cees J. (1984) *Cultural Autonomy in Global Communication: Planning National Information Policy*, New York, Longman.

Hedebro, Goran (1982) *Communication and Social Change in Developing Nations*, Ames, The Iowa State University Press.

Hodge, Francis (1971) *Play Directing: Analysis, Communication, and Style*, Englewood Cliffs NJ, Prentice Hall Inc.

Horn, Andrew (1980) 'African Theatre: Docility and Dissent', in *Index on Censorship* 3/1980.

—— (1982) 'The Theatre of Zakes Mda', paper presented at AUETSA Conference, Pietermaritzburg.

——— (1984) 'Public Health, Public Theatre: A Report from Southern Africa', in *Medicine in Society* (London), Vol. 10, Nos. 1–2.

——— and Gregory G. Davenport (1985) *Theatre in Community Development: Project and Conference Report*, Roma, National University of Lesotho.

Inayatullah (1967) 'Towards a Non-Western Model of Development', in D. Lerner and W. Schramm (eds), *Communication and Change in the Developing Countries*, Honolulu, East–West Center Press.

Isaac, Stephen and William B. Michael (1983) *Handbook in Research and Evaluation*, San Diego, EDITS Publishers, 1981/83.

Jones, Eldred (1979) (ed.) *African Literature Today: Drama in Africa*, London, Heinemann.

Kamlongera, Christopher (1989) *Theatre for Development in Africa with Case Studies from Malawi and Zambia*, Bonn, German Foundation for International Development.

Kasoma, Kabwe (undated) 'B.F.A. Theatre Arts Programme', unpublished letter to Dr M. I. Mapoma and Dr A. W. W. Tamakloe, University of Zambia.

——— (1983) 'Participatory Communication and Development', in *Journal of Adult Education*, Vol. 2, No. 1.

Katz, E. and P. F. Lazarsfeld (1955) *Personal Influence*, Glencoe, Free Press.

Katz, Elihu, Jay G. Blumler and Michael Guverich (1974) 'Utilization of Mass Communication by the Individual', in *The Uses of Mass Communication: Current Perspectives on Gratification Uses*, Beverly Hills, Sage Publications.

Katz, Elihu and George Wedell (1980) *Broadcasting in the Third World: Promise and Performance*, Cambridge, Mass., Harvard University Press.

Kerr, David (1981a) 'Didactic Theatre in Africa', in *Harvard Educational Review*, Vol. 15, No. 1.

——— (1981b) 'An Experimental Popular Theatre in Malawi: The University Travelling Theatre's Visit to Mbalachanda (July 1981)', Chancellor College Staff Seminar Paper No. 18, University of Malawi.

——— (1982) 'Commentary and Replies' in Harvard Education Review, Vol. 52, No. 1.

——— (1983) 'Nchira wa Buluzi: The Process of Creating a Popular Vernacular Play', mimeographed paper, February.

——— (1988) 'Theatre and Social Issues in Malawi: Performers, Audiences and Aesthetics', in *New Theatre Quarterly*, Vol. 4, No. 14.

——— and M. Nambote (1982) 'The Malipenga Mime of Likoma Islands', Chancellor College Staff Seminar Paper No. 26, University of Malawi.

Kidd, Ross (1979a) 'Liberation or Domestication: Popular Theatre and Non-Formal Education in Africa', in *Educational Broadcasting International*, Vol. 12, No. 1.

——— (1979b) 'Folk Theatre: One-way or Two-way Communication?', in *Development Communication Report*, No. 28, October.

——— (1981) 'Folk Media, Popular Theatre and Conflicting Strategies for Social Change in the Third World', in Ross Kidd and Nat Colletta (eds)

Tradition for Development: Indigenous Structures and Folk Media in Non-Formal Education, Berlin, German Foundation for International Education and International Council for Adult Education.

—— (1985) '"Theatre for Development": Diary of a Zimbabwe Workshop', in *New Theatre Quarterly*, Vol. 1, No. 2.

—— and Martin Byram (1981) *Demystifying Pseudo-Freirian Non-Formal Education: A Case Description and Analysis of Laedza Batanani*, Toronto, Mimeo.

Klapper, J. (1960) *The Effects of Mass Communication*, Glencoe, Free Press.

Kumpukwe, Joyce (undated) 'S. M. Mbewe, Creator and Producer of Malawian Radio Plays', mimeograph.

Laedza Batanani (1974) *Organising Popular Theatre: the Laedza Batanani Experience*, Gaborone, Popular Theatre Committee.

Lambert, J. W. (1977) 'Politics and the Theatre ', in *Drama: The Quarterly Theatre Review*, Spring.

Lambert, Pru (1982) 'Popular Theatre: One Road to Self-Determined Development Action', in *Community Development Journal*, Vol. 17, No. 3.

LDTC (1987) *Survey of the Potential Media in Lesotho*, Maseru, Lesotho Distance Teaching Centre.

Lee, John A. R. (1976) *Towards Realistic Communication Policies: Recent Trends and Ideas Compiled and Analysed*, UNESCO Reports and Papers on Mass Communication, No. 76.

Leis, Raul Alberto (1979) 'The Popular Theatre and Development in Latin America', in *Educational Broadcasting International*, Vol. 12, No. 1.

Lent, John A. (1977) *Third World Mass Media and the Search for Modernity: The Case of the Commonwealth Caribbean 1717–1976*, Lewisburg, Penn., Bucknell University Press.

—— (1982) 'Grassroots Renaissance: Folk Media in the Third World', in *Media Asia*, Vol. 9, No. 1.

MacBride, Sean (1982) 'Two Years After', in *Media Asia*, Vol. 9, No. 3.

Malamah-Thomas, David Henry (1989) 'Innovative Community Theatre for Integrated Rural Development in Sierra Leone: The Telu Workshop Experience', in *Ifda Dossier* 70, March/April.

McAnary, Emile G. (1980) *Communications in the Rural Third World: The Role of Information in Development*, New York, Praeger.

McCloy, James (1989) 'Privy Secrets: The VIP Latrine is the Spoilt Child of Sanitation', in *Sethala*, Vol. 3, No. 23.

McCroskey, James, Carl E. Larson and Mark L. Knapp (1973) 'Interpersonal and Mass Communication', in Joseph A. DeVito (ed.) *Communication Concepts and Processes*, Englewood Cliffs NJ, Prentice Hall Inc.

McLeod, Jack M. and Lee B. Becker (1974) 'Testing the Validity of Gratification Measures through Political Effects Analysis', in Elihu Katz and Jay G. Blumler (eds) *The Uses of Mass Communication: Current Perspectives on Gratification Uses*, Beverly Hills, Sage Publications.

McQuail, Denis and Sven Windahl (1981) *Communication Models*, London, Longman.

Mda, Zakes (1983) 'Commitment and Writing in Theatre: The South African Experience', in *The Classic*, Vol. 2, No. 1.

—— (1986) *Marotholi Travelling Theatre*, Roma, National University of Lesotho.

Meier, Gerald M. (1976) *Leading Issues in Economic Development*, New York, Oxford University Press.

Mlama, Penina Muhando (1991) *Culture and Development: The Popular Theatre Approach in Africa*, Uppsala, Nordiska Afrikainstitutet.

Moitse, Sindie (1989) 'The Ethnomusicology of the Basotho: A Study of the Cultural Institutional Basis of the Music of Basotho', seminar paper presented at the Institute of Southern African Studies, National University of Lesotho, May.

Moore, S. (1983) *Music for Life's Sake: The Media of Roles and Rules of the Media; Education Through Music in Industrially Developing Countries: Priorities and Policies*, The Hague, CESO.

MTT Report (1987) Vol. 1, No. 2.

Murray, Colin (1981) *Families Divided: The Impact of Migrant Labour in Lesotho*, Johannesburg, Ravan Press.

Nambote, Mike M. (undated) 'The Growth of Popular Theatre in Malawi: A Thumbnail Approach', mimeograph.

Nasiru, Isaac Oluwalalaaro Akanyi (1978) 'Communication and the Nigerian Drama in English', Ph.D. thesis, University of Ibadan.

Ndebele, N. S. (1984) 'Theatre for Development, Commendable Performance at Matsieng', in *National University of Lesotho Weekly Newsletter*, No. 39, 27 September.

Ngugi wa Mirii (1980) 'Literacy for and by the People: Kenya's Kamiriithu Project', in *Convergence*, Vol. 13, No. 4.

Ngugi wa Thiong'o (1983) 'Language and Literature', in *The Classic*, Vol. 2, No. 1.

—— and Ngugi wa Mirii (1982) *I Will Marry When I Want*, London, Heinemann.

Palmer, R. and N. Parsons (eds) (1977) *The Roots of Rural Poverty in Central and Southern Africa*, Berkeley and Los Angeles, University of California Press.

Pavlich, George (1988) 'Re-evaluating Modernization and Dependency in Lesotho', in *The Journal of Modern African Studies*, Vol. 26, No. 4.

Phororo, D. R. (1988) 'Keynote Address', unpublished paper presented at the Lesotho Development Seminar, Thaba Khupa Ecumenical Centre.

Pool, Ithiel de Sola (1979) 'Direct Broadcast Satellites and the Integrity of National Cultures', in Kaarle Nordenstreng and Herbert I. Schiller (eds), *National Sovereignty and International Communication*, Norwood NJ, Ablex Publishing Corporation.

Pratt, Cornelius B. and Jarol B. Mannheim (1988) 'Communication Research and Development Policy: Agenda Dynamics in an African Setting', in *Journal of Communication*, Vol. 38, No. 3.

Radke, N. L. (1978) 'NFE and Entertainment', in *NFE Exchange*, Michigan State University, Issue No. 12.

Rogers, Everett M. (1973) 'Mass Media and Interpersonal Communication', in Ithiel de Sola Pool *et al* (eds) *Handbook of Communication*, Chicago, Rand McNally Publishing Co.
—— (1976) 'Communication and Development: The Passing of a Dominant Paradigm', in *Communication Research*, 3, pp. 213–40.
—— and F. Shoemaker (1973) *Communication of Innovations*, Glencoe, Free Press.
Rostow, W. W. (1960) *The Stages of Economic Growth*, Cambridge, Cambridge University Press.
Schiller, H. I. (1976) *Communication and Cultural Domination*, New York, International Arts and Sciences Press.
Schipper, Mineke (1982) *Theatre and Society in Africa*, (trans. Ampie Coetzee), Johannesburg, Ravan Press.
Schramm, Wilbur (1973) 'Channels and Audiences', in Ithiel de Sola Pool *et al* (eds), *Handbook of Communication*, Chicago, Rand McNally Publishing Co.
Shannon, C. and W. Weaver (1949) *The Mathematical Theory of Communication*, Urbana, University of Illinois Press.
Shore, Larry (1980) 'Mass Media for Development: A Re-examination of Access, Exposure and Impact', in Emile G. McAnary (ed.) *Communications in the Rural Third World: The Role of Communication in Development*, New York, Praeger.
Sitas, Ari (1986) 'Culture and Production: The Contradictions of Working Class Theatre in South Africa', in *Africa Perspective*, new series 1 and 2.
Smythe, Dallas W. (1979) 'Realism in the Arts and Sciences: A Systematic Overview of Capitalism and Socialism', in Kaarle Nordestreng and Herbert I. Schiller (eds), *National Sovereignty and International Communication*, Norwood NJ, Ablex Publishing Corporation.
Steadman, Ian Patrick (1981) 'Culture and Context: Notes on Performance in South Africa', in *Critical Arts*, Vol. 2, No. 1.
—— (1984) 'Alternative Politics, Alternative Performance: 1976 and Black South African Theatre', in Daymond, Jacobs and Lenta (eds), *Momentum on Recent South African Writing*, Durban, University of Natal Press.
—— (1985) 'Drama and Social Consciousness: Themes in Black Theatre on the Witwatersrand Until 1984', Ph.D. thesis, University of the Witwatersrand.
Stefanova, Malina (undated) 'Communication in Theatre', in Michael Herzfeld and Lucio Melasso (eds), *Semiotics Theory and Practice Vol. II*, Berlin, Mouton and Gryter.
Stempel III, Guido H. and Bruce H. Westley (1981) *Research Methods in Mass Communication*, Englewood Cliffs NJ, Prentice Hall Inc.
Sweezy, Paul M. (1981) 'Centre, Periphery, and the Crisis of the System', in P. M. Sweezy (ed.) *Four Lectures on Marxism*, New York, Monthly Review Press.
Tomaselli, Keyan (1981) 'The Semiotics of Alternative Theatre in South Africa', in *Critical Arts*, Vol. 2, No. 1.

Tonnies, Ferdinand (1957) *Community and Society (Gemeinschaft und Gesellschaft)* (trans. and ed. Charles P. Loomis), East Lansing, Michigan State University Press.

Transformation Resource Centre (1988) *Lesotho Can Develop Herself: An Analysis of Rural Development Strategies in Lesotho*, Maseru, TRC.

Traore, Bakary (1972) *The Black African Theatre and its Social Function* (trans. Dapo Adelugba), Ibadan, Ibadan University Press.

Van Zyl, John A. F. (1977) 'Towards a Socio-Semiology of Performance', in J. A. F. van Zyl and K. G. Tomiselli (eds), *Media and Change*, Johannesburg, McGraw Hill.

Vogel, Susan (ed.) (1981) *For Spirits and Kings: African Art from the Tishman Collection*, New York, Metropolitan Museum of Art.

Wang, Georgette and Wimal Dissanayake (1982) 'The Study of Indigenous Communication Systems in Development: Phased Out or Phased In?' in *Media Asia*, Vol. 9, No. 1.

Willett, John (1966) *Brecht on Theatre: The Development of an Aesthetic*, London, Eyre Methuen.

Work for Justice (1989) 'The Traps of Dependency', in *Work for Justice*, No. 22, September.

Index